The Power of Projection

When Storytelling Becomes a Business Norm

Copyright © 2019 by Hisham Ezzat

All rights reserved. No part of this book may be reproduced, scanned, or distributed in any printed or electronic form without permission. Please do not participate in or encourage piracy of copy righted materials in violation of the author's rights.

https://wwwhisham-ezzat.com

First Edition 2019
ISBN: 9781799259640

All praises be to God, the Lord of the worlds...

Index

The Hitchhiker 1
Chapter One 5
The Magic of Stories 5
The Magic of Stories 6
The Projection 13
Why Stories? 18
The New Business World 23
The Dual Processing Story 26
The Mirror Neurons 33
The Mental Image of The Story 41
Zulu Echo 5 46
Complex Sciences 53
Handful of Hormones 56
The Chess Manager 62
The Best in Influence 67
A Step Back 71
The Camel Projection 77
Chapter Two 82

Types of Stories 82
    Goal 86
        Who am I 89
        Why am I here 98
        Vision 101
        Value 107
        Decision Making 126
    Source 146
    Path 147
    Delivery 160

Chapter Three 166
The Story that Never Ends 166
The Unbearable Story 167
The Bearable Story 175
    Ping Pong 176
    Zeigarnik Effect 180
    Repitition 186
    Contrast 188
    Numbers 195
    Ambiguity 197
    Sound 199

Silence 204
Gestures 206
Messages of the Eyes 214
Humanize It! 220
Influencers 233
Ending 236
Unexpectedness 239
Details 260
Handful of Words 262

Epilogue 265
References 267
About the Author 274

The Hitchhiker

I was amazed at my friend's obsession with the adventures that come with hitchhiking. He tells me that he derives pleasure in summertime not in the many places he visits whether Italian beaches or Spanish islands but rather in hitchhiking. He passionately explains how this obssesion of his is incomparable to any other — leaving home knowing he doesn't have enough even for a cab or even a bus. So he does his best to stop a car and convince the driver to get him to the next town or the farthest possible to get him near his destination. And by that, he traveled from east to the west of the European Continent. The journey that took several weeks with just as many stops as the many towns and villages. But that is the beautiful consequence of hitchhiking, he insists, to head wherever the car owner was going to. No agenda, empty itineraries and no appointments. If you're late, no one is impatiently waiting, and if you come on time, no one cares because there is no schedule to keep anyway! No blame! This is the hitchhiker life.

What amazed me more is that my friend comes from an aristocratic and wealthy family. He certainly has the money that will afford him to travel in business class and to stay at any luxurious hotel he fancies but when asked why he chooses hitchhiking over comfort traveling, this was his answer:

> "Believe me, the thing that I adore in such trips, lies in the uncertainty in each moment; passing through a highway day or night; walking against a car's path for minutes or even for several hours till one cars appears running in my direction and all I have to do is signal it. If it stops, I get in and if not, I keep walking."

Even more surprised, I asked him, "So, where is the pleasure is in such suffering and uncertainty?"

He looked to me with a faint smiled and said, "They don't teach these things in engineering school, but I'll teach about it."

He drinks the last sip of his coffee then leans on the table with his elbows and places his intertwined fingers before his face moving toward me and saying:

> "When I walk alone all this distance, with backpack on my shoulders, looking to the extent of my sight and seeing one of those vehicles coming from a distance, at that particular moment, I see the future that still I know nothing about it except that it is approaching as I am to it and once its driver passes me by with no intention of stopping, in a blink of an eye, we lock eyes and that's it. That is the present that never stays to be present in its presence. Once this snapshot is over and the driver speeds on his way then comes the…"

I interrupted him saying, "The past".

He said, "No, then comes the story…".

Silence.

My friend continues:

> "When a vehicle passes by, it turns to a story like hundreds and thousands of stories of other vehicles. There are cars that stopped and picked me up and there are those that sped away and wouldn't care less about me and my plight in the a long stretch of highway. And this is life, a future that I don't worry much about as long as I'm walking toward it. Like thunder, it just goes. So all that is left for me is the past. That past that always hides beneath the cloak of a story. It covers me. It flows into me as water flows downhill multifurcating between folds of sands it in my canteen accompanying me in my hitchhiking which I never know when will end nor where it shall lead me.

I asked him, "So what do those stories represent to you?".

He said:

> "It represents life. Wherever and whenever I go to the highway, I gain. After the suffering of walking, waiting and waving are the stories. There is wisdom and lessons in a completed route which I may never go through again and that is the path that I'll never deviate from. When I begin my hitchhiking and I walk in that long route that I percieve to be neverending then all of sudden is completed, shows me how fleeting life is. It stretches forth when you believe it is short and abbreviates when you believe it is long. That's why there is nothing that quenches my thirst like the stories that I come to know in my hitchhiking. It's all that I carry in my backpack that if I lose it, it would be as if I never left my small house... and never went a day to the path"

Before I could ask more questions, my friend whom I just met, bade farewell, carried his backpack, left the rest house and went back to his hitchhiking life...

******

My friend was quite truthful, the endeavor of a human being including his experiences, passions, searches and the outcome of his deeds ultimately are nothing but a faint and buried memory or a present story to be told. In dozens of interviews that I attended, one common question comes up, *"Please! Tell us your story."*. Amongst hundreds of research that I skimmed, all were about a certain story of some kind. Researchers narrate. The *Big Bang*, after all, is the story of the universe and in *The Theory of Evolution, Darwin* tries to narrate the story of the beginning of existence up to the theory of *parallel universe,* which is another attempt in narrating the story of other worlds, a story that might or never happen. Even our daily personal lives are nothing but a story that made an impact or a story awaiting its impact. When we lose the drive to save our personal heritage or leave a legacy with our many stories, when our tongues and hearts are heavy to narrate our stories then there will be no difference between the day we came into this life with the day of our departure from it.

Stories are the only witnesses that we were ever here. It's the witness that presented, propagated and projected. The aim of this book is to narrate a story that influences life, especially in managing daily routines and activities. With the support of stories, concepts and ideas are clearly projected that provide motivation and propel not to mention inspire ultimately getting work done in its best shape and manner.

Chapter One
The Magic of Stories

The Magic of Stories

Gold…The perpetual dream of mankind – to horde as much as they can of that precious metal and so man strives hard to acquire it. It would still not be enough even if one day man wakes and finds out that the mountains surrounding him turned in to gold and was owned by him. Instead man will wake up the next day hoping to see earth and sky turned to gold possessing it still. Then one day, the man awoke, got out of his bed, walked toward his door and when he turned the door's knob, it had turned to. The man was shocked and fell on the ground looking at the golden knob. After collectiing himself, he stood and kept switching his eyes from his hand and the golden knob and back again,

"It's gold, gold, gold…."

The man kept repeating in surprise, not believing at what had just happened. Immediately, he scans left and right and saw a small hair comb and so he grabs and stares at it passionately. And in just seconds the comb turned to gold. Surprise quickly turned to happiness and fulfillment like he had never felt before. The man went out of his room and kept touching all he could in his way and everything turned to gold. Every piece of furniture inside the house, the man turned to gold. He kept thinking that this was a fortune that even the wealthiest kings never had, not even the most wiley merchants! But the man was insatiable so he went out to the garden and began touching trees, plants, rocks and sand! In no time, all the garden turned to gold that its sheen under the morning sun could blind the eyes.

The man returned inside his house exhausted but feeling happy. Hungry, he reaches for an apple from a bowl on the table. Salivating, he hastens to bite a fresh green apple. A tremendous pain ran through his skull. He felt his teeth grind in to the apple which turned to gold in a blink of an eye. The apple, shiny gold, very heavy but very much inedible as well. He tried another apple and once more it had turned to gold. He tried another and another and another but was futile. He took a cup of water to quench his thirst but it, too, had turned to gold. The man began to realize how awful this situation could be. If things don't change, he may die in days. And while the man sat in the middle of his golden garden, reflecting at what had just happened; whether it was blessing or curse. And while he was immersed in his thoughts, he heard a voice calling and approaching,

"Dad, dad!"

She is his lovely daughter running over to hug him and in an instinctive reaction, he picks her up and gives her a warm hug. Her laughter and her little body suddenly froze. The man felt he could not carry his daughter's weight. She was turned to a golden statue.

The man stared at his daughter's golden figure. Shock and tears are welling up in his heart and his eyes. His dream had come true and already it took his daughter and he is soon to perish. Here he is owner tons of gold making him the richest on the face of the earth but he can't even drink a sip of water or eat a morsel to save his live. The man looks at everything around him, his eyes scan all the gold including his daughter then all of a sudden he faints and falls to the ground.

The man rolls over his bed and falls on the floor waking up abruptly. He stands up and quickly goes to his mirror checking his face and his hands. Nervously, he touched the hair comb, he waits for a moment and nothing happens. He grasps other things and nothing. He lets out the deepest sigh of relief he ever did in his life. He smiles and whispers, *"Thanks! God!"*. Then he rushes out of his room to wake his beautiful daughter and to give her the longest, tightest and warmest hug ever.

What would you do if you were such man but instead of influencing inanimate objects, you had the power to influence people? No one escapes from your persuasion trap. You can close sales with 100% success rate. Everybody believes your side of arguments and no one refuses your requests. Do you take that as a life goal? If your answer is yes, beware of a similar fate to that of the man in the story. Influence can be a blessing and it can also be a curse. Allah almighty says in the Quran, *"And man supplicates for evil as he supplicates for good, and man is ever hasty"* Al-Isra 11.

When you aim to sharpen whatever skill, you have to know that evil could dwell in what you believe is an absolute realm of good.

So now, what if we omit the previous story and we proceed to narrate the following lesson without any reference to the man? For sure, the impact of the message would radically differ, also the wisdom would quickly fade from our memories, maybe in couple of days you wouldn't recall the whole thing. A story is retained longer in the memory compared theoretical or even factual information. In influence and persuasion literature, there is nothing more powerful than telling a story which holds within it the message or request. Stories used to be a major element in books of religion and it also has been the most common tactic of teaching and disciplining children and nowadays it has a growing interest in business and most professions relating to information transmission.

It was the eighth class and I was thirtheen then. I neither recall the teacher's name nor which class it was. I don't even recall who was seated to my right or left. Details escape me but I can still picture the teacher sitting on the top of the desk, watching all of us. Our teacher was absent so he was a substitute and he decided to do that in a marvelous way by telling us a story. It was like a scene from a movie: The lovely teacher seated on the top of the desk, telling a story, looking at each one's eyes as if he was just focusing on one. All we saw in this scene was him. Everything around him blurred. We were captivated.

The teacher began by saying, *"I'll tell you a story, maybe it's real and maybe it's not. This your own decision to make..."*

The story took place in the era of pharaohs. A young Egyptian hero witnesses the execution of his own brother in the hands of the oppressors. He goes down to the arena where the execution took place when everybody had gone. He collects the macabre carcass of his brother. Kneeling, he started grabbing pieces of clothing and some body parts and clung them to his chest whilst embracing his dead brother making a vow to avenge him. Just when the plot began its rising action to the climax, the bell rings signaling the end of the school day.

Although our mental image of the ring was that of a savior ultimatley freeing us, poor kids from protracted boredom inside the classroom; the extreme power of the unfinished story completely altered our paradigm from that old and fixed mental image to hating that bell which ended one of the most pleasurable moments I've ever experienced in that class, in that school and maybe in my entire educational experience. I neither recall the anatomy of an ameoba cell nor the date of the Battle of Waterloo nor the locations of the African savannas, but I clearly recall that story, that day and that substitute teacher. And to this day, that story holds a special place in my heart as nothing else I've ever heard or seen inside the premises of that school.

A story has an incredible influence on both the heart and the mind. A study on the retention and impact of a story indicates that recall is more lasting than abstract and bullet point information. In an experiment, a lecture was conducted to a group of students. Information was transmitted in the form of numbers, through statistics and graphs. To another group, they conducted the lecture but in the form of a story. After a couple days, they tested both groups based on the lecture's content. They found that the first group recalled only 5%, while the second group recalled 65% of the lecture. *Steven Denning,* the author of the book *The Leader's Guide to Storytelling,* claims that storytelling contributes by 14% to the United States's GDP, that if the story represents half of persuasion, it means that the annual value of storytelling exceed one trillion dollars in the US market.

Who Got the Monkey at the Blue Ocean?

We were preparing for a training program for professionals called *Manager-X* aimed to equip junior as well senior managers to cope with their new positions and to teach them various skills any manager would need – like dealing with information, decision making, managing and risk and uncertainty, etc. I spent long time designing the program. I needed to look up quite a number of big punch, bestselling books and articles to enrich the program and one of the best resources I used was the prestigious journal of Harvard Business School *HBR* that was first published in 1922. The most influential figures of business and management worldwide participated with tens of articles that made *HBR* one of the most influential business journals worldwide. Out of hundreds of very professional and beneficial unique articles, my deepening interest drove me to trace the best among the rest and I found two articles, *Management Time: Who's Got the Monkey?* and the second one, *Blue Ocean Strategy.*

I read both with indefatigable drive and passion to figure out the connection of the title to the content of both articles. To my surprise, both articles were easily summarized in about hundred words. *Who's Got the Monkey?* focused on the workflow of the whole team /organization. It suggests not to keep pending items at your desk. Tasks that are dependent on other tasks that fall on your desk / scope of work should go to the next step in the process or event.

Blue Ocean Strategy focused on the area of competition. Suppliers of goods and service providers are often confined in a small *Red Ocean*. Red because of the bloodshed brought about by the very tough competition among the the many who fill that ocean or a particular market leaving almost no space for newcomers. *Blue Ocean* on the other hand has a huge and almost unlimited space no one will ever reach its frontiers. It has many opportunities and new products that competitors at the *Red Ocean* have no clue about.

I was amazed at the simplicity and maybe the naivete of both ideas and I was more amazed that both were the two bestselling articles in the history of these journals. I assumed that many who have read the articles respond by saying, *"So, what?! What novelty do these articles present?"* But after reflecting on the content of each article, I realized that it wasn't the content that made them so famous but it was solely the exceptional projection both made. The articles projected a crucial meaning that was absent from many readers's minds although prominence of another meaning easily came into their minds leading to more awareness of the first meaning and more motivation to realize it and to drive it to real action and that's what both articles succeeded at.

We all know how frustrating it is when a task gets stuck with one person, while other staff or departments with dependency in the particular task lie and wait hampering personal or departmental productivity and deliverables. And we all know how gratifying it is to get out of the monotonous cycle of competition of traditional goods and services and to invent new products and provide different services. We all want to get out of this tough rat race but we lack a psychological push to get those meanings to surface on our minds and turn them into action plans in order to finally to execute and seek the best results.

Many people see those kinds of of articles and books that posit management issues or mental creativity but seem to never bring any new to the table. They just put axioms together that everybody knows already one way or another. But what makes a book or article better than another is in the ability of the writer to project this *"Axiom"* on an imaginary surface or even a tangible surface that is in another dimension and in so doing revolutionizes people's awareness which makes the reader reconsider this abandoned axiom. One example of these axioms is the topic of the collective innovationut of business organizations. *Prof Vijay Govindarajan* released his latest book *The Three Box Solution*. The book discusses the importance of having three conceptual frames of any organization by setting up three separated boxes. The first one cares about the present, which is the focus on implementing the daily working routines and executing strategies that were already planned. Then the second box relates with the future, like plans for developments, ideas for new products, unprecedented marketing strategies…etc. Finally, the third box deals with the past, how to vanish its negative consequences that curb the other two boxes from achieving their targets. This is the whole idea of the book, of course in addition to many examples of organizations that applied such idea and noticed a substantial growth. Although the basic idea is so simple and didn't present something new, the projection of the main idea on the three boxes acted like the spinal cord the book that contributed to its success and to the flourishing of that theory.

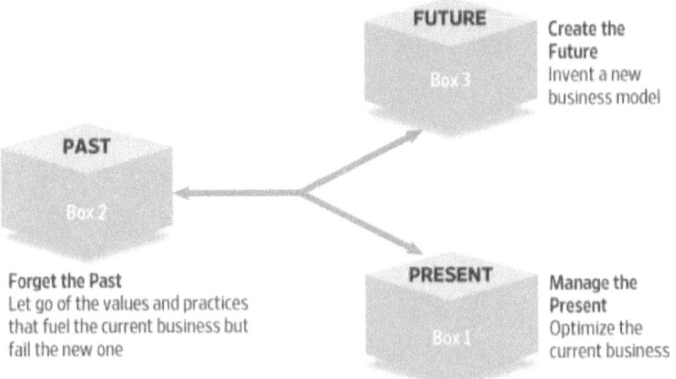

THE THREE-BOX SOLUTION
By balancing the three boxes, managers can resolve the inherent tension of innovating a new business while running a high-performing business at the same time.

The Projection

College stood as the most important transition in my life. It was the preparation for my professional life. Hard work began on day one. Studying engineering is sweat, breath and effort taking you to your breaking point. The first semester is an introduction to various disciplines related to engineering. Students have a plethora of classes in mathematics, physics, programming, chemistry, mechanics... etc. I remember how perplexed and bewildered my friends and I were! We were thinking what purpose was there in studying all these subjects. Eventually, we trained oursleves to get used it and more importantly not to ask or argue anymore but to focus and overcome these so-called obstacles and pass exams. Then the "obstacles" escalated and elevated us to the monster that is drawing and it was called Descriptive Geometry, *the widow maker*. This drawing class was both ambiguous and complicated. From the beginning until we finish a drawing assignment and look at what we just did or attempted to do hoping that at least a handful of surrealism artists would understand, we'd still ask ourselves, "*What the hell did I just draw?*".

I remember how most of us felt after each physics lecture. We walked out of the room and whoever had the will power – the most stamina walked out hypnotized at best while the rest looked more like newly contaminized zombies. But that class actually brought us ecstatic relief realizing for the first time that earth is actually a sphere. We used to leave mathematics lectures wondering how dumb we were and how brilliant the professor was but wondering even more at how strange it was to see the lecturer continuously writing equations upon equations on the long board even when everybody had already left the class. I also remember chemistry lab where we had so much fun than we ever expected. We found out in our experiments that producing smells that were worse than fart was a serious challenge. Lab class inspired many of us and was probably the reason for many to shift careers and move to international terrorism.

But no adventure could be compared to workshop class where we saw all those machines we studied such as lathes, welders and piercers. I often wondered why students from behavioral psychology frequently came to the class in their neat white coats looking at us while taking notes. And then I found out that they were getting first hand and very rich data for their social interaction analysis. They were observing us, engineering students, in our blue workshop coats chasing one another with a welding torch burning at 1000 degrees Celsius trying to prove the professor's claim that it could cut a body in half and still some students trying to trim their friend's hair on the lath machine was the funniest to date.

But all those experiences and hilarity pales in comparison to the elation when students finish Descriptive Geometry class.

At those particular moments, heads bow down, pacing slows down, eyes roll the same way *Frankenstein's monster* did upon dying and still others would fill the corridors sitting down on the floor embracing their thighs to their chest. The scene is similar to that in concentration camps and it seems all mumble one thing, *"Is the boiling sound inside my brain normal?"* while others ask, *"Is the world going to be a far better place if someone had just assassinated the inventor of Descriptive Geometry?"* I felt so confused in this particular class, I kept asking myself if it had any practical benefit or is the dean just killing time by filling the gaps with meaningless classes.

And one time while I was talking to myself asking these questions, I saw one of the lecturers of Descriptive Geometry pass by so I chatted him up. Although had the look of a وقار، and with the knowledge, I thought, he must have; I still couldn't help but feel that he wasn't the one to answer what was bothering me. But I had no one else to ask so I politely stopped him and with subtle frustration said:

"Excuse me ,sir, why does everything look ambiguous and unclear in this place? We will learn a great deal, we are told and that is why we study our subjects but what is the purpose? And to top it off is Descriptive Geometry! Yes, we are able do it and we get good marks but it's soley because we follow the steps and we practice hundreds of times to pass periodic tests. And yet if a small child asks me why I do it, I have answer. We are supposed to design machines, not be the machines..."

The man looked straight into my eyes for a long while. He seemed to be thinking intently for an answer or maybe he was aready thinking how he was going to flunk me in his class because of how rude I was. I didn't wait much longer till the man smiled and looked up for a moment and then said:

"It's projection, son!"

"What?!" I asked in confusion.

The man continued, saying:

> "Each profession in this world has an outward and inward aspect. The outward aspect is manifested in the influence of its science – its logic or the art and execution of a particular profession seen and often understood by the commoners while the inward aspect is what commoners do not perceive except for the artisan who dedicated his life to such profession. The physician, the author, the maestro, the chemist, the engineer and many others are the people who understand the inward aspect of each sciences. But what differentiates a creative physician, author, maestro, chemist and even a creative engineer over a regular one is in their ability to turn this inward, ambiguous and hidden aspect to a glaringly clear and simple scenario to commoners.
>
> The author who inspires millions with his writings is the one who could skillfully project his ideas and opinions on printed words. The amazing maestro is the one who succesfully took the notes, the rhythm and harmony that resonated deep inside his mind and projected it on instruments and his staff. And finally the creative engineer is the one who took complex equations and figures that no one else envisioned and projected it into simple and executable drawings turning an idea – a dream into a plain truth – tangible material, turning the impossible to hope and turning paper sheets to real construction. You're a creative engineer if you become a plain mirror for the commoners. Once a difficult and hard thing is placed before it, it projects back a simple and lovely truth to people. If you are not like a mirror, you will only serve as voice that no one understands. And maybe you, too, may not understand although you are speaking it fluently. Your ability as an engineer is bounded in your skill to project... and this is the secret of creativity."

The man went away and eventually the semester ended but the exceptional grade I achieved in Descriptive Geometry had a different weight than the others I had in other subjects. It held more meaning than the high mark written on the certificate. It was a point of departure from the outward to the inward – it was a start to build up an indispensable skill. Whenever I encounter people who have difficulty in accepting or digesting an idea, I remind myself of the man who taught me how to let them see that will allow them to accept and digest… It's the power of projection…

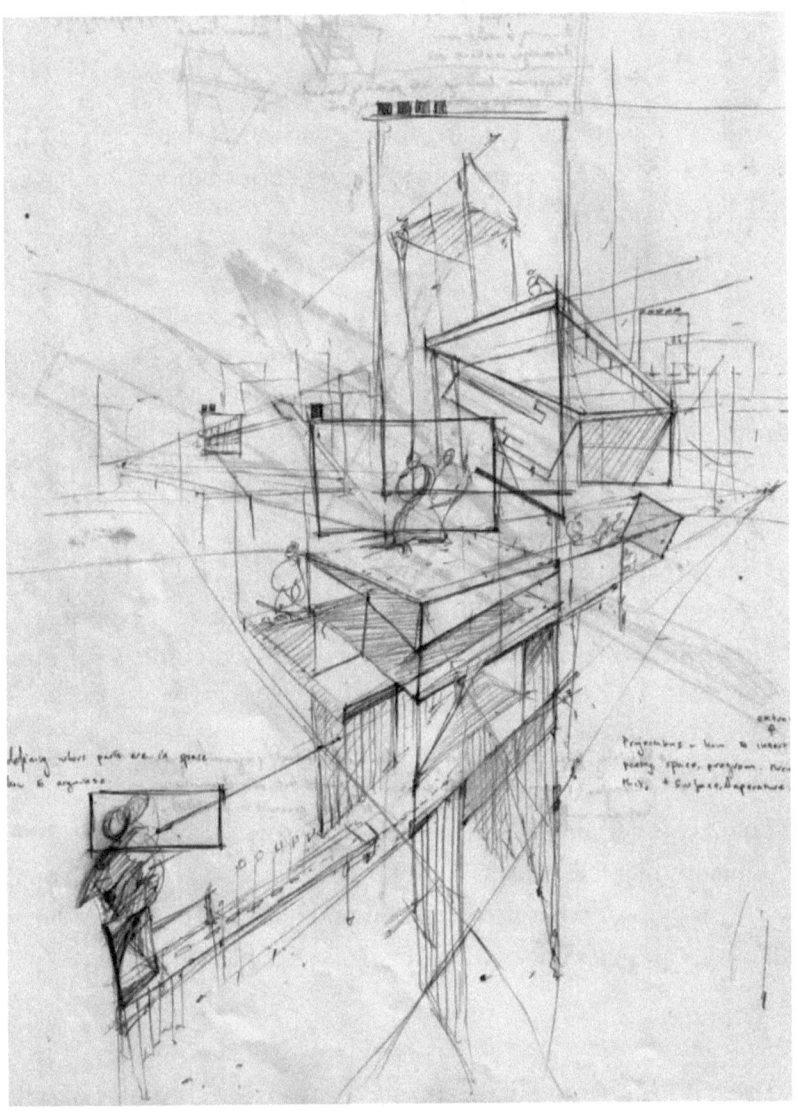

Why Stories?

Allah says in the Quran:

"So relate the stories that perhaps they will give thought."

Al'Araf-176

"And [We sent] messengers about whom We have related [their stories] to you before and messengers about whom We have not related to you."

An Nisa-164

"And recite to them, [O Muhammad], the news of him to whom we gave [knowledge of] Our signs, but he detached himself from them; so Satan pursued him, and he became of the deviators."

Al'Araf-175

"That is from the news of the unseen which We reveal to you, [O Muhammad]. You knew it not, neither you nor your people, before this. So be patient; indeed, the [best] outcome is for the righteous."

Hud-49

"There was certainly in their stories a lesson for those of understanding. Never was the Qur'an a narration invented, but a confirmation of what was before it and a detailed explanation of all things and guidance and mercy for a people who believe."

Yusuf-111

"Thus, [O Muhammad], We relate to you from the news of what has preceded. And We have certainly given you from Us the Qur'an."

Taha-99

"We relate to you, [O Muhammad], the best of stories in what We have revealed to you of this Qur'an although you were, before it, among the unaware."

Yusuf-3

All books of religions were reinforced with stories within its chapters and the stories in the Quran represent almost one third of the whole book. Listening and narrating stories were a divine order as they motivate people to think and reflect. The story that was repeated the most in Quran is the story of Prophet Moses "Peace & blessing be upon him." and his struggle with pharaoh and his quest with the clan of Israel. A reason that such story is repeated maybe because it's a universal story that encompasses various human struggles that continue till today. From the persecution of ethnic minorities, to a mother's grievance over her baby and her dependence upon her God to save him is a universal theme. Hook type scenes emerge from the water that saved a child Prophet to the water that took out the oppressor, from a heart full of mercy and compassion that allowed the sister of Pharaoh to adopt the child to the exodus of an entire clan escaping from merciless hearts of pharaoh and his soldiers, from helping the weak and helpless women to fulfilling promises with their father, from the daring confrontation of an oppressor to the sudden change from the oppressor to following the true God, from keeping steadfast in the truth to crucifixion and death for the sake of the belief.

The Quran contains various tales that occurred to man which apply to present situation. These stories from a past experience serve as a guide for mankind on how to confront similar predicaments based on the wisdom of the stories in the Quran. Allah almighty says,

"And We have certainly diversified for the people in this Qur'an from every [kind] of example, but most of the people refused [anything] except disbelief."

Isra-89

"And We have certainly diversified in this Qur'an for the people from every [kind of] example; but man has ever been, most of anything, [prone to] dispute."

Kahf-54

For thousands of years, stories were the main way of communication between peoples whatever their culture or background. Ancient Egyptians used to inscribe the stories of their battles and personal lives on the walls of temples in a narrative style. The most important literatures of the Greeks were mere stories like *Iliad & Odysseus* and the caves of France and Mexico witnessed the inscriptions of the early men depicting their lives – stories in a series of pictures and drawings.

No doubt that emotions constitute a major part of how we make decisions and the real power of a story is in its ability to induce emotions from people's hearts more than any other tactic or influence. A story can transmit logic in a seamless way that abstract information cannot do as a story is something fast, powerful, free, natural, persuasive, entertaining and quite unforgettable. That is why some people claim that personal stories and rumors represent more than 65% of our daily conversations and once you begin focusing on the content of people's conversation, you'd notice even a bigger percentage.

We are naturally drawn to acquire information through stories. When a child does something wrong, dads come and quite naturally asks for details saying, *"Tell me all that happened."*, *"Tell me the whole story from the beginning"*. The same natural phenomenon happens in workplace between friends and even in exchanging general news – people aren't attracted to abstract information, rather they need to listen to some sort of a story, and out of its context, they will pick up the details that form a general concept of what is being said.

I recall when I saw a program on TV about an Australian man who decided to defy the limits of his brain by developing it. And so, he travels to many places worldwide and meet neuroscientists to learn from them techniques to develop his brain faculties. In doing so, he meets with people with exceptional minds as well. Among them, the former playing cards memory world champion. This man can recall playing cards even in random patterns. Our Australian friend decides to participate in a contest but miserably fails even to recall a small number of cards. The former championship began teaching him the secrets he employs to master his skill. The man tests himself again and this time he makes an incredible performance.

The secret was nothing but turning the sets of playing cards into sets of stories. For example, if the first four cards are as follows, five clubs, six spades, two hearts and seven diamonds; the man comes up with a story about those four cards. It goes like he enters his room to find the four cards placed on a small table so he puts them in his book then goes to the bathroom and he finds on the floor four other cards and so on till he has one story for all the cards sets. During the competition, the man principally begins recalling the story not the cards themselves as they form just the context of the story. He begins entering his room and finds four scattered cards on the table, which are five clubs, six spades, two hearts and seven diamonds and then he goes to the bathroom and so on so forth.

How come a story could have this significant impact in increasing human memory? The human brain, with training, can develop the ability to associate information with a mental image. New neural synapses (connections) are established between the input and the mental image. Depending on the strength (with training) of such synapse, the information is easily retrieved when recalled. And what determines the quality of the synapse (connection and association) is the condition of the brain when the information was received and the how the different types of inputs flow. A story has a role in connecting chains of information that consequently creates connected chains of synapses so when the brain recalls one piece **information**; it immediately associates another bit so to speak another or a second one which is already connected by association to the first information and so on and so forth. Connecting scattered information by means of a story is like connecting pieces of scattered pearls in one chain. The story or narration per se is the most common projection media that produces immense influence or impact. The story is the most utilized to project reality onto various dimensions where imagination can flow and accept what it couldn't in reality.

The New Business World

The world of business today has a completely different shape than a century ago. Each decade has its demand, conditions and criteria that differ the previous one. The beginnings of the twentieth century witnessed tremendous changes in industrial manufacturing. For the first time in modern history, the world lived through unprecedented rates of productions. Private companies which have thousands of workers on full time payroll was something completely novel to emerging economies worldwide. From there, modern principles of business management made its first steps to offices and halls of companies and factories. Management was mainly trial and error. Once a theory surfaces based on some study or research published in renowned journals which aims to improve management of people and resources, businesses were ready to try it out for the sake of increased output. But sooner or later managers who readily adopt such theory and put it in action find out it wasn't the best option for them with adverse outcome not to mention its ramifications almost readily ditches it out.

The same case happened in other fields like in medicine, for example. In the fifties, some physicians in the United States recommended smoking for health benefits because of some studies conducted.

In the 1960s, Prof. Douglas Mcgregor introduced what he called Theory X and Theory Y. The traditional Theory X states that people, in general, are lazy, idle and chaotic so the best way to manage and motivate them is to put them under a strict and continuous surveillance, to seduce them with periodic incentives for their good work, and to face their mistakes with strict penalties so to avoid their repetition. Theory Y, according to Mcgregor supports the instinctive nature. Humans have enthusiasm and passion to develop, they are driven by competition and achievement of success and are naturally motivated to work so there is no need to motivate because the true aim management should be to maintain and protect those natural human

tendencies – it's not about motivating people rather to avoid *De-Motivating* them. (1)

One of the famous debates about the economic theory is the old belief that people make their economic decisions in a logically after analyzing inputs objectively and that Supply and Demand are the main forces that stabilize the markets. But in the seventies, other theories were introduced refuting the former as obsolete. More and more academics tended to believe that people are mainly irrational in their decision in general. Prof Don Ariely wrote a book discussing this issue and he named it, *Predictably Irrational: The Hidden Forces That Shape Our Decisions*. He discusses how emotions and cognitive biases dominate our thinking while making decisions. (2)

Those new researches led to the flourishing of a new discipline that merge psychology and economics which later was called *Behavioral Economics*, where it focuses on the psychological and emotional influences on people in making their economic decisions. It became popular that emotions are the main factor of a purchase decision and that the ability to control and manipulate emotions will be the main concern of thousands of organizations in order to fnd the best way to influence the consumer behavior toward certain products or services. From then on a new revolution has erupted affecting how to display, promote and position products and services. All gave little concern on the logical aspect while targeting emotions. Many researches and books were published to discuss the nuances of consumer influence and market demographics such as man, woman, child or adolescent as each differ ways persuade and influence decision.

Later on, storytelling began spreading in business as its growing power to influence were clearly noticed. Many marketing agencies adopted various techniques to present products in narrative way.

Many were extremely successful because the stories presented were so captivating while others couldn't trigger enough if not any emotions at all in their target audience / market. Narrative ads shown on TV may take no more than ten seconds on screen which demands more creativity to craft and present. From the ambiguous first scene to the escalating events up to the unexpected end, each should contribute to fix in the memory the product or service offered which will result in sales.

In this era where products are getting more and more identical in features, quality and price due to stiff competition, influence becomes the third factor that guarantee superiority and success in the marketplace. Marketing departments and ad agencies have new roles and challenges in a world where attention of customers is so limited if not so scarce. And so the need for a well-crafted story becomes indispensable for those who aim to go through the new business world.

The Dual Processing Story

When I was ten years old, I used to watch a program about movie festivals. In the show, after each movie, they open the floor to directors and critics. A girl in her twenties stood and made a very unexpected commentary. She said that she didn't enjoy movies as other people do or like she did in the past. The presenter inquired. She explained that her father is a famous director and took her along while shooting movies. Immediately, the experience turned from a captivating one where her imagination would flow wherever it wanted to a somewhat dissected form of watching the anatomy of the whole process of movie making. When events reach climax and the protagonist faces a complicated situation and audience almost can't take a breath, the focus of the girl is drawn to the positioning of cameras and figuring how the cinematographer utilized such and such lighting to create a certain effect on the scene. When a king is stabbed and falls on the floor of his palace, the girl never weeps as others in the cinema; rather she is impressed by the ability of the cameraman spinning around the king's cadaver to creating dramatic effect.

This girl lost the joy of the commoners who readily leave the control to the directors to lead them wherever he wants keeping up with him till the end of the movie. And then after, they return to reality where they regain control. But things are different for those involved in this work of movie making. They are never dragged into the movie as the spectators. It may seem that these people lost their innocence to enjoy and be influenced by the story because their (system 2) has jacked their (system 1) making them a *storyless* human beings.

William James, the father of modern psychology, whi died in 1910 is considered the first scientist to present what is known as *Dual Process Theory* wherein he proposed that the human mind has two different modes of processing information. The first one is *Associative* while the second is *Reasoning* so when planning or designing, the reasoning mind leads the process connecting the dots in a logical way and when thinking of something personal, the associative mind dominates the process which connects the current idea or information with some other stored and historical memory. (3)

The following decades, other psychologists set proposals about the function of the human brain and most of them based on the dual processing function of the brain like *Jonathan Evans,* who proposed two paths of thinking, *Heuristic* and *Analytic.* Evans says that the natural thinking begins with the heuristic path where the person chooses which of the presented information is more identical with the current situation and then he goes to the analytic path where he takes the applicable or practical information and begins to analyze it separately. (4)

In 2004, *Fritz Strack* and *Rolan Deutshc* published a study titled *Reflective and Impulsive Determinants of Social Behavior* where they proposed that humans use reflective path to make decisions by analyzing the objective information, while the impulsive path is used to make decisions from a pre-determined plan or old ideas and beliefs already set up in the mind regardless of the current status quo. (5)

Finally, *Daniel Kahneman* proposed how our brain works in a very simple way. He collected his previous works and put them in his groundbreaking book *Thinking Fast and Slow.* In his book, he wrote about theories of cognitive biases and heuristics. Also he spoke about his research that earned him a Nobel Prize in behavioral economics. Khaneman referred to the dual processing functions of the brain by the intuition and the reasoning or *(system 1)* and *(system 2).* He explains that all those cognitive biases and heuristics are the causes of our reliance on system 1 majority of time. (6)

System 1 is what the human mind uses to manage its daily functions. It is the fast and intuitive mind that sees things in general and abstract way. It is the mind the never wants to dig into complicated details. It is the mind that saves its energy through superficial thinking. It is the mind that takes a fraction of a second to answer "4" when the question is 2 x 2. It is the mind that responds fast once it acknowledges a common name. It is the mind that acts fast to protect its owner when a fast moving car is about to hit. It is the mind that orders your facial muscles to cringe for a split of a second upon seeing something disgusting. It is the mind that doesn't take much time making judgement on a person you met for the first time.

System 1 is the mind that goes to a thrilling adventure in a nearby galaxy where everything is possible and there are no limits to your power or your dreams. When the lecture begins and the speaker drags on boringly, everyone in attendance switches to system 1 to trigger his imagination and go away to some place else to a faraway galaxy. This is the system human beings loved ever since. It has many benefits to save human lives in time of danger but acts as the main reason for laziness and incapacity of a human being to produce more and be persistent in reaching goals. Also it prevents humans to acquire and scrutinize information in a critical way.

System 2 is the mode of thinking that inflicts humans with headache and exhaustion after being activated for couple of hours. It is the system that makes computer programmers feel hungrier than a martial arts practitioner working for the same amount of time. When the brain works continuously, it consumes the biggest portion of the body's total stored energy – the brain alone consumes about 25% of total human energy.

Khaneman refered to system 2 as the slow mind that takes a general situation and dissects and scrutinizes every bit of detail in a serial and focused manner. It is the system that gives the answer 391 after some analysis and calculation when the question 17 x 23 is what. It is the system that is activated when fixing cell phones. It is the system that tries to make sense of system 1 which was suspicious of the person you just met today. It is the system that controlled your facial muscles from showing contempt and and allowed you to fake a smile upon seeing your manager whom you never liked by chance in the mall. It is the system that drives and pushes you to take note of every letter the boring lecturer says and writes on the board for the next three hours because that boring but kind-hearted lecturer promised the students that the content of this lecture will form a major part in the final exam.

System 2 takes back control when reading a book or writing dissertations because system 1 triggered meandering on the internet, e.g. the news, Facebook, YouTube where headlines are no more than just one-liners and details are set aside. Maybe what afforded Facebook it worldwide success is the feature of showing crumbs of news that are updated constantly and continuously which is what triggers system 1. Although humans are not capable to activate system 2 for long periods of time as it consumes a considerable amount of energy, it still the system that dictates the success and personal development for every human being.

One of the amazing ways to activate system 2 for a longer amount of time with less exhaustion is in what psychologist *Mihaly Csikszentmihalyi* called *Flow* which is total immersion in the thinking process till one reaches the stage of seamless flow, with neither desire nor want to stop or quit a task and to completely forget any interferences or interventions that may disrupt the task. Mihaly demonstrated flow as in the following figure, (7)

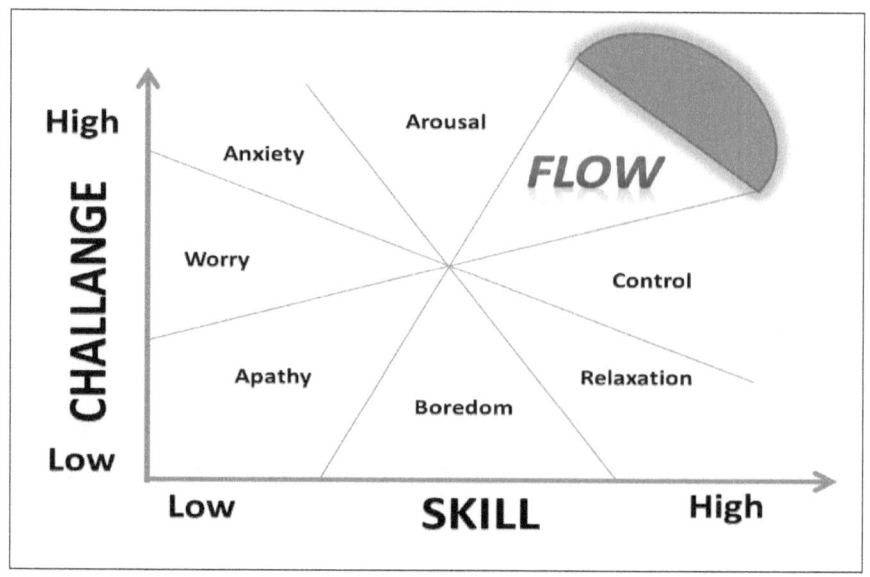

Whenever a concern to a particular person fails to necessitate or trigger any skill nor elevate his passion with a clearly defined challenge, it leads to a state of apathy while doing that task. And when the task encompasses a big challenge but that person doesn't have the necessary skills to solve, it creates a state of anxiety for the person. And when the challenge of the task is simple and the skill needed is available, it leads to relaxation. Finally, when the challenge is big and the skill required is considerably high, in this case, the person goes into a state of flow while executing that task. In storytelling, the real challenge is inducing a thrill, ambiguity while injecting deep meanings. The skill is the ability of the audience to understand, reflect, and to be influenced by such story. The more these challenges and skills go high, the more the audience reaches rapidly to the flow state which is the best state for storytelling.

Generally system 1 is the one dedictated to receive the story and to enjoy it from beginning till end. It is the system that leaves the storyteller to handle the bridle of the mind to drive wherever it wants and this is the main factor of the success of any story whether auditory or visual is to keep system 1 active the longest time possible. That is why there are numerous factors that make a story pass through system 1 effectively. But once a storyteller stutters or uses a non-conducive voice tone or pitch, or the plot is weak, or someone had previously told the story and how it shall end, these particular moments, the mind which was enjoying the story through system 1 will involuntarily move to system 2 that does everything that has no relation with being enjoyed with the story, like focusing on the storyteller himself rather than focusing on the content, or verifying his credibility, or guessing what the following scene would look like without any concern to the story and its meanings.

Finally, I've realized that Arabic language widely demonstrated the dual process theory of the human brain, a language that I certainly believe is the origin of any existent language, a language that was revealed from God, and no humans contributed to bring it up from the nowhere. God almighty said in the Quran,

"And He taught Adam the names - all of them."

Al-Baqarah 31

God taught Adam the names of all that existed in the universe and naturally God gave them the best names that described their nature which are the most concise that no other language could compete with. Digging for a certain name and to check its derivation, we find it carries prestigious meanings of this thing or that attribute.

The word brain or mind in English isn't derived from other words that can infer to their functions or to be related to other deeper meanings. But the word brain in Arabic *"Akl"* is derived from the verb *"Akala"* which means to stop, confine and hold. I was amazed from those precise meanings that reflect the main role of human brain in Arabic language. The much intent of psychologists to describe the mind as *analytic, reasoning, reflective, system 2,* they all lead to the meaning of holding and controlling the act of the mind and preventing its irresponsible and dispersed flow into a precise, meaningful and result-oriented thinking. In the first case, the event is the leader of the mind as it imposes on it what to think and where to be immersed, while in the second case, the mind is the one who choose what to think about and how it interpret things, and what to focus in and what to focus out in that story. That mind is the one who will decide to immerse whether the details of the story or its peripheral aspects.

That's why, I believe that the best stories that we watched or listened are those who could activate our both systems 1 and 2 respectively. The successful story is the one that let the audience to flow into it using their system 1 from the beginning and toward the end, then the story ends up with the great surprise, or the great wisdom, or the unexpected solution of that riddle, and here system 2 gets activated in order that the mind reaches the peak of its concentration to analyze this great climax, so it helps the audience to reach ecstasy of the story content and to keep it as an unforgettable memory.

The Mirror Neurons

Have you ever thought of the reason what makes you panick when you see a gory scene in a horror movie? Have you ever felt that tingling sensation from your spine that crawls and transfers to the arm of the friend next to you? And when you see someone sipping on a piece of lemon enduring its sourness, what effect does it do to your face? And what makes someone grab his crotch upon seeing someone being hit at the exact same spot? Even when just listening to a story about someone being hit there, your hand involuntarily flies over to your crotch with facial expression and all. If these things happened to other people, why do you react as if it happened to you?

In the last century, Medical Sciences have substantially developed, and currently we now know much more of the nature and functions of the brain. And one of the top discoveries about the brain is this huge network of brains cells called *Neurons* that principally acts as memory cells and decision making units by producing electric signals which travel through billions of conductors called *Synapsis* that transmit these signals to the nerve endings that exist in each part of the human body to execute orders, like muscle expansion and contraction, blood flow, sending warning signals,...etc.

In the 70s, a groundbreaking device was invented *MRI (Magnetic Resonance Imaging)* which led to a revolution in recording brain activity determining more precisely the parts of the brain that are responsible for certain functions or reactions like knowing which parts is responsible for fear or happiness and also determining the hormone secretion locations in the body. The concept of the MRI is that our tissues contain water which already contains protons that rotates and generates a natural magnetic field. The MRI generates an artificial magnetic field to stimulate protons to align parallel with the magnetic field then it generates a radio wave that alter the position of the protons at different degrees, and once the radio waves are shut down, those protons release certain amount of energy as it goes back to their original state. Time lapse for each proton to return to its original state would differ according to the tissue type and status producing a 3-D image according to these information.

Then in 1992, a more advanced device, *fMRI (Functional Magnetic Resonance Imaging)*, which it measures signals produced by the brain. Its working concept is based on the fact that when the neurons are active, it needs more oxygenated blood, creating a more intense blood flow in the veins increasing diameter surrounding the neurons. The device generates a magnetic field with a magnitude ten thousand times more than earth's magnetic field. This causes the oxygen protons to align with that magnetic field and then generate radio waves the same way in MRI. The lapsed time for protons returning back to their original states would differ according to the amount of activity each one had. The active parts of the brain will contain protons that will take more time to be idle comparing to the other less-active parts so that a clear picture can be taken (although it's not yet very accurate) which show the response of each part of the brain for each stimuli such as action, movement or emotions.

One of the results fMRI revealed about the human brain is the renowned discovery of the different functions between the right and the left hemisphere of the brain. It had been observed that the right hemisphere is more active when a person does creative tasks like drawing, talking, contemplating while the left is more active when a person focuses on analytical tasks like solving mathematical equations or brooding over a logical issue. That is why, they noticed, left-handed people are more creative in arts, sports or just about any task because the right hemisphere is dominant over the left part of the body leading to more activities for the right hemisphere and in order to strengthen the synapse, using the left hand and the left leg more stimulates the development of the right hemisphere.

Although some researches refute the accuracy of *fMRI* results and only acknowleges it as a nascent field of science. But combining repetitive observations with the results gives an encouraging and promising data. For example, observations show that the right hemisphere is more responsible for creativity; although *fMRI* is still inaccurate in determining exactly which brain cells are responsible, it shows clear activity in that part of the brain. This is quite enough to build a credible basis in the theory.

In 1996, machines like the EEG (electroencephalography), PET (positron emission tomography) and TMS (transcranial magnetic stimulation) were used for the purpose of observing brain activities when subjected to a certain stimulus. Researches performed an experiment on monkeys and and made them perform actions like picking up a banana or jumping and then they made other monkeys watch the action that the first set of monkeys were doing. The observed neurons that were active while the first set of monkeys picked up the banana and jumped were the same neurons when they were quiet and watching the other monkeys performing the actions. The researchers concluded that the same neurons were activated in both groups of monkeys – the group performing the action and the group watching. Later, they named this phenomena *Mirror Neurons*.

Other experiments have been conducted to study the mirror neurons. In one of these, they brought monkeys and made them watch a hand of a man grasping a banana which they called *the visible condition* and in another case, they show monkeys a hand reaching to grasp an object but before it does, the hand disappears behind a screen which they called *the hidden condition*. In the second situation, the monkeys do not see where the object disappeared to. In the first situation, mirror neurons of monkeys activated normally while in the second, it did not so they removed the screen in order for the monkeys (in the second situation) to see what the hand will grasp i.e. a banana and then they replaced the screen. Mirror neurons (this time) activated at that instant the hand disappeared behind the screen. This was proof that showing what the hand was grasping (in the second situation), the monkeys expected the next event (hand grasping the banana) which led to the activation of mirror neurons.

Researches then took it to the natural direction which was to observe this phenomenon in humans. Researchers began making monkey-like experiments on human subjects and the obvious result they obtained is human beings, too, possess mirror neurons. The human nervous system is responsible for giving orders to the human body to execute various actions like moving muscles, walking, jogging. When researchers situate human subjects to relax while watching another perform activities, they found out that the same neurons that are responsible for the action have already fired by just watching and the phenomenon repeated when they showed someone getting hit on the forehead which provides additional proof of the occurence of mirror neurons even before the invention of the *fMRI*.

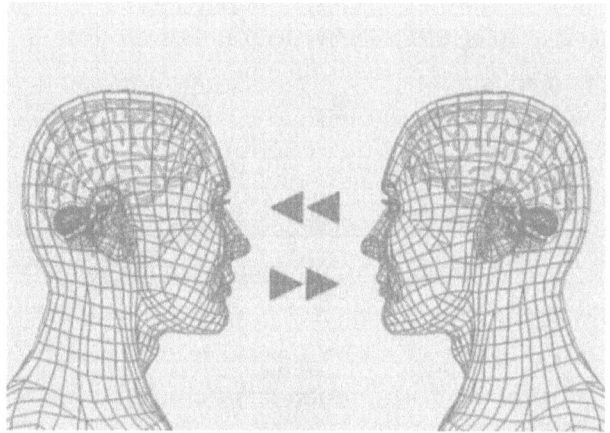

In these fractions of a second where mirror neurons get activated, the sole controller of the mind is system 1 which translates what you are watching or listening to one of the most important emotions human beings have: *Empathy*. This condition makes us human beings, it is the main trigger point of a plethora of emotions like, mercy, warmheartedness and cooperation. The source is empathy. It becomes mutual feelings of pain, needs, happiness, destitution between human beings. That's why the majority of the human race can't watch someone suffering physical torture and they rush to take action to stop it. This is one of the greatest acts resulting from empathy – to stop peoples' suffering.

Man stays in this utopic state full of empathy and mercy until system 2 interferes and spoils his ideal situation. When your friend breaks in your room in the middle of thriller movie with the intent of ruining your viewing by telling you how the protagonist will be stabbed and will struggle to his death in a hospital; you won't be able to experience any activation of your mirror neurons. Consequently, your empathy for the protagonist will malfunction because system 1 was interrupted triggering system 2 that will inhibit the flow of your mirror neurons and alter thinking. And the same thing will happen if I tell you that our approaching friend will come to tell you the story of his brother who had just been hit in his genitals. Once he comes and narrates the sequence of events, your hands wouldn't rush to cover your crotch and your face wouldn't grimace in pain because system 2 is in control of the situation.

A study has been conducted on children who suffer autism. The study cited that autistic children have a malfunction in their mirror neurons as compared to normal children resulting to lack of empathy to their peers or their environment thus they tend to be more isolated. Needless to state that there are normal people who could dampen the function of their mirror neurons that is why it comes as no surprise when there are people who have mastered torturing and killing in the most heinous way. These people once felt disgust, pain and shivering at the site of such acts for the first time and even more so as they are subjected to macabre practices with their own hands. But with repetition, system 1 subsided more and more and system 2 took its place and turning a once emphatic human being into an executioner. That's why whoever tries to rip empathy off from his heart and mind that God implanted, Allah has in store a great torture. Prophet Muhammad (Peace and blessings be upon him) said, *"There are two types of the people of Hell that I have not seen, men with whips like the tails of cattle, with which they strike the people…"*. Those people who decided to abandon mercy and empathy from their hearts, so in this was their deed in this life, and that was their retribution in the hereafter.

The reason why you get immersed in a story you watch or listen to is mainly because of your mirror neurons. They transmit to you all the emotions which happen in the context of that story. It does not let you be in the story but allows you to be a character in it so that what the character suffers you also suffer and what the character gains you also will gain. Your entire entity will merge into the story from the beginning to the end, penetrating your heart and your brain and imprints in the memory in your mind, and finally it will lead to influence your attitude and the way of your thinking in the long run.

That's why Allah prohibited a believer to listen to gibberish. Allah says in Quran,

> *"Certainly will the believers have succeeded. They who are during their prayer humbly submissive. And they who turn away from ill speech"*
>
> Al-Mu'minun 1-3

> *"And when they hear ill speech, they turn away from it and say, "For us are our deeds, and for you are your deeds. Peace will be upon you; we seek not the ignorant.""*
>
> Al-Qasas 55

This small talk always comes in the form of a story or anecdote and once you get used to listen to it (even if you refuse it), it indispensably infiltrates your heart and mind and will own a stable and fixed territory there. And your mirror neurons will involuntarily project yourself in this small talk and make you the main character in it. That is why Allah said in the Quran,

> *"And it has already come down to you in the Book that when you hear the verses of Allah [recited], they are denied [by them] and ridiculed; so do not sit with them until they enter into another conversation. Indeed, you would then be like them. Indeed Allah will gather the hypocrites and disbelievers in Hell all together"*

An-Nisa 140

The saying of God *"Indeed, you would then be like them"* may not just refer to the similarity in sin but also to the similarity in thinking, influencing and recalling the small talk inside the mind.

A study was conducted in Ohio University in 2014 titled *The Power of the Mind: The Cortex as a Critical Determinant of Muscle Strength/Weakness*. They brought three sets of participants to undergo wrist-hand immobilization for four consecutive weeks to induce weakness. Another group also underwent four weeks of immobilization, but they performed mental imagery of strong muscle contractions for five days a week. Mental imagery has been shown to activate several cortical areas that are involved with actual motor behaviors. A control group, who underwent no intervention also participated in this study .(8)

After one month, they found out that the physical power of the wrist-hand of the second group almost doubled compared to the first group, and the surprise was that the physical power of the second group outweighed the control group who had their wrist-hand free the whole month. The results of this experiment demonstrated the faculty of neurons to imagine a muscular movement of a limb, and to transmit electric signals to that limb causing more blood flow to it - exactly the same as physical training does to the limbs of our bodies.

Therefore, mirror neurons can get all your bodily functions into a story. That is why stories have this incredible power to influence people. Each word, situation and incident that the narrator speaks has the ability to let all sensations and limbs of the listener feel those words as if he was experiencing it himself.

But not all stories whether visual or aural ones have the same power to stimulate mirror neurons. Throughout history, people saw and listened to stories that they found as silly, weak and unattractive. This is because people leave a story the same condition they enter it. But an impressive story is the one that lingers in our minds. These are stories that make system 1 lead the brain throughout watching or listening process. It is the kind that worked up our mirror neurons to its peak. It is the kind of story that made its audience jump on a white horse and go to the heart of the desert. It is the story that successfully stimulated our tear glands because the protagonist's dear friend is dying. It is the story that made the audience hold their breath because the hero is struggling underwater. It is the story with the hero winning in the end making you feel ecstatic as if you were the hero yourself.

The true challenge of your story whether in business or in any other field is about how much it stimulates the mirror neurons of the audience. That's why using lots of visible details and sneaking other details is what will determine the quality and the influence of your story. A story that has well-crafted events and underlying meanings may be ruined with horrible vocal narration or maybe some unrehearsed and impromptu gestures will increase the attractiveness and the engagement of the audience. Later on we will discuss these things much further.

The Mental Image of The Story

Each word that comes into the human ears establishes for itself a mental image imprinted in the brain. The word "garden" carries many of the personal experiences that are being associated with happiness and tranquility. The word "torture" also has various mental images of agony and pain that was experienced in a lifetime. Such aversion is associated with the word because of the pictures that it represents in the brain. However, some words have various effects on people whether positive or negative depending on what a specific word means to that person. Words like school, home, family, work...etc. may carry a positive mental image for one person and conversely so for another. Some of us may associate the word "home" with a happy memory, while to others, it may carry misery and suffering. Now what about the word "Story", what kind of mental image pops when we hear someone say, *"Let me tell you a story"*.

What mental image we do have for a story is a combination of all that relates with human identity and feelings. It relates to our happiness, pains, challenges, failures and successes. That is why human beings have a natural tendency to tell stories, to listen to them and to go and look for them: a story of mother who puts her baby to sleep with a nice story, a story while we were sitting at our desks and anxiously listening to our teacher while he narrates a great fable, a story we used to spend our money on by buying in a book fair spending sleepless nights reading and immersing in them, a story of fairytales we listened to on the radio about a great hero where we used to imagine all the scenes as we listen to the narrator. The word "story" signals the start of a joy for the heart and the mind. A well-crafted adventure, acts as stimulus for our mirror neurons to work in full capacity allowing you enter and engage into the plot to live the entire story from beginning to climax until the end.

In 2006, a study was published in the Journal of NeuroImage which is dedicated to researches on the brain. In that study, the researcher asked the participants to read some words linked to a special odor, like coffee, perfume and the like. Then he let them read other words with no relation to odor like chair, key, etc. The participants were subjected to fMRI while doing the experiment. The researchers noticed that the cortex responsible for distinguishing odors called *Olfactory Cortex* was fully activated and blood was flooding to that area while the participants read the first group of words but conversely so in the same area reading the second group of words which was not associated with odor. (9)

Other researchers conducted a similar a study in the University of Emory in the United States but this time they subjected the participant to metaphorical sentences that refer to sensing textures like a singer with a soft voice or a person with rough hands. They detected a notable activity in the sensory cortex area which is responsible for textures while words in phrases like "a singer has a beautiful voice" or "those hands look strong" did not trigger any activity in such region. (10)

In a third experiment conducted in France, at the Laboratory of Language Dynamics, the participants read phrases referring to motion like "John grasped the object" or "Pablo kicked the ball". Scans revealed an activity in the motor cortex area that is responsible for the coordination of body movements and muscle contraction and relaxation. (11) Therefore, the mental image that imprints into the mind of the story recipient is a combination of various feelings, interconnection of the olfactory, sensory, and motor cortices that ultimately cause a total immersion in the realm of story. This happens if the storyteller is aware of the most optimal phrases that stimulate those three cortices. Words should aim to generate images that are already stored in the brain to be summoned and associated. Words should come in consecutive order to generate consecutive mental images which are interconnected to generate a stream of coherent events turning the mental images and words into a story.

In 1870, John Tyndall wrote an article titled "Scientific Use of the Imagination", where he wrote, "Some have gone so far as to suggest that images are best understood to be, by definition, a form of inner, mental or neural representation" (12). He infers that a human receives the words and external stimulus and decides which mental images shall be associated with such input. Some researchers showed that people identify themselves in stories or novels they hear or read. That is why the best way for humans to be receptive to words and external stimulus in a seamless order which will in turn cause a series of mental images that will ultimately influence his decisions and his life in general is to group input in a form of a story which has a sequence from beginning to end. Stories should have wisdom and lessons, surprise, tragedy, and survival. That way, the mental images influence in a positive and productive manner better than any other way of delivering information.

After many years of using stories handling issues from my social and even in my business, I affirm that the story you heard from a friend in camping or at the beach which everybody loves and earnestly listened to, does not differ by any means to a story narrated in the meeting rooms of a multinational company. The story that aims to transmit a certain idea such as managing a marketing campaign, or setting up a new sales plan, or adopting a new management system demonstrate that certain feelings can be induced with its recipients – the same itch, hankering and joy as if they were sitting on the beach or in a boardroom about to do business. This what makes storytelling crucial in the business arena and continues to gain ground with notable numbers.

Leaders and public speakers who always fascinate their audience raise an important question about the reason for their captivating talks and at how people get hooked right away with what they say. What causes their overwhelming charisma? Maybe you didn't notice it before but now you can start to notice the great care these leaders and professional speakers in making stories play a quintessential element in their speeches. They are expert in telling stories and use them to turn their requests, plans and even their personal and professional errors into a dramatic plot wrapped in the cloak of an exciting story that captivate the audience's emotions. Such story ends with a decision that necessitates support or the request that necessitates cooperation, or an apology that is commanded by sympathy. The compliance or follow through rate is much higher as compared to just addressing issues in an abstract, emotionless manner.

Many books about storytelling in business or storytelling in leadership become boring upon reading although the main skill it addresses is storytelling which is ironic. Anyway, what I noticed missing and really focused on in those books I studied are two things. First, the Types of Stories according to its usage for each and every different situation like stories for motivating people to act, stories that aim to inculcate values, etc. Second, Stories that Occupy / Activate (all my) Mirror Neurons, grabbing my whole attention and infiltrating my senses and emotions. And that is what I found rare in many of the books and lectures in my research (except for a chosen few, of course). I realized that the skill of storytelling to influence requires a lot refinement, focus, training, and continuous observation in order to build a personal model of storytelling that serve my if not the purpose. Storytelling is a scarce skill that demands that you to become the one to invent and develop various tactics to influence others.

The speeches and talks that I delivered which had a very powerful influence on people were the ones with stories whether I created myself or real events that happened to me or others. Maybe experiencing the events of the story and actually being immersed in it is what gave the story that extraordinary power and made it a vehicle for me to deliver an incredible message. Adding body gestures and facial expressions which tend to intensify power in the process of narration captures the emotions of the audience converging to your own. If you get to reconcile and merge various elements from choosing the right story to tell and drafting it well and delivering it the best you could, you will then get unbelievable results. Results which may come later when you receive a call some days, week, month or even years from people you do not know professing that the story you told helped them to get low to high, from failure to success, from death to life.

Zulu Echo 5

In the early 90s, our local media broadcasting bought several documentaries showing the natural habitat of sea creatures, worlds in different planets and animals in the forest. It began as very interesting TV shows showing the day to day interactions between animals which was a new thing to most people particularly urbanites which spiked viewership of such shows at that time. Although the new concept those programs presented were very relevant, people quickly got bored with the content and viewership went down as it did in my country. So a revision was needed and many production companies hired marketing consultants to find the best way to increase if not regain lost viewership.

BBC and Nat Geo are two of the most influential networks in the early 20th century. These two media moguls have a vast reach. They produce high quality documentaries. No wonder we see scientists, psychiatrists, neurologists, sociologists, statisticians among many others working in different teams for different productions. All work, sometimes, in single frame to find the best way to explain and thereby grab attention and excite viewers in their broadcast. From the cinematography to the musical score, everything is interwoven within the show which may seem trivial to the viewers but those details had passed scrutiny and deliberation by a group of professionals who approve what is to be shown or omitted all for the sake of keeping viewers interested if not engrossed.

The efforts paid off. Viewers returned to their couches watching the programs of animals on land and the deep oceans only this time with unprecedented viewer ratings since the invention of television. And the sheer volume of viewership escalated to unforeseen figures. Definitely, cinematography and camera trickery and technique in shooting was employed and many other suspense and thrilling elements contributed to the success but the content and subjects were the same and unadulterated – unrehearsed and unchoreographed. But, in my opinion, the main reason for the breakthrough success of the programs can be credited to employing a very old technique in a fairly new genre. It is the way which made millions of viewers all around the world forget the old productions of animal shows, but those same millions kept recalling it today: *Zulu Echo 5* & *Foxtrot 1*.

The show began as an ordinary animal documentary, the title was "Crossing the Deadly Mara River". Mara River passes through three countries: Uganda, Kenya and Tanzania. The documentary began with herds migrating from the dry south to the rainy north. Animals travel the great distance to reach the dense pasture and flowing waters from Tanzania to Uganda. The deep voice of the narrator explains the setting and necessity of the migration which occurs twice a year from south to north and back when the seasons change. The trip is full of danger because of the distance and the predators along the way of the migration. Technology heightens nostalgia and a touch of suspense with cameras mounted on drones which allows a spectacular aerial shot of the herds spread hundreds of meters across the marvelous land. Cameras mounted on small electric cars capture the herds from ground level shots of running hooves and paws which are quite arduous for cameramen.

The narrator tells each event in an engaging fashion leading the viewers to a herd of zebras with an amazing color of black and white stripes under the sun. It is here where the plot takes an interesting turn by singling a certain zebra called Zulu Echo 5. The narration focuses on Zulu whether it would reach the northern boundary of the Mara River or end up being killed and eaten by one of the many predators in the journey. The viewers shift from just following the herds in general to focusing on Zulu, from a general compassion of the hardship of the animals to a specific sympathy for Zulu. Emotions escalate with the addition of one more player, Foxtrot 1, the little foal of Zulu looking too small and meager for such a dangerous but necessary journey because if its mother abandons it or dies along the way, none of the other zebras will breastfeed it and death will be the only option left whether from starvation or the jaws of the predators.

The cameras shift from the migrating herds and Zulu and Foxtrot. Then the escalation of events begins in a very intriguing way, exactly as what Joseph Campbell mentioned in his book "Hero's Journey" which we will tackle later on. The herds had traveled a long distance and reached a lake. They gather at the banks sipping the water when all of a sudden a huge crocodile emerges from the water opening its giant jaws and bites the head of one of the zebras. It drags its prey to the deepest part of the lake drowning it. The herds look on to what is depicted as a bloody and horrifying scene but at the same time, cameras also record Zulu and Foxtrot. The cameras capture mixed reactions of wanting and hesitation to drink. The narrator tries to interpret what is going on in the minds of the zebras as if learned in the language of zebras. Shall they continue drinking and subject themselves to the danger or shall they move on and risk dehydration?

The herds reach an open area to spend the night. At about midnight, lions and a pack of hyena approach and attack the herds. Another killing and blood shedding takes place. The massacre does not end till dawn. The camera finds Zulu and Foxtrot who were among the fortunate zebras to escape the carnage of the previous evening. The journey continues to the northern banks of the Mara River. If the herds safely cross, all suffering would end and life begins anew full of hope and renewed energy. But all the other herds' suffering cannot be compared to what the zebras will have to face at Mara River. Hundreds of hungry crocodiles prepare for this migration twice a year. This day they will not hunt but rather store for the coming months. A crocodile will drown a zebra one after another. Today is the great carnage. Zulu has had enough experience to know how to go through but Foxtrot only has its instincts.

The zebra herd lines up at the riverbank in a spectacle that resembles Middle Ages battle phalanx while the crocodiles with bobbed heads patrol the waters waiting for the first zebra to cross. The scene, quiet but heavy in a moment of silence till the bravest and the most miserable zebra decides to be the first one to break the silence and jump into the water. The first zebra swam slowly to the opposite bank at least a hundred meters away which seem much farther. Although the scene intensely thrilling, the camera turns toward Zulu and Foxtrot for viewers to observe while both look on as one of their kind is about to disappear under the water for good. Crocodiles slowly approach the crossing zebra as it nears the other side of the bank. Then one of the crocodiles opens its jaws to catch the zebra but in a fraction of a second, the zebra escapes the deathly grip and with exquisite movement, kicks the crocodile in the head and kicks at the mud on the river's bank in order jump off and walk safely on the other side. A moment of triumph and rejoicing – the zebras, narrator and the millions of viewers heave a sigh of relief! Women shed tears of happiness – a happiness for the survival of the brave and fortunate zebra.

But the moment is fleeting and eyes go back to the two heroes that, instinctively, join the herd and jump into the Mara River! And now zebras jump into the water as crocodiles begin swooping on zebras' necks and do the death roll. The epic scene is filled with blood and drowning and survival of zebras that successfully waded to the other side. In the chaos, the cameras lose sight of Zulu and Foxtrot. Are both lying deep at the bed of the river, lifeless and torn to shreds or did they make it across?

Foxtrot emerges from amongst the herd still in the water and swiftly jumps to the bank fleeing from an open jaw of a huge crocodile but the riverbank is about three meters of mud just before hard and dry land and only big zebras can pass the clay obstacle with effort. Those trapped could still be attacked by the crocodiles. Foxtrot exerts maximum effort to wade through muddy obstacle. The narrator adds more gravity to the situation commenting "little zebras get fatigued easily and quit moving just waiting – for death." For sure millions of viewers around the world like me and exclaimed in excitement at the narrator, "Shut up! You stupid narrator! Go! Foxtrot, try one more step… please!"

In those critical seconds, all zebras that survived crossing had made it to the flat land but Foxtrot still trapped within the mud wall. The water surface is broken by a couple of crocodiles from different corners going toward Foxtrot. The tempo of the soundtrack picks up and millions of viewers hold their breath hoping the narrator does not spoil it for Foxtrot. Foxtrot tries to climb out the mud blocks but falls on its back near the water's edge as the crocodiles approach its exhausted little body almost in the water. Suddenly Foxtrot jerks. It appears that he made an oath that day not to end up as meal inside a croc's stomach. He stands up and instinctively runs to the shallow part of the muddy bank and leaps with all the power he had left but a croc reaches the muddy edge with jaws wide open ready to snag the leaping Foxtrot as soon as it lands and within seconds, Foxtrot is falling, but not in the jaws of the crocodile. Rather, he falls on the flat and dry land. And the soundtrack calms down. Feeling hungry, thirsty and helpless but most importantly alive, the young Foxtrot portrayed the climax of the story in the best way ever that even Gustav Freytag could have imagined. Sorry, we shall discuss it later.

Foxtrot rejoins the herd waiting peacefully on the other side. He looks for his mother, Zulu. The cameras, the narrator and viewers all search with him. Foxtrot begins braying to his mother. The narrator adds, "Foxtrot has not fully survived yet. Maybe he will die in the herd in a couple of hours if he doesn't find his mom to feed him because…" (In that moment, I believe that for sure they fired the narrator.)

The scene cuts to a drone hovering focusing on a fresh carcass of a zebra lying on the grass. The controller of the drone says on the monitor, "It seems to be the carcass of Zulu. Over." Another responds, "Approach the carcass and verify." The camera draws near the carcass and circles it then announces, "Negative. Over."

Suddenly, the herd diverges showing a beautiful zebra running from a distance to the source of the braying. Yes, it is Zulu! Both caress each other feeling extremely happy for their survival as they continue walking toward north safe and secure. The episode ends up with a scene of the herd walking in the direction of sunset continuing their journey while Zulu and Foxtrot follow behind once in a while glancing back to the Mara River as if knowing they will cross it again soon. But for now, both have long months ahead to live and for other adventures. Yes, it's a tough life, where the survival is always for the fittest but Foxtrot will grow bigger and stronger and maybe his mom will die before the next migration but no one is certain. Zulu and Foxtrot are lost in the herd just as their memory except their special names – tags really... Zulu Echo 5 and Foxtrot 1.

I believe there is no need to explain any further how this particular documentary has succeeded to gain millions of dollars in revenue. The migration of animal herds has been covered hundreds of times in old documentary films but once it took the shape of a story; where the focus was on certain characters possessing special names, with a tight familial relationship, adding to it a well-crafted narration, motivated viewership. Waiting to know the fate of the zebra mother and her son, although they are like any other zebra in the herd, makes it special because of the magic of the story that enriched the scene and made it more vivid and unforgettable.

N.B.

The mother zebra and her son were traced by electronic GPS chips, and finally, they received the sad news. Zulu Echo 5 has died.

Complex Sciences

"Perceive science as an art, and perceive art as a science"

-Anonymous

I read that quote in my childhood and it implanted in my mind because, in my opinion, it is very succinct. Although I do not recall the author, maybe Da Vinci, still the words are concise to direct one who swims in the ocean of science to notice the its artistic perspective. At first glance, complicated and difficult but by viewing it as an art, it becomes enticing to the senses – attractive even. The same for artists, they have to look at the scientific aspect of (their) art to have a more realistic or pragmatic view which enriches (their) art. Once Albert Einstein said, "If you can't explain it to a six-year-old, you don't understand it yourself". Einstein had that balance between art and science as he was both a physicist and a violinist. By staying in the middle of both disciplines, he could reach with his imagination much further than any other scientist in his time coming up with the Theory of Relativity, although he did not even step into a laboratory while working on it.

Richard Feynman, a noble laureate in physics was called The Great Explainer, because his lectures in physics inspired millions around the world. He contributed to change people's perception about science as something complicated to perceive to something simple, pleasurable, challenging but full of excitement and still full of the moments of surprise, dazzle, laughter and joy. The way Feynman explains natural phenomenon leads the listener to envision a very simple picture for such phenomenon like how the atoms of Oxygen would have a tendency to stick to carbon atoms and when those two atoms adhere, they jiggle and dance. And when with enough temperature, more atoms join the party and adhere to them. At that point, disaster happens – fire. This is the way fire ignites.

Scientists and lecturers exhausted themselves and bored students and audiences trying to explain the Theory of Relativity till Einstein explained it in the simplest and clearest way. He projected it by describing someone sitting with another person who is a good conversationalist and after, the first person would ask how come time went by quickly while, when sitting with a boring conversationalist, minutes pass like hours. Feynman and Einstein were among the smart people who found the missing link between science and people's perception and that is projection! Being able to project the hard, the vague and the abstract (subject) on another plain which is clear and easy is exactly like projecting atoms and chemical substance on a glass slide as it is so that any eyes that look into the microscope will see if not understand the nature of the substance being projected. Sciences like physics, mathematics, quantum mechanics and many others are not complicated by nature rather the true complication is the inability to project it in a manner simple and easy to be understood. That is why the one who could project these sciences in a manner ordinary people would understand deserves to be called a scientist because of the awareness of the nature of a particular branch of science.

Mathematics in its nature is nothing but natural and physical phenomenon that have been projected on a piece of paper with symbols. So many teachers failed to let their students appreciate math because they lack one more phase – that of projection. Projection transfers / transcends these vague symbols into something people in general or students in this case would understand and enticed with. I used to go to different schools and conduct interviews with some of the best math students. I ask various questions like what is the purpose of studying math and what does differentiation and integration mean? Answers were shocking because no one knew what those things meant although they had an exceptional ability to solve equations of differentiation and integration and they even got top scores in exams! But still they could not see beyond theory. They actually turned to robots walking in a predictable and predetermined path. What shocked me more was the fact that they didn't know the definition *Function*, meant. None of those exceptional students who were about to enter university was able to define function and its practical application. The last question which I thought was unimportant to ask, after my disappointment, was if the students even liked math. How can I expect any of them to like something they never understood and could not decide what to do with it in professional or personal life.

Those students were not dumb, on the contrary, they were the cream of the crop but what they really missed was the projection of that unknown and vague in mathematics to what they know, taste and even like – to what they were familiar with. We invited those students to watch a cartoon video narrating a nice story. It was a scene in a factory that produces processed meat where the cow is put on a conveyor. It enters the factory and then it comes out in cans at the other end. Another cow enters but it goes out as it is – still a living cow. A sign appears on the screen reading the machines are switched off, thus $X = Y$. Another cow enters but this time two cows come out. Another sign appears on the screen, $X = 2Y$ and so on till the end of the short movie. Afterward, we asked the students again, what a function is. And this time, we got answers, answers we were expecting – different answers than before. For the first time in the life of those students, they could give an answer to such questions. And step by step, the students began to look at mathematics with a different perspective. This experiment was a vivid example for students who missed the value of projection, and once presented to them, so the facts reveal, science took a different shape and taste which its recipients can distinguish, enjoy and even crave.

Handful of Hormones

The goal of any living person is to satisfy his Lord, and then to satisfy himself, quenching his desires, and seek to feel happy and fulfilled, also to be away from pain and misery. With the advancement of science, researchers discovered the hormones responsible of stimulating emotions. In his renowned book, *Leaders Eat Last,* Simon Sinek speaks about four major hormones, which cause human beings to feel good, and they are Endorphin, Dopamine, Serotonin, and Oxytocin. The Endorphin is the hormone responsible to block feeling pain when you exert physical activity, so the more you exceed your body limits, the more it numbs the body feelings, so to feel less exhaustion. Then the dopamine, which is the hormone of ecstasy and satisfaction of what has been done, it's the hormone which for its sake, project managers invented what is so called *Milestones,* the worker who removes from his To-Do-List what he has done in his daily working routines, by doing so, he seeks more secretion of dopamine to flow in his blood so to feel fulfilled for doing more steps ahead even if it's a fraction of a step. Therefore, we always listen to those Life Strategists advice people to write down their goals, and to keep staring at them from time to time, also management consultants usually advice companies to state clearly vision, mission, and strategy, so everybody in the organization can see and embrace. Jack Welch the former CEO of General Electric used to focus on making the companies vision memorable by every single worker in the organization. (13)

It seems that the experience of those people made it clear for them that visual goals area a must to increase motifs to achieve those goals - in another meaning, those visual are the means to force Endocrines to brings more drops of dopamine that push humans to get his tasks done. That's why the outstanding speech I have a dream of Luther King had the biggest effect to let millions feel to the secretion of dopamine that pushed the entire American society for a true change in the human right issue. Repeating the phrase *I have a dream,* that were placed in various contexts, like mentioning that he has a dream of seeing colored kids playing with white kids, that he would see discrimination is disappeared from the entire US. The repetition of this phrase had a notable effect to transmit those words into a visual picture, each listener would visualize, and finally results of a feeling fulfilled. Personally, I couldn't get done writing this book if I didn't divided to very tiny parts, and making sure to mark with bold yellow on the title of each section I finish writing, if not so, those fingers wouldn't be able to keep writing, rather going away and obeying system 1 to scroll in some social media websites that that doesn't consume much of the brain energy, and doesn't call for hormones secretion.

Then, it comes the hormone of Serotonin, it's the hormone of pride, dignity, and sense of self, it's the hormone that pops out after four or five years of university study, at the moment of getting your graduation title, it's the hormone that makes you feel happy when someone praise the work you did late night at office. Then, it's Oxytocin, it's the hormone of love and sympathy which flows out when facing a situation that stimulates your positive emotions, and this a very beneficial hormone for the body organism, so many physicians advice people to exchange hugs and physical touching so to stimulate the secretion of that hormone. Finally, the Cortisol, and this hormone is at the opposite side of the other four happy hormones, it's the hormone of anxiety, tension, and worry that takes place in the sad and dangerous moments, and it's a quite harmful hormone for the body, so the people gets tensioned a lot usually suffer from a set of diseases, beginning from high blood pressure to diabetes, and heart attacks.

There are lots of other hormones that contribute the stimulation of various emotions to the human being, like the Testosterone which is responsible of the feelings of vitality and vigor, and there's the Adrenaline that pops out from a glandular that is situated above the kidneys, and it's the hormone that turns the ordinary person to a superman with exceptional physical ability when he feels a threat looms over.

Now, I expect the majority who read all this brief about hormones would ask what it has to do with the story. So, here we strongly confirm that the unforgettable story that was narrated for tens of years is the story that made a success to pop out as many hormones, especially the ones related with happiness. In one experiment, they brought sets of participant and they put on their heads fMRI sensors, then they played to them a visual story of a child and his dad playing around, while the voice of the narrator mentions the warm relationship between both, and the happiness of the son that his father share with him a time to play, while the father doesn't feel inside the same happiness, because his son has a cancer, late stage, and most probably, he'll not live for long, maximum six month.

While participants were listening to that story, they watched cartoon images of son and father, so fMRI scans detected more secretion of Oxytocin and Cortisol in the brains of the participants. The Oxytocin was a result of the demonstration and empathy of the father toward his son, while the Cortisol was due to the dramatic change in the events, from the normal and ordinary scene to the sudden shock knowing the disease of the son .(14)

So, when they showed the same movie for another set pof participants, but this item, it only contained the first part of playing togther father and son, without mentioning about nthe disease, so they detected no secretion of any kind of hormones, whether Oxytocin or Cortisol. It meant that, even when the scene is happy and cheerful, it still not enough to stimulate emotions, there must be a problem, crisis, turn that can stimulate emotions and pops out hormones. It seems that the amount of hormones produced depends of the story plot, it's a proportional relationshimp, the more the story is powerful and influential, the more hormones comes out wether the story is about happiness, tragedy, thrilling, or even comedy.

Science revealed a very tiny discovery of hormones and their sources, still reasearches hve many work to do to reach conclusions about a precise measurmnet of the influence of each elemnt of external stimuls on the increase of specific hormone secretion. In the next couple of years, we would witness some studies that discuss the use of some visual aids, acoustics, phrases, and body gestures that all contribute to pop out a certain hormone.

Now, you may change your view about the naivety of the people who adore attending horror movies, where they jump off their seats out of fear, whoever seeks to watch those kinds of movies become gradually addicted to high doses of Adrenaline, which acts later on as burden on the health of people, because this specific hormone was designed to pop out at critical times and not most of the times. Also, one main reason people addict to drugs and Nicotine is because of the addiction of the dopamine. Marijuana and Hash deliver a high sense of happiness and tranquility for the abuser, as consequence of that, all the cheerful events wouldn't let him feel happy like straight people, because the amount of dopamine those nice events has aren't reaching the threshold of the dopamine amount he gets when is high, so all cheerful event wouldn't move his cheeks to smile or to feel nice. Some ladies also got addicted to the Cortisol, she always needs more of it, so ladies hunt those moments when their husbands come home tired at night as he represents for her the riches source of Cortisol, so she would begin reminding him late night of all the tragedies they have faced and may face and may not ever face.

Although the hormone of Cortisol isn't [referable to many, yet it still a very effective element in the good stories, because if there is no problem, so there is no story, and the problem means stress and anxiety that should be transmitted to the audience, and the griever the problem the heavier the stress. So, by presenting the company's history and showing the richness of their portfolio along with mentioning its pitfalls and finishing with overcoming those obstacles, so this is well-crafter business story that pops out various types of hormones, from the Cortisol that pushed the audience to feel momentary agony and pain that is followed with empathy and satisfaction.

The Chess Manager

When we were working on Manager-X program, we wanted to introduce through sets of articles and videos, but one of the difficulties was how to summarize this new and different training program to their target customers, especially that training aimed to solve a notable problem that many organization suffer from, which is the good selection of the qualified manager and to developed his skills progressively, so we had to choose attentively a good way and strong words that grab attention to the problem that Manager-X solves, and after researching many articles that address the topic of managers and how they add value to the organizations, we found a very brilliant article in HBR with the title *What Great Managers Do,* written by, *Marcus Buckingham,* so the first article of Manager-X series had no option but to quote the words of that brilliant author,

Manager-X: The Difference between the Talented & the Mediocre Manager

A manager role remains as one of the most sophisticated jobs at any organization, mainly because of the ambiguous needs such job necessitates, to the wide varieties of skills a manager should have. But, what makes the job more and more complicated is the unclear job description and unclear goals demanded from that manager. Some organizations would associate the manager's success with a mere increase in profits, but profits might get increased due to other factors where the manager performance wasn't a direct cause of it, rather he/she had an obvious awful performance that lead to less profits. In another cases the success of a human resource manager would be associated with lower rates of staff turnover, but with deep investigation, they may find out that the sudden depression that affected an entire industry was the real reason the staff stick more to their jobs as less offers they get and more instability emerges. Finally, the performance of a sales manager would be measured by a certain target of annual sales, and this might happen at the short timeframe, and after though it's revealed that such increase in sales was due to some illegal transactions and unethical agreements, that finally will lead to a significant drop in sales at the long timeframe.

Hence, what qualities a manager should have so he/she would grant sustainable results for his/her department and for the organization as a whole? And what are those crucial skills that qualified that particular person to be titled as a manager?

When observing the main traits of the two managers, the brilliant and the mediocre one, it won't be quite easy to snatch a certain repetitive pattern that distinguishes both of them. The brilliant manager would attribute his peak performance due to using some sort of complex algorithms while making important decisions. But the mediocre manager might know and use the same algorithms but still not achieving good results. The inability of controlling emotions is one prominent trait of a mediocre manager, rather the brilliant manager sometimes fail to control his/her emotions. The brilliant manager is someone who got a piercing insight of the possible future changes, while many mediocre managers may have the same unique insight, but they couldn't adapt to changes, and finally scored poor results.

Therefore, attributing success or failure in management based one or two elements wouldn't be a very accurate thing to do. That's why the best analogy that differentiates between the brilliant and the mediocre manager that I've ever encountered was the analogy made by Marcus Buckingham, in his book, "First, Break All The Rules: What the World's Greatest Managers Do Differently" and that was also mentioned in his article that was published in Harvard Business Review titled "What Great Managers Do", where he gave an example of the mediocre manager as a checkers player, where he sees all his pieces (team) as a one thing, having the same capabilities and with no difference in qualities or traits, he moves all of them the same way, he got very few strategic options to implement as many of them are already known and practiced and have never been altered or developed .(15)

While the brilliant manager is a chess player, he deals with each piece he has as a very unique piece. He knows that each of them has both, a point of strength and weakness. He knows well that the most vulnerable piece can cause a marvelous advancement because of its good positioning, while he also believes that defeat can be a cause of one of the strongest pieces he has, but is located at the worst possible position. He knows that checkmate is neither a coincidence nor a fate, but a series of smart moves and accumulated small winnings that the opponent couldn't expect or deal with. The various scenarios of the next move of pieces would exceed a probability of fifty thousand different moves. A professional chess player thinks attentively in successive moves and sets up a separate scenario for the consequences of each, all simultaneously inside his mind, and finally, he alters his main strategy according to the current situation maybe more than once during the same game.

The traits of a chess player is a very close analogy to the traits of a brilliant manager that his subordinates would feel his influence during the shortest time frame, but so few would grasp the source of his faculties that made him that brilliant manager. This type of a manager uses multidisciplinary approaches to tackle the problems he faces. He masters various skills that all combined work in synchronize to create an awesome management style that leads to awesome results. That kind of managers acts like the symbol x, in mathematics, where as many of variables and equations mingle together till finally finding out the true value of x, that solves the dilemma. The brilliant manager is the one who can master all those variables, equations and rules so to turn all the complex problems into a great and optimal solution. Only thus, such a person deserves to be titled, Manager-X.

*****

To resemble the good and weak managers with checkers and chess players is one of the best projections that expose meanings and clarifying visions. So, to project meanings on various dimensions isn't an easy mission, it requires contemplation, reflection, and testing for more than one time, so to result in a projection that is similar to the one made by *Marcus Buckingham,* that thousands around the world read and kept it clinging in their memories.

The main power of projection is that it drifts away the attention of the listener or the reader from his current dimension to other one, from a narrow space to a wider one, from vagueness to clarity. The role of a manager is one of the most sophisticated roles in any organizations, many wouldn't understand for which reason that made that manager to get all this salary that overweighs his subordinates, even some managers don't have the ability to describe their role in simple phrases, except few who already have a special talent that should exist in any manager, which is the ability to let his subordinates to understand and perceive what goes inside their manager's head, in another word, he is the manager who is expert in projection.

When one of HP junior executives fidgeted from their new CEO who earns lots of cash, so he dared to ask him why he would earn all that amount, while he and his colleagues are the people who got the majority of the work burden, while his CEO wears the best tuxedos, setting in a luxurious office, travelling in first class. The CEO had to prove to that junior executive the true value of his role in the company, so it was just one phrase that made a great echoing in the entire company as he seemed to master the art of projection, so he said, *"If you screw up, you lose your job, but if you screw up several thousand people lose their jobs"*

The Best in Influence

One of the many traits given to human beings is the instinct to continuously evolve and the active pursuit to reach the top – surpass it even which man has done repeatedly. He always seeks to go higher and beyond. Man is not considered normal if he does not seek to want more of what he has whether be it money, knowledge or pleasure. That is why people have a drive within to best or surpass someone who has set a record or did something no one has done before. Therefore, published works that try to rank the best of anything have a wide reach. Take for example the work of *Michael Hart*, "The 100: A Ranking of The Most Influential Persons In History", which piqued people's curiosity. (16) Also, curiosity drove many to search for the most influential books in human history, so an author like *Martin Seymour*, wrote a book with the title, "100 Most Influential Books Ever Written", where he tried to classify books according to the substantial ideological change it had on readers. (17)

Although there are quite variety of these kinds of books, we find that authors have commonly chosen books that have made radical impact on human intellect. A book by *Nicolaus Copernicus* "On the Revolutions of Heavenly Spheres" which sparked a revolution in the Roman Catholic church which believed the earth is the center of the universe. Works like "Principia" by *Isaac Newton*, "The Origin of Species" by *Charles Darwin*, "The Prince" by *Machiavelli*, which contain many political views, "The Interpretations of Dreams" by *Sigmund Freud*, "The Muqaddimah" by *Ibn Khaldun*, which formed a basis for social science and "The Wealth of Nations" by *Adam Smith*, which stated the theory of the modern economy, wherein he called for the withdrawal of the state from controlling the economy and leaving it to balance itself by the factors of supply and demand have, in more ways than we can surmise, influenced the world of today.

When I went through the lists for the first time I was surprised. The majority of the books that influenced the masses and led to a change in perceptions, habits and laws were not scientific, political or sociological; rather these were novels – historical narratives about people and nations. Stories, in a variety lists, constituted more than 80% and still in other lists about 40 books out of 50 were purely stories.

In the east, Russian novels like "War and Peace" by *Tolstoy* played an important role in influencing the Bolshevik Revolution and it became one the finest novels in the entire history that presented the lifestyle of Tsarist Russia with the historical background of the Napoleon invasion. "Ana Karenina" also by *Tolstoy* and "Crime and Punishment" by *Dostoyevsky* presented a special view of good and evil and how the criminal perceives them.

Still in the east, "One Thousand and One Nights" and "Kalila and Demna" are like two shining stars in the history of novel that reflect the mystery of that part of the world. The novel, "The Improvement of Human Reason: Exhibited in the Life of Hai Ebn Yokdhan" by *Ebn Tophail* discussed in a fictitious adventure the meaning of God, monotheism and the natural instinct of human beings to believe in the one God. "Kitab al-Aghani: The Book of Songs" by *Al-Isbahani* took from its author fifty years contained a huge number of stories and news of that epoch.

European literature contributed more than its ample share even if we only count the Renaissance and the Industrial Revolution periods. "Les Misérables" by *Victor Hugo* depicted the contrast of the rich and the poor prior to the rise of the bourgeois and the French Revolution, "The Count of Monte Cristo" by *Alexandre Dumas* highlighted concepts of injustice, revenge and vengeance. The works of *William Shakespeare* such as "Hamlet", "Othello", "King Lear" and "Macbeth" offered societal criticisms. *Charles Dickens's* "A Tale of Two Cities" sold more two hundred million copies worldwide reaching and influencing many readers. The thriller novels by *Agatha*

Christie like "And Then There Were None" which sold more than hundred million copies since its first publication in 1937 has far-reaching consequences. *George Orwell's,* "Animal Farm" is still relevant. "Harry Potter" series by *JK Rowling* has become a franchise to be reckoned with.

Then the new world in the west shared great novels that influenced both sides of the Atlantic. "Hundred Years of Solitude" by *Gabriel García Márquez,* and "Love in The Time of Cholera", also "The Alchemist" by *Paulo Coelho,* which was translated to more than 69 languages offer insights to the human psyche. "Uncle Tom's Cabin" by *Harriet Stowe* had a huge influence in the initiation of the American Civil War by raising the issue of slavery and the sufferings of slaves in the form of a story that we will mention about it later on. Finally, "The Da Vinci Code", "Inferno" and "Angels and Demons" by *Dan Brown* made millions of sales around the world offering a new take on conspiracy theory on the Catholic church.

Moreover, books on biography have a high ranking in book sales. A most recent addition is the biography of *Steve Jobs,* the founder of Apple. All this shows the nature of human beings to gravitate toward stories. People look to stories. They escape the midst of the grind – from "everyday" reality through stories. And as presented, major social and political changes were paved by stories that projected the misery of that juncture in time on ink and paper hoping ignite action among the people. It had been said that revolutions begin in hearts and minds first. Those same hearts and minds require motivation to move toward change. That motivation must be disguised so as to delve into the sick hearts and the rusted minds to cure it and reignite passion to evolve. That is why stories represented a source of fear and anxiety for many corrupt regimes that already know that just one good novel is enough to defeat all their propaganda. Therefore, many of those authors were subjected to subjugation – jail time, exile and even assassination. Still others were seduced with money and power so as to employ their stories to the benefit of the ruler and to distract the attention of the people away from the cause of their sufferings.

Stories may have significant influence to change the course of history but still stories and anecdotes do offer a vital importance in our daily routine. Storytelling can change the way we manage our businesses in certain if not all aspects. And the second millennium holds many signs of that rising trend. The endeavor to get funding for budding ideas, inventions and projects may end in success by a strategic or well-placed anecdote in the presentation that project the same values as the investors. Now products and services present their own stories if not testimonials of loyal or even new customers on social (over the internet) or traditional media narrating the benefits of such product or service over another. Nowadays, keeping skillful and experienced and trained employees is one of the crucial tasks of a successful organization. This necessitated the development of the skill of storytelling for top management in order to spread an atmosphere of compassion and understanding within the company while continually driving the mission and vision to the hearts and minds of employees.

History and the present have proved that the story is the centerpiece of change. It is that drop of water that ripples the stagnant pond and turns it into a raging ocean. And the future will prove that the story is main drive for the development of ideas and the evolving of values from one generation to another.

A Step Back

One of the toughest moments I have ever faced in my life was when I was in great need of money because my child fell ill and if I could not pay for the treatment soon, I would lose him in a couple of months. It was no help that I had a serious financial problem during that time and so on a daily basis, my wife and I revised, calculated and revised our financial plan thinking of ways to pay our arrears in addition to the house expenses that never end. One day I was so engrossed in my work while at the same time thinking of ways can I do to save my family from this predicament. It would take a miracle that solve my situation. A miracle has never happened to me but it is about time for such a miracle. All of a sudden, a loud crash jolted me from my thoughts and rushed to the window. There I saw my colleague's car crashed with another one and from the looks it, no one would survive the accident.

Everybody rushed out heading to the scene hoping to save anyone involved in the crash and so I hastened out of my office located on the 10th floor and ran to the corridor. I passed by the accounting office which was completely empty. The devil did not waste a fraction of a second to tempt me out of my would be chivalrous act and divert my attention from lending a hand to our colleagues to stepping into the deserted accounting office with an open safe due to the commotion at the crash site.

I stepped into the deserted office and carefully shut the door behind me. I approached the safe and opened its door and began to take as much cash as I can in bundles and stuff it into the pockets of my jacket. While I was doing so I turned my head to the left and it was like a thunderstorm inside my head as I saw the guy in charge of the safe standing by the window, stunned and staring at me. In my heedlessness I did not notice that he was standing few meters away from the opened safe didn't leave the office like the others. Those next seconds passed like days while the man's eyes were fixed at my hands holding money that I did not own. He looked me straight in the eyes and it was as if he was talking in his silence, blaming in his silence and scolding me in his silence for my treachery. All of a sudden, his facial expression altered from surprise to anger and wrath. He turned his head to the window. I realized that once he screams, it would be my end. And so, with no other thought and with no other way out, I rushed toward him in the speed of light and I did what I never thought I would do in my entire life.

Yes, I pushed my friend Sam out of the window with the all the power I had and within seconds, he hit the ground with a horrific and macabre thud. I concealed myself below the window and crawled out of the office and the building. All the way back to my home, my tears flowed. I was looking at my hands I could not believe how I took an innocent life and stole money. My entire life, even in extreme poverty, I never stole a morsel and yet here I was with an act which entails putting my neck in the gallows. Anything that would save the life of my child is the only cause and justification I shall present to my Lord so he may forgive my sin.

Those awful thoughts kept looming in my mind till I stepped into the entrance of my building. I slowly went upstairs and found the door of our apartment wide open and surprisingly I saw many of our neighbors inside. I rushed inside and found my wife wailing at the doorstep of our son's room. Involuntarily, I dropped all the money in my hand and stepped over it while I approached my son's room filled with anxiety and fear.

I kissed my son and closed his eyes. I wiped his face from my tears that filled his cheeks. And in my grief of this tragedy, I heard a sound that I have never heard so close to reality. It was the police siren. I listened for footsteps coming upstairs. I am finished, my son is finished and everything was finished because of my stupid act. I gained nothing out of it except shame and more misery. And while cops were heading to the apartment, I said to myself, "*I have to end all this stupidity right now...*" An officer barged into the room with his arms stretched out to accost me but before he could do it within few centimeters, I ran toward the half-opened window, and jumped off, smashing its gla...

It seemed I was swimming heading to the ground. I saw my little son lying on the ground with a bloody face and a wide open mouth. As I fell towards him, I noticed his sharp teeth looking that of a hungry shark awaiting for me to fall inside. It was as if my son was hitting me for the shame I inflicted on him and his mother. I kept falling and nearer and nearer I came to the mouth till...

I cried like never before. I shook tremendously on the cold floor I fell on. I stood up still weeping and I went back to my bed. I sat on it and cuddled my knees saying, *"Oh God! Protect me from doing evil and from dying the death of evil ones".* Then I prayed in the idleness of the night and I went back to a deep sleep.

****

This type of dream has been a recurring phenomenon throughout my life. Mostly I used to have awful nightmares but in the passing of time, I came to realize that these dreams become a strong and effective deterrent of evil acts which allows me to take a step back and reflect. Dreams like these are like full-fledged stories in themselves and although I appear to be the author, protagonist and somewhat the director of such dreams, I am only a watcher for that particular story. Even more strange, even as I watch the events unfold, I still am surprised and affected with tragic endings and conversely elated with the happy ones.

Dreams are nothing more than a story the mind stitches into a fabric while sleeping. Prophet Muhammad spoke about dreams and said, *"Dreams are of three types: one good dream which is a sort of good tidings from Allah; the evil dream which causes pain is from the Satan; and the third one is a suggestion of one's own mind"*

So, the dream fabricated by Satan is the one we always find to be ugly, meaningless and without value or lessons except anxiety and fright. And no human being misses or cherishes those kinds of dreams because Satan uses them as a tool to intimidate or discourage sons of Adam.

The other type of dream which in Arabic is called "Ro'ia" is a message from God that He sent to whoever He chose to glad tidings whether in this life or after, Such dreams come to people in some kind or form of a marvelous story yet ambiguous requiring some consultation with people of insight for its interpretation.

One of those Ro'ias is what Aisha, the wife of Prophet Muhammad, mentioned. In that dream, she saw three moons falling on her lap. The Prophet told her that three precious people on this earth will be buried in her room. And it became true. The Prophet and his two best companions were buried in Aisha's room.

Finally, the third dream is a story someone fabricated for himself in his sleep. It is the story that a person uses to escape from the miserable and harsh realities of his life. Those who suffer psychological pains and on the verge of depression because of a hard truth they cannot deal with and so they prefer to sleep for longer hours – sometimes for half day. In reality it is not always because of laziness, rather it is a conscious attempt to live out another story which is better and far removed from pain and intrigue. So people who are fed up with their real and harsh life become experts in fabricating stories as a way to cope and in their long sleep, they choose the life they want live, becoming the author of their stories and their lives.

Daydreams

Some studies were conducted to measure the total amount of time someone spends in the obscene, in other words, daydreaming. Researchers found that a person daydreams almost two thousand times a day, on average 14 seconds for each daydream. (18) While we walk, or sit, or while performing our jobs, we retreat and go into a different world where some story awaits us like thinking of another way we could have handled the last phone call we took – modifying and rectifying such scenario. A guy walks on the street and sees a certain girl on the sidewalk and so begins to weave story of a married life with this beautiful young lady and how she will get into a love spat with him over forgotten diapers for their newborn then quickly breaks out of his reverie when the girl passes by him. And begins anew.

We all have our favorite storylines when we daydream where we consciously make ourselves to be great heroes. Daydreams resemble sleeping dreams because it also serves as "a step back" we take. And we usually do this after experiencing something particular in our daily life – a situation we went through. Whether we were satisfied or otherwise about how we responded to it, we tend to rethink the situation and re-live it with several stories. And we dismiss daydreams as quickly as we started it if we find ourselves in a not so favorable scenario like a car crash. We leave it voluntarily if we find another story that grabs our attention. In those moments of boredom and idleness that strike your audience, daydreams are nothing but an intent to escape from a current story jumping to another one and you will not be able to bring them back to your realm unless you present a better story – a story that tops their daydreams bringing them back to your reality – your story.

Finally, the main reason why humans adore stories is because they daydream about one third of their lives but still those daydreams are quite dangerous for humans. Such daydreams in most cases are called heedlessness and delving into heedlessness is destructive for people's productivity as it wastes their lives and energy and the only cure for heedlessness is reflection – to reflect in what you witness and see permanently. Allah praised people who snatch themselves out of daydreams to reflect in the creation of God when he said in Quran

> *"Those who remember Allah while standing or sitting or [lying] on their sides and give thought to the creation of the heavens and the earth, [saying], "Our Lord, You did not create this aimlessly; exalted are You [above such a thing]; then protect us from the punishment of the Fire."*
>
> *Al-Imran 191*

So that discipline they made for themselves to reflect in God in all their states has sieged their daydreams and limited its adverse ramification.

The Camel Projection

One day a Bedouin came asking the Prophet for financial help. The Prophet gave the man something and asked, *"Have I been good to you?"* The Bedouin said, *"No, you have not and you have not done well."* The Muslims got angry and was about to do the Bedouin harm. The Prophet motioned his followers to hold off, got up and went into his house. He then called for the Bedouin to add something to his gift and asked, *"Have I been good to you?"* The Bedouin replied, *"Yes, may Allah repay you well in family and tribe."* The Prophet said, *"You said what you said and that angered my Companions. If you like, say what you said now in their presence so as to remove what they harbor in their breasts against you."* He replied, *"Yes."* They went out and the Prophet addressed his followers, *"This Bedouin said what he said and then we gave him more. He claims that he is content. Isn't that so?"* The Bedouin answered, *"Yes, may Allah repay you well in your family and tribe."* The Prophet said, *"The example of this man and mine is like a man who has a she-camel which escapes from him. The people chase it and they only drive it away farther. The owner calls to them to stay clear of him and his she-camel saying, 'I am more compassionate and better to it than you.' He goes in front of it, takes some clods and drives it back until it heels and kneels. He then saddles and mounts it. If I had given you permission when the man said what he said – if I had let you punish him, he would have entered the Fire."*

Desert life mostly is made up of tending to livestock and camels, in particular, are very essential if not indispensable creatures to desert inhabitants. The time a shepherd spends with his sheep or camels may exceed the time he spends with his family. Prophet Muhammad said, *"The tranquility is among the owners of goats and sheep, and pride and conceitedness is among the uncivil owners of the camels"*. So, it seems that the physiological traits of camels transfer it to their owners as is for the owners of goats and sheep. And because of their relatively small size, inherent quietness and tranquility transmit to their owners.

Prophet Muhammad once said, *"Allah is more pleased with the repentance of His believing servant than a person who loses his riding beast carrying food and drink. He sleeps (being disappointed of its recovery), then gets up and goes in search for that (riding beast) until he is stricken with thirst. He comes back to the place where he had been before and goes to sleep completely exhausted placing his head upon his hands waiting for death. When he gets up, before him his riding beast and provisions of food and drink. Allah is more pleased with the repentance of His servant than the recovery of this riding beast along with the provisions (of food and drink)."*

Such a projection is enough to release a good batch of dopamine for the Bedouins who hear this story. When you focus on the stories going around today, you'll find that many of them use transportation like cars, motorcycles and planes as a medium for projection as they can convey meanings efficiently. This kind of projection aids people in learning the kinesthetic skill of driving. Do you recall the first day of your driving lessons? The instructor began by going through a checklist of all the necessary steps; from adjusting both side mirrors as well as the rearview, how to hold the steering wheel, turning on the engine in neutral, putting your foot on the clutch pedal then engaging the first gear, releasing the clutch slowly while gradually stepping on the accelerator, finally driving from the parking lot to the curb. And while in the middle of all the things running in your head, switching your feet from clutch, gas and brakes not to mention minding the handbrakes, right and left signals and other cars which seemed quite easy to the instructor while all hell is breaking loose on your side of the seat!

Your brain and the pupils in your eyes get hotter and hotter moving at the speed of light while keeping track of the instructor's reminders. You are driving but you cannot focus on anything except holding the steering wheel tightly with both hands completely forgetting to check your rearview as you change lanes then the horrified shout from your instructor wakes you up because a car coming from behind almost crashed to your rear end.

And a whole year from your first lesson, you see yourself driving 100 kilometers an hour without a care – your right hand holding your cellphone texting, the left switching from the wheel and a meatball sandwich while your eyes dart to the rearview mirror to check the road behind and back to the road ahead until you reach your destination safely. The example above traces the path your brain takes while learning any skill for the first time. Take another example like learning a second language. At first your brain needs to activate (System 2) for a certain period in order to stimulate new neuron cells to function as memory cells for new vocabulary and grammar. And then you begin focusing on the synonyms, tenses and conjugation. Your brain then builds connections of millions of synapses carrying information of the new synonyms, tenses and conjugation and relates these with pictures or words of your native language or other things that may have a connection to be established. In the process, disruption and fatigue take place which results in boredom and sometimes despair but by the time you speak the second language fluently, disruption, fatigue, boredom and despair are becoming less if not gone. And you begin speaking the second language without overthinking. Another channel (System 1) is responsible for the transmission of the second language from your brain to your ears, tongue, mouth and hands therefore, you practice the language without any tiredness or restlessness. That is how the skill gradually goes through (System 2) which you endured the suffering of training and practice then goes into (System 1) where you actually enjoy results.

I've used this type of projection multiple times and each time I saw how audiences digested and enjoyed it because driving and learning a second language is something majority of people are doing more and more. Recalling the suffering of acquiring such skills and reminding the enjoyment after the ordeal causes the release of hormones that make stories like the two examples a meaningful projection that drives the listeners to be motivated and subsequently take action.

Tony Robbins is one of the few good motivational speakers who use stories in a natural way that induces emotions and leaves an impact. Maybe Tony has mastered all the techniques of storytelling that we will mention later on, and one of those impactful stories is what he narrated when he went to visit his friend, a racecar driver, who shared the secrets of driving racecars. So, Tony took the steering wheel and beside him sat his friend. Tony began driving at high speed on the racetrack. Tony's friend noticed that he was drifting near the concrete barrier and it was getting quite difficult for him to keep a straight path. Every time the car started to drift to the barrier which Tony feared he might crash in to, he focused on it in order to avoid it. Every time he did so, his friend harshly reminded him, *"Look at the road, not to barrier!"*. And whenever Tony came close to the barrier, his friend would warn him again and again. Finally, the ride was done and his friend told him, *"When your car drifts toward the concrete barrier, your natural reaction is to focus on it thinking you can avoid it by doing so. However, if you keep focusing in the area of your fear, you'll unconsciously move toward it. And your end will be there. Professional race drivers know too well that a driver drifts unconsciously to where he focuses, and because the life of race drivers are always on the verge, they ignore everything and focus solely on the racetrack."*

When Prophet Muhammad said, *"What do I have to do with the world! I am not in the world but as a rider seeking shade under a tree, then he catches his breath and leaves it"*. It had a very deep influence with his companions who knew very well the value of a tree a traveler, in the middle of a desert, finds. He can estimate the time he would spend under the shade before reaching the final destination. Every human and every time has its own camel which greatly influences it. As a storyteller, you have to bring that camel to surface and project on its hump whatever value and message you want to convey so that your story becomes an unforgettable experience to its listener.

Chapter Two
Types of Stories

Storytelling can be classified as short stories or anecdoetes that serves business issues, while long stories like legends and fairytales are more benefical for educational and entertainment purposes.(19)

THE STORYTELLING SPECTRUM

There are many classifications of stories. For example some classify stories according to plot and others classify depending on the ending whether happy, sad or mysterious. With so many possible classifications, it is therefore important to follow one in order to utilize it properly. The best way to do so is to set up a criteria that will aid in grouping stories. So, ask yourself. Why shall I tell my story? How shall I tell it? To whom shall I tell it? Who is the protagonist? How shall it end? Answering these questions will provide a clearer way to categorize your stories. Finally, place each story in each category and present it.

In this book, we won't go far as to classify narrative in its entirety. We won't touch upon novels, movies or commercials. We will concentrate on stories that take place in the workplace. We will limit the classification to stories that you may share in corporate or team meetings, your professional life – your daily grind in general. By asking yourself the purpose of your story will lead you to know the goal of such story, asking the way you narrate it will lead you to classify according to presentation and your question as to who will receive it will lead you to choose the right story for a particular audience ultimately serving your purpose.

With this we have four classifications for business stories: The Goal, The Source, The Path and The Display. What is the purpose of your story, which source your story will emerge, what path shall your story follow and lastly, by what means shall your story will be displayed or presented to your audience.

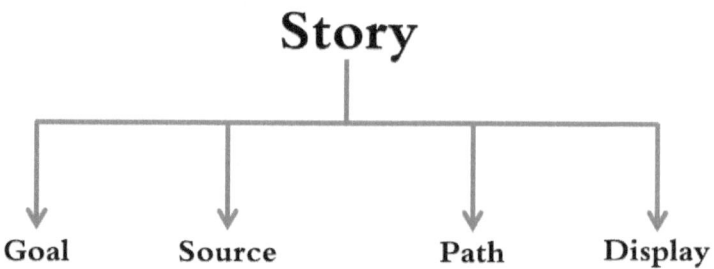

Upon finishing this section, you will be able to make a simple scheme filling it with a goal, a source, a path and a display. You will then come up with each story and projection that has been mentioned in this book and put it under a sub-category of each of the four main classifications which we will tackle in the following sections. By then, managing a story will turn from just an instinctive talent to a professional skill. You will become more dynamic in retrieving or recalling as many stories stored in your memory under specified categories. And with it, you get the right story that serves its purpose. With this new tool, day after day, you will begin hunting – noticing stories that otherwise just pass you by and to store these in "story lockers" for you to use at your will.

In the long term, you may remove or add to the four classifications according to your specific requirements – according to what suits you because it is, after all, about your personal conclusions mixed with experiences and opinion that made come up with your classifications for your story in the business arena from management, sales, marketing, leadership, decision making, etc…

Goal

Initially, you may stumble to know the real goal of your story. When asked to present results of your work in the last quarter, you can choose a story that aims to highlight the volume sales that you and your partner achieved or describe the sacrifice that you went through or resourcefulness you came up with due to the scarcity of resources. In job interviews, you may choose the best story that conveys who you are. The list will seem daunting not to mention endless if you do not have specific goals.

In his groundbreaking book, "The Seven Basic Plots", *Christopher Booker* studied stories man used from the beginning of history – from the stories drawn on cave walls and carved on temples and epic stories of Greeks and even stories of postmodern era in movies and commercials. He classified them in to seven basic plots. The first one, *Overcoming the Monster*. This is where the protagonist seeks to overcome a series of evil forces aimed to kill him then finally facing the master of all evil incarnated in a fairytale creature or a big boss of some gang or even his manager at work. The second type is *Rags and Riches*. The protagonist elevates himself to power and authority after suffering some setbacks and sometimes losing achieved power only to regain it like the stories of Aladdin and The Conte De Monte Cristo.[20]

The third is *The Quest*, where the protagonist seeks to retrieve a prize which necessitates going on a long trip riddled with hurdles like "Harry Potter". The fourth is *Voyage and Return* which is about leaving the place of birth, living in a new land where the adventure will take place and then the hero goes back to his homeland bearing treasure or wisdom. So is the story of Prophet Muhammad – *peace and blessing be upon him* – where it began in his hometown Mecca then expelled out of it so as to live in Medina then finally returning back to Mecca as a conqueror. The fifth is *Comedy* which has a sole purpose – to make people laugh. The sixth is *Tragedy*. In this is, the hero commits many mistakes in search of (any) good and usually ends the demise of the hero. This is because the purpose of tragedy is to allow the audience experience the state of depression of the hero and leave the story with a lingering sadness within. The last is *Rebirth*. This is a story where the hero, in the part, is completely different from what he shall be in the latter part – it is a transition from evil to good, from failure to success, from denial to belief.

Maybe all the stories we've listened to our whole lives does not fall into any of these seven plots though this is highly doubtful. But what about the business story that desperately needs a rehash to fit some if not one of these plots because the work environment is very unique in its continuous endeavor for humanistic communication. The workplace needs stories to trigger emotions – stories that grabs attention or to distract from something else.

Building trust between workmates is one of the toughest tasks, a team leader has to perform. Here, the story acts as a catalyst to enhance and accelerate the process. It helps in spreading the warmth of camaraderie – ensuring the acceptance of unintentional and sometimes inevitable errors and mistakes encouraging innovation, resourcefulness and helpful opinions. These need a push, momentum, motivation and stirring of emotions that a good story can provide. Also, a story can work to remove hatred and reduce negative emotions resulting from the competition between individuals which can easily end in conflict whether short lived or permanently.

Grabbing, not to mention keeping attention nowadays is hard. Period. The older generation was saved from the so-called technology invasion. People had time to converse and listen but now things are different. This is why many developed the skill of presenting their issues and products and what not in a fast and frugal way. Now we have the elevator pitch where you have less than thirty seconds to persuade and get that "Yes". That's why the short but persuasive stories become indispensable. Five goals of the story that serve such purposes are as follows: Who am I, Why am I here, Vision, Value and Decision Making. In the following sections, we will introduce each goal with an example that shows the importance of each in composing a heart-capturing story.

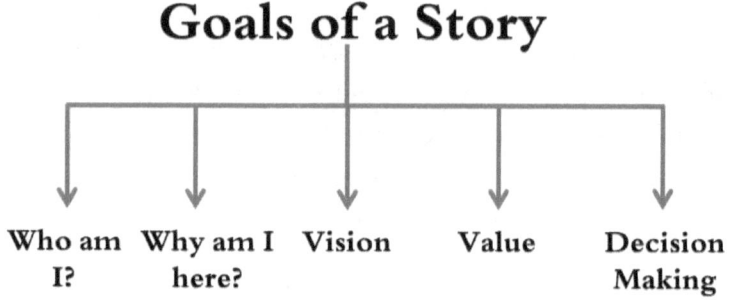

Who am I

Humans fear most what they do not know and what man knows the least of is his future, so he prefers to live in the past. At least he knows his past because it is neither ambiguous nor uncharted – he has lived it! But the past is full of agony and misery so man settles for the present and ignores what lies death and without a vision, he becomes depressed and lost. Ignorance is a principal source of worry and anxiety. When the man fails to understand or even misses signals of people around him, he tends to be cautious, vigilant, and prudent – guarded even suspicious of what others say or how others act UNTIL he takes time and effort to know enough to reveal, open up and surrender his trust.

Weak communication between parties happen in the workplace that sometimes lead to major loss or even catastrophe. And the main cause of this inefficient communication is of trust. The cause for this lack of trust is the negligence of answering important questions: "Who am I?", "Who are you?", "Who are they?" and "Who we are?".

Your ability to introduce yourself and let people know who you are as fast and as clearly as you can may shorten the route of miles to a few feet. I always hear people claim that the main reason they are encouraged or able to work someone is because of trust or because he knows his partner better than any throughout the time spent together. Trust is the elixir – the catalyst to execute fruitful business allowing for crucial decisions to be made in equally crucial times. *Stephen M.R. Covey* wrote "The Speed of Trust". It is about the value of trust in an organization and how it leads to better business. As more trust culture prevails in an organization, more positive results emerge. (21) The opposite is true with an organization with a distrustful culture. Trust facilitates the decision which needs to pass a hundred people for a hundred signatures in an instant.

The BP oil spill disaster in the Gulf of Mexico was caused mainly by lack of trust between employees and the top management. BP engineers avoided mentioning to senior managers installing a valve that could cost the company half a million dollars. The failure of which eventually caused an environmental disaster resulting in billions of dollars in losses and many of the senior managers lost their jobs including CEO *Tony Hayward*. (22)

Many of us have experienced giving our trust to people who deserved it which led to mutual success, and also, many of us experienced trusting people who did not deserve it resulting in loss and sometimes pain.

I once worked in a company where the top management didn't really care about encouraging the culture of trust among the employees. Top management did not bother to introduce newcomers. So, gaining the trust much less, getting a sense of the work environment was the newcomer's obligation. Given the situation, I witnessed a significant amount of problems and dilemmas which translated to financial loss which every individual in the company suffered. People generally thought they knew and trusted each other, but later on trust issues to surface. I went to another company with an awareness of the importance of trust among workers. Periodic and informal friendly meetings were held to encourage everyone to be open and to address problems, share ideas and sometimes even personal stuff if needed and so, trust is cultivated and strengthened. I noticed how problems are nipped in the bud in that company.

In the past few decades, the business environment has tremendously changed. The percentage of workers who do business from home has substantially increased due to the technological advancement and many companies utilize the so-called *Virtual Collaboration* to manage many of the business operations through the internet. This advancement has brought new spectra of business opportunities but it also came with its own set of problems that never existed in traditional offices. One is the manner of working with the absence of trust among virtual coworkers. *Karen Sobel* mentioned this in the opening of her article on HBR entitled "The Subtle Ways Our Screens are Pushing Us Apart". She asked a former U.S. Navy Admiral in charge of a fleet of aircraft carriers how he felt about collaborating with people through email, computers, smart phones, etc. In response, he told her the following story:

> "I would never send a rookie pilot to land a fighter jet on a carrier deck in the middle of the night, in the middle of the ocean on a new moon. It's pitch black. You can't see your hand in front of your face. The pilot has all of his instruments ready. He always knows his exact altitude, speed and distance from the ship. But he doesn't have the one crucial thing he needs to land safely. He doesn't have depth perception. And that's how I feel when I "talk" to people online – I have no depth perception." (23)

Recall memories at work – your interactions and evaluate your efforts in allowing your mates and friends to really know who you are in order to reach the peak level of trust which pays off. The one who truly knows who you are is you and you know what is good and the not so good. So, you are the best person to let people know you according to your own timing. In many cases, you will find that you did not do enough to let people know you to the degree that encourages them to trust you. The question is what is the best way you could let people know you so you could gain their trust. Normally, the seed of trust grows between two people and it may take years to bear and enjoy its fruits. So how can we cut this growth period short?

Recall people in your life whom you instantly trusted (of course some of them may have been scam artists). Have you asked yourself what common attribute those people shared that made you feel you have known them for years. A majority would most probably be professional storytellers. They tell amazing stories like it was all they do in their lives. They are expert in telling stories about themselves, about their heroism, their successes, their epics and they keep doing so till the bridge of trust is constructed – well established between you and them. So, once you get accustomed in introducing yourself through stories, you'll find lots of listening ears. Whereas, if you are used to introducing yourself the traditional, abstract, ballpoint information manner which does not don the cloak of emotions, trust may take time in finding its way between you and your audience. Humans are wired for stories, especially the personal ones, the true ones – stories that are narrated by the hero himself.

The plot of a "Who am I" story changes from one situation to another. The story you tell in a public lecture will differ from the story you tell in a job interview which will also differ from the story you tell to your new customer when you are selling something as it will also differ from the story you tell to your family or friends. Your "Who am I" story will have to suit the event, the listeners and the goal to achieve biggest possible impact. So, when closing a sale, your story must be about how you became a successful salesman who withstood all difficulties and challenges. Your story in a job interview should be about introducing who you are in terms of being driven always seeking success. To raise awareness for an imminent danger, you may tell a story about how you saved yourself and your family from a similar situation by being disciplined and prepared compelling your audience to follow.

The time frame for a "Who am I" story varies from a minute to several depending on your ability to hook your audience.

One of the good lecturers in business is a young man *Ty Bennett*. He is good in choosing personal stories which he narrates hundreds of times always producing such an incredible influence to his sales. It is as follows; (24)

> *"Bill Gates was nineteen when he did his first successful project. He had the trust and enthusiasm that made him certain that he could fulfill his promise and dream, and let every home own a personal computer. It's not necessary that I reach the same success of Bill Gates, but I'm certainly sure that I have the same trust and passion of Bill Gates to do this project and to get it done..."*

This is a very powerful and influential story due to the elements of contrast and comparison where Ty shared with Bill the same passion and enthusiasm, so the listener could place both in the same picture – Ty, the storyteller and Bill, the successful business magnate. Automatic matching and association will imprint on the recipients. Bennett mentions that the story was the reason so many of his meetings were a success. This is a one-minute story, very short but with strong recall in the recipient's mind. And this is the real power of storytelling – to turn little words into deep and influential moments. This is the simplest "Who am I" stories, where you speak about your aptitudes and persuade your audience that you really have those characteristics.

Another story which is very easy to narrate in various situations is the chronological story. Narrate your story from birth to the present leading up to your actual talk in an orderly, rapid and brief succession focusing on aspects and parts that will serve your purpose of persuasion. This type of personal story is very easy and quite fast. And people like it because they like order that they minds can absorb and digest quickly. This is an example:

> *"My name is Rix Swaggart. I was born in 1986, was raised in Birmingham, lived there till high school then returned to California, went to university, studied computer science, earned my degree and began to do progamming from home. I married last year and have a lovely baby*

named Sara. I build e-commerce websites and I am here to offer one of them to your esteemed company."

The "Who am I" story has a vibrant resonance with the audience when composed and delivered well. The "Who am I" story may show one aspect of your personality you seek to share whether it be your strength, patience, stamina, etc. It is a descriptive story that can have a simple plot which clearly describes who you are. If someone asks you to describe yourself in a single sentence, you have to evaluate and anticipate what the questioner really needs to know most about you. Here, we will see some projections of "Who am I" that have a more powerful impact than your CV. We will reveal the trait that the questioner wants to know and based on it will be your answer.

I: *Who are you in one sentence?*

A **(Stamina)**: When the sun rises in the early morning in the forest, the weak deer runs faster than the fast lion to survive and the strong lion runs faster than the slowest dear in order not to die of hunger. Maybe I am neither stronger than the lion nor faster than the deer, but once the sun rises every morning I just run with all my stamina and all my strength never stopping till I achieve what I seek.

I: *Who are you in one sentence?*

A **(Courage)**: Maybe nothing is special about me to be said in one sentence except that I am a person who always refuses despair and motionlessness and this is the reason which made me sit in front of you, applying for a job and answering the question of "Who am I".

I: *Who are you in one sentence?*

A **(Extroversion)**: Do you have an electric mosquito trap?

I: Yes, why?

A: I'm like a mosquito trap but I just attract and never harm.

I: How come?

Showing a cell phone,

A: In the short time I sat outside, I made acquaintances with 5 of your staff and got their numbers and quite possibly hang out with some of them this weekend.

I: *Who are you in one sentence?*

A **(Ability to learn)**: I am 2.5 Beta byte.

I: What?!

A: I am 100 billion neuron cells, 100 trillion synapses and 2.5 million giga bytes of memory cells who seeks to get and digest anything new. All in all, 2.5 Beta bytes that can make miracles come true.

I: *Who are you in one sentence?*

A **(Obeying orders)**: I am you.

I: What?!

A: They say that people embrace the religion of their kings and I say that the best people embrace the same religion of their kings if they are truly virtuous. So, if my manager is virtuous, I will be as what he wants me to be.

I: ***Who are you in one sentence?***

Getting a cell phone, handing to the interviewer,

I: what shall I do with it?

A **(Innovation)**: Take a picture of me.

I: What?!

A: It will answer your question.

I: So, tell me the password.

A: You guess.

Interviewer tries various combinations but fails.

I: I can't.

Taking back the phone.

A: You tried many combinations to get the password but it never crossed your mind that I may not have one. And this is how people perceive me – ambiguous even strange like the supposed password to this phone. But once they see me in different situations, they get to know who truly am I.

I: ***Who are you in one sentence?***

A **(Persuasion)**: I'm a fig leaf.

I: What?!

A: The bee pollinates the leaf and produces honey, the sheep eats the honey to produce milk. So, wherever I am, I work to get the best out of people.

I: **Who are you in one sentence?**

A **(Intelligence)**: My mom answered this question thirty years ago.

I: How come?

A: She named me bliss.

I: Hehehe, but this not your name on paper.

A: But, it's my name in action.

The "Who am I" story is very dynamic. You can create hundreds of personal stories conveying your message effectively at the same time making an impact on your audience. So, begin by preparing your personal stories – real ones that showcase values you want to transmit. Ask yourself, what story shall I tell that shows my professionalism or what story shall project my calmness and self-control in the midst of crises. What stories will show your enthusiasm, passion, simplicity, ambition, etc?

Why am I here

After you answer "Who am I", the next question that comes to mind is "What am I doing here". Why have you been assigned for a particular job? Why are you lecturing us? Why you selling us this and that product? Why have you summoned us to this urgent meeting? Man's nature makes him reluctant to change even in simple things like attending a lecture, or a change tasks or assignments, or buying a new product. The "Why am I here" story eases change and exit from comfort zone. In any event, you can give reasons for your attendance with a simple and persuasive story like the following:

"I'm honored to conduct this lecture about what changed the course of my entire life. In the past, I used to speak about success and how to persevere reaching it but recently, I've changed – a hundred and eighty degrees. Today, I decided to talk to you about failure. Yes, failure. It's the most important experience that you have to taste and get immersed in to. Why? Why is failure a more solid experience and more beneficial than success? Let me tell you a story of a man – a man who failed early in his life – in his business, his love life with his fiancée's untimely demise shortly before their wedding, his nervous breakdown and finally his bid for office when he ran for parliament but failed again and again and for a third time failed. He ran for vice-president and failed, ran for parliament again but failed. But this time, failure was quite different. It was the last entry of failure to be written in his book. All the past failures began to pay off. He became one of the most influential characters in American history. The man won the elections of 1860 and became the sixteenth president of the United States of America and was called The Great Emancipator. He led his country in during The American Civil War. He is Abraham Lincoln, the man who invested

> *in his failures to make a remarkable success in politics and war in American history. Perhaps Lincoln would not have attained such success without scaling the ladder of failures the way he did then finally getting a broad view of the situation from where he was on top of the ladder of success."*

Beginning your lecture with such story would help in hooking your audience because they know (at once) why you are there and what you shall deliver.

We are witnessing a revolution in the service business like taxi services, reservations, hospitality, etc. These services make lots of noise on the internet. And now other companies offer services that guarantee visibility and traffic. When I check one of these websites, I get distracted with their landing page. I feel it does not let me know what the business is about in brief so my eyes immediately run to the *About us* tab.

The more competition of such websites, the more visitors go and check the *About us* page. When I do so, I get even more confused after reading the first couple of lines. This page should provide concise information precisely the kind of service or product they offer. Although, publishing the purpose of a company's existence in story form is very catchy, only a few websites do so. Maybe some believe that a story in the *About us* tab will be boring. But Uber presented a new and different initiative that made a fuss worldwide. They re-named the page and called it *Our Story* and it is as follows:

> "On a snowy Paris evening in 2008, Travis Kalanick and Garrett Camp had trouble hailing a cab. So, they came up with a simple idea – tap a button, get a ride.
>
> What started as an app to request premium black cars in a few metropolitan areas is now changing the logistical fabric of cities around

the world. Whether it's a ride, a sandwich, or a package, we use technology to give people what they want, when they want it.

For the women and men who drive with Uber, our app represents a flexible new way to earn money. For cities, we help strengthen local economies, improve access to transportation, and make streets safer. When you make transportation as reliable as running water, everyone benefits. Especially when it's snowing outside" (25)

Vision

While we were preparing the training program, *Manager-X*, and picking up modules, studying and refining them; I met one newly hired employee. I quickly noticed that he was confused and bored so I talked to him to get a sense of what was going on with him. He began complaining about his continuous distraction and that he almost never begins a task without getting distracted away from it. After, I talked to his manager and I realized that the root of the problem was with the latter. He never bothered to let the guy understand and digest the value of what the guy was asked to do and what it did to contribute to the prosperity, if you will, and the development of the entire company. The manager never let him integrate the vision of the company. So, what we did was remind the employees what the company expects from them – from the vision to the tiniest of details of everyday work. And we formulated this message into a simple projection that carried lots of meaning which the manager can convey to his subordinates:

> *"The first day I came to this company was the day I entered a long dark tunnel. The entrance, where everything began, was my first day leading the way for everybody who followed me. And its exit is the biggest success everybody seeks to reach. Each step we make inside are the long days we spend behind our desks, not really knowing when or what happens when we get out; whether we exit at the other end to the right destination or find ourselves in a place we did not even consider on the first day at the entrance of the tunnel.*
>
> *Everybody found a foothold in various places inside the tunnel. Some stood by the entrance for a swift exit in case of an emergency where the tunnel collapses, others decided to be in the middle they can't see their hands in front of them, others lost inside but keep discovering new places, others who got so exhausted walking in the darkness and sat down and stopped altogether, and finally, two persons reached the exit. The darkness they endured for so long vanishing behind them while the light outside was blinding.*

The first one goes out happily seeing the rays of the sun but the other one looks back at the dark tunnel and he decides to go back inside. He runs and yells calling to his friends and colleagues and blindly bumps in to one of them. Hysterically laughing in happiness, telling the good news that he finally reached the exit, he guides his friend and then goes for another to save and to lead out before they quit and go back on their heels leaving the tunnel from the entrance... or never leave it at all.

Soon, everybody was out of the tunnel waiting for the last man, the man who led them. Everyone was in a jovial mood so they sang and danced celebrating their success reaching and exiting the other end but in the middle of the party, they see the person who exited the tunnel first. They found him motionless – dead. Although he was the first one to exit, he couldn't survive outside alone and became exhausted. He stopped moving, sickness overcame him and finally died...

They mourned him, buried him and then continued their journey entering the next tunnel before sunset... This is the philosophy, the strategy, and the vision of this company. We shall enter the tunnels one after the other, all together and leave it all together, we succeed all together and we celebrate all together."

The vision of a company for employees should be like that of the hope of meeting a lover. If this hope is gone, so is the lovestory. Making the vision crystal clear and as bright as the sun's rays is one of the main qualifications of a skillful manager. Making the worker to see the path of the company as well his own and where the two paths lead to is the main catalyst that motviates an employee do his best. If the vision is sidelined, neglected, or monopolized by top management; distraction, hesistation, boredom and less intrinsic motivation develop.

The employee who seems to breeze through the long working hours are those who have a clear and piercing vision of the big picture. The more tasks they accomplish, the more satisfaction they get out of it and in turn, their brains pump more dopamine motivating them to "go the extra mile". There is a growing favorability to *Intrinisc motivation* over *Extrinsic motivation*. The latter like the stick and the carrot. This is an easy motivation technique which does not require skill from managers because it does not take more than raising the stick and hanging a carrot on it. But engendering an internal motivation necesitates a special type of person, a manager that has a special ability to exploit the inner power of his employees to lead themselves. This kind of management needs a continuous mental effort but leads to achievments that the stick and the carrot technique can never bring. (26)

This is why successful managers advise their subordinates to make the vision the first and the last thing they see. Discuss and contemplate on it throughout the day. Write it down, memorize it and inculcate it in work processes. But still the story is the most powerful tactic to instill a vision and make it almost tangible. The capabilities of the story indicated earlier qualifies it to be the best method to convey a vision.

In his book, "Winning", Jack Welch, the former CEO of General Electric, wrote that one of the main roles of top management to their employees is to teach the vision of the company and to let them know it by heart so all the plans, proposals and decisions meet at the tip of that vision; otherwise disruption, conflict, attrition of talent result because of the failure to teach the vision. (27)

One big Egyptian company suffered from neglecting to share its vision. Their vision for the next five years was to increase production and stock value as much as they could to take advantage of the tax cuts they had been offered exlusively. But this was not transmitted well to the different departments. R and D had its own microscale vision aimed at developing and testing many new products keeping assembly lines occupied most of the times adversely affecting production rate of existing products. While R and D was very vital to the company, the failure to transmit the vision to the different departments down to all the workers caused conflict which rapidly translated to significant loss in terms of cashflow. Sharing the vision to everyone is not an easy job. Only companies with a high awarness of the strategic importance of vision care to do so and sadly, also companies that suffered loss because of the lack of vision sharing.

Lots of companies began to use stories to inculcate the vision to their employees like in periodic meetings, trainings and even in their publications. Some companies conduct periodic testing for employees to make sure they are aware of the company's vision and how to implement it in the day to day activities.

Steven Denning, in his book "The Leader's Guide to Storytelling", shares the time he became interested in sorytelling in business. He was manager in the World Bank in the mid ninties and sought to point out to his subordinates in his departement the importance of managing information effictively which was something new and unusual at the time. Denning shares that he presented many infromation that support his claim. The result was unconvincing so he utilized *PowerPoint*, visual aids, graphs and everything that could enhance his message but nothing worked. He was about ready to use anything to get his point through to his people then in 1996, Denning used a different method. He told them this story:

"In June of last year, a health worker in a tiny town in Zambia went to the website of the Center for Disease Control and got the answer to a question about the treatment of malaria. Remember that this was in Zambia, one of the poorest countries in the world, and it was in a tiny place six hundred kilometers from the capital city. But the most striking thing about this picture, at least for us, is that the World Bank isn't in it. Despite our know-how on all kinds of poverty-related issues, that knowledge isn't available to the millions of people who could use it. Imagine if it were. Think what an organization we could become."

Although Denning realized later on after he consulted professional storytellers that the story of Zambia was a weak one and had missed many of the elements such as suspense and attractiveness, he confirms that this simple story filled with flaws contributed much in helping the workers of the world bank imagine and digest the vision he presented them. Denning continues that later on the information department became one of the top priorities of the top management. Denning adds that since then he used stories with more professionalism and excitement to support the vision of top management and seamlessly spread it to the workforce. (28)

Many companies suffer the difficulty in establishing the importance of continuing studies and development to its workers improvement and growth. Here we present a very simple story, easy to deliver which helps in increasing awareness in the importance of learning, development and seeking new ideas:

> *"When I was about, 14 my Dad took me to football every week. We would stand in the outer perimeter and being smaller than everyone else, I often missed out on the action. One week we decided to bring along an old milk crate we had lying around to stand on. It was great – I was finally head and shoulders above everyone and could see the whole game. The following week, we brought along the milk crate again but this time we noticed that a few other people had also brought along their milk crates. We were actually a bit impressed that we had started a trend. Unfortunately, within a few months nearly everyone had a milk crate and I was literally back to square one, back with the rest of the pack. My experience at those matches reminds me of what we are trying to achieve with the war for talent. We can't be happy with starting a trend and taking an early lead, we need to constantly be on the lookout for our next milk crate."*

Now, let us shift to the one they called a storyteller first and a president of the United States second, Barack Obama. That politician who loved using stories to pass his vision and influence to voters. He used to get harsh critiques with his excessive use of stories during his presidential campaign but it seems that it was one of the top reasons why he won and became the first African American president of the United States. He also used (his) skin color as story to convey the amount of suffering African Americans experienced through decades in their struggle to gain social rights. He told that they were on the verge of historical change by turning the dream into reality. And finally, Obama succeeded in investing in his stories to influence voters to elect him.

In his presidency, Obama faced a fierce opposition from the Republicans in passing bills and projects including his Obamacare which aims cover more people under the Act. The Republicans were about to smash the project. Obama's administration conducted several campaigns to convince the people of its feasibility. Obama gave a speech in the garden of the White House speaking to the American people about the project where he subtly used a fascinating story. Healthcare coverage is an issue for ordinary citizens. This is why Obama and his administration were keen on delivering a speech that has a strong social theme to be directed to all Americans regardless of ethnicity, gender or status. So, in the background they placed a white beside an African American, in the front stood a few old ladies. They also brought a white buxom girl which represented the demographic of American women to create a balanced mental image for the viewers. Then Obama began his speech. It was as follows:

> *"Let me just tell you, folks, a few stories that are represented here today. A few years ago, Amanda Barrett left her job in New York to take care of her parents and for a while she had temporary insurance that covered her multiple sclerosis... But when it expired, many insurers wouldn't cover her because of her MS. She ended up paying $1200 a month. That's nowhere near affordable. But starting today, she can get*

coverage for much less... because today's new plan can't use your medical history to charge you more than anybody else.

Sky-high premiums once forced Nancy Beagle to choose between paying her rent or paying for her health insurance. She's been uninsured ever since... So, she pays all of her medical bills out of pocket, puts some on her credit card, making them even harder to pay... Nancy says, "They talk about those who fall through the cracks; I fell through the cracks 10 years ago and I've been stuck there ever since". Well, starting today, Nancy can get covered just like everybody else.

Tranaise Edwards was laid off from her job a year ago today. Six months ago, she was diagnosed with a brain tumor... She couldn't afford insurance on the individual market, so she hasn't received treatment yet... Her daughter LeNaise, a student at the University of Maryland, is considering dropping out of school to help pay her mom's bills... Well, starting today, thanks to the Affordable Care Act, Tranaise can get covered without forcing her daughter to give up on her dreams...

So, if these stories of hard working Americans sound familiar to you, well, starting today, you and your friends and your family and your co-workers can get covered too."

The program became more popular to the masses and finally Obama succeeded in passing it into a law in Congress. It added to his achievements and earned him a second term.

Value
One of the most noble missions of any parent is to raise a a child with good values like honesty, trustworthiness, humility, generosity, love and respect. The direct method to inculcate such values is notably less effective in youngsters than in adults general. Instinct drives man to follow someone he feels is a leader, an example. This is because of man's inclination to imitate and match the actions rather than compliance to orders.

The following graph shows the development of the human behavior with the devolvement of human age. The blue curve represents compliance to direct orders from parents or other significant figures which tends to have a moderate influence at childhood. The red curve represents emulation in acquiring values until reaching age of maturity where there is more tendency to follow a direct order because of the development of reasoning, ability to analyze and scrutinize.

Corollary, at age 60, saturation for emulation is reached, so the curve slopes down at this age. Of course, there is a deviation from this trend depending on the development of mental and emotional maturity of some people. Some young people refuse to emulate behavior if they are not convinced that the emulation is sound and conversely, some old people tend to blindly emulate others in whatever behavior as long as it will bring them happiness.

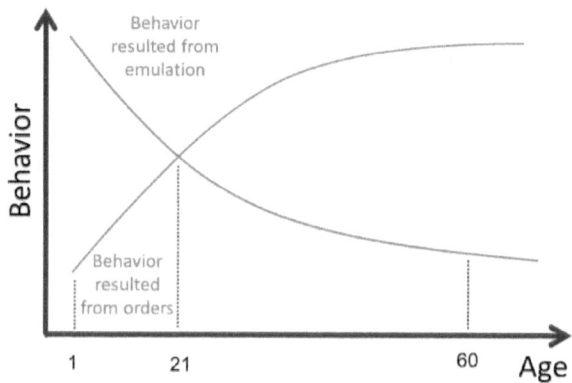

The point is how to strengthen the power of the direct order to penetrate deeper into the heart and the mind of the recipient because emulation is not always an available option. As stated, nothing is better than directing orders in the form of a purposeful story as storytelling had been used as a common way of transmitting values through millennia. When mentioning a value like honesty and trustworthiness, many would recall the story of Prophet Muhammad when he planned to secretly migrate from Mecca to Medina. He assigned Ali, his cousin, to remain in Mecca until he gives back all the belongings of the people which Muhammad kept in his custody. In lying, millions would recall the story of "The Boy Who Cried Wolf". One nice and brief story but with a big impact is about the Great Wall:

> *"When the Chinese wanted to live safely, they built their great wall. And after, they thought no one could succeed breaching it. But during its first hundred years, China was invaded three times and each time the enemies did not have to climb the wall or to destroy it. All the invaders had to do was bribe the guards at the gates. Chinese were busy with building the wall, meanwhile they forgot to build the people. And building men must be done before bricks and walls."*

The next story I usually use at the end of my lectures. Read it then we discuss its values.

> Faraway in the Himalayan Mountains, there was a small village with monks as the majority of the population. They had a wise old man, Tao Su. All the men and the women of the village went to him, learning from his wisdom. He had a secret talent. He knew what people hid in their homes and in their minds as well. It was enough for him to look at any one of them to explore thoughts and secrets. One day, two young shepherds were tending to their sheep in a far mountain. One told the other, 'This Tao Su is just a fraud and I have a plan to expose him in front of the entire village'. His friend asked him, 'And how would you do so?'. He said, 'I'll hide one small bird between my palms then I'll go to Tao Su while everybody is gathered around him and I'll ask what I have between my palms. If he says a small bird, I'll ask him the second question. Is this bird is alive or dead? If answers it is alive, I'll squeeze it between my palms and show everybody a dead bird and if he answers a dead bird, I'll release the bird to

fly. Everyone would know that Tao Su is a fraud'. The other shepherd was impressed of the idea and they decided to descend the mountain and confront Tao Su.

The young shepherd pushed his way through the crowd circling Tao Su and shouted that he will expose the wise man. The people got furious and were about to grab him. However, Tao Su spoke in a deep voice and ordered everyone to calm down and said to the boy, 'Come over! Don't be scared and say whatever you want.' The people looked on with anger. The boy approached Tao Su and showed closed palms and said loudly 'What do I have inside my hands?' The wise man didn't look at the boy's hands but rather looked into his eyes for a moment then calmly said, 'It's a small bird' The boy to worry and the people were delighted at the man's wisdom. The boy quickly followed up, 'Now, tell me, is it alive or dead?'. The people muttered in anger so the wise man ordered them to be quiet and looked back at the boy with a faint smile. He approached him and gently held the boy's hands and with a voice full of care and wisdom he said, 'It is up to you, little boy… you who will decide whether this small bird will live… or die'. Seconds passed like ages while the boy stared at Tao Su's eyes. All the people were stunned in silence until the wise man cut the silence saying, 'But I…'. And all of a sudden he opened up the boy's hands and the small bird flied out of his sweaty hands and Tao Su continued, 'I prefer it alive'".

I close saying, "And now, after all the information you learned in this lecture, you have to know that it is like the small bird in the palm of your hands. Only you shall decide whether it will vanish and be forgotten as other information have or it lives and prospers in your hearts and minds. Choose now…"

Usually, I finish a training session with the story above. I remember encountering a group I met in other lectures I gave a couple of months before. So, I asked them if they remember anything from my training. As expected, the majority did not recall. Then I asked if they remember the story in the Himalayas. Their answer stunned me, "Of course, Tao Su". They did not remember the story in general but certain details stuck. The incident illustrates the recall of a story over abstract information and how it can instill values much deeper than direct orders.

****

Unity with God is a primary value any Muslim should learn and understand. It is the main pillar of the religion. And in this time we live in where principles are relative in many societies, using stories that convey values could help people live them.

> A father decided to take his nine-year-old son to a picnic one weekend outside the busy city. He wanted to teach his son how to live, survive, and enjoy in the desert. They went to a remote part of the desert. Both stepped out of the car and the father said 'Let's pitch our tent as the weather is getting very hot'. The son answered with enthusiasm, 'Let's go'. They took the tent and tools from the truck and began pitching the rigid fabric. They formed square with the four stilts and placed a fifth one in the center.
>
> After they finished, they went in as the weather was reaching 50 degrees Celsius. After resting a while, the son said, 'Oh my God, who could stand staying under this scorching son?' The father answered, 'Then, our survival means we should stay inside'. The son answered, 'Of course.' The father then stood up, took a big machete and said, 'So, if I go to that corner and chop off its stilt'. As the father was talking, he hit it but it did not break. The son, in panic, said, 'Thank, God,

it did not break'. The father hit it again and a quarter of the tent collapsed. The son exclaimed, 'You collapsed a quarter of the tent but we still have shelter!' The father went to a second stilt, hit it gently and asked, 'And now?'. the son, more nervous, said, 'I'm afraid that the tent wouldn't hold with two fallen stilts'. The father hit it and broke it saying, 'Let's see'. And half of the tent fell. Stunned, the son asked, 'Dad, are you okay? We just have half of the tent'. The father did the same with the third and the fourth stilt. The son crawled to the center stilt holding it tightly and said, 'Oh father, this is the last place in the tent we can stay otherwise we will die in scorching heat outside'. The father asked, 'You think I can gently hit part of this slender stilt without it collapsing?'. The son said, 'Impossible dad, it's very thin. If you hit it just once, it will break. Dad, what are you doing? Did you fight with mom this morning!'. And before he finished, the father hit the last stilt and the tent collapsed.

Driving back to the city at sunset, the son was speechless. The tent with its broken stilts in the back of the truck. The son broke the silence and asked, 'Why did you do that, dad?'. The father looked at him and said, 'I wanted to teach a lesson, but I was sure you wouldn't get it if we were in the middle of the hustle and bustle of the city, so I decided to go where there is no one except you, me and God'. The son asked, 'And what's it about?' The father answered, 'Each time I chopped one silt, you thought we had a chance of survival until I chopped the center pole. You lost any hope of survival and went outside to suffer the scorching sun'. The father paused then continued while keeping his eyes on the road, 'This tent, son, is your religion. And the safety you felt inside is Paradise while the scorching heat is the torture of hellfire. The four stilts are The Four Pillars: Praying, Fasting, Charity and Pilgrimage. When you fail in one of them, it's like chopping one of the stilts. You are still safe but each time you chop one of the stilts, your area of safety becomes more and more confined'. More curious than ever, the son asked, 'And what about the center pole, dad?'. The father looked at his son and said, 'If you learn it, will you live it?'. The son quickly replied, 'And I'll never forget it as long as I live'. The father said, 'The center pole is the unity with God. When you fail doing any good in your life, you still have it as your lifeline to survive. And if you miss it, absolutely nothing will save you. Always remember to maintain the center pole in your life and never break from it nor hurt it.'

*****

We Already Know

I still remember this story although I heard it fifteen years ago. He narrated his journey to the United States carrying his PhD in Geology. Looking for a job at one of the universities, he was told that hiring for the first semester had already closed and he had to wait for the next one. He could not wait several months without a fixed income, so he went to whatever university, then at research centers and after sending about 120 letters; one research center replied. So, Dr Faruk Albaz worked as a geologist in NASA.

This was the time John F Kennedy pledged publicly that the United States will land a man on the moon and bring him back safely before the end of the decade. NASA was racing against time to get this done and called it "Project Apollo". One of their tasks is to study moon terrains to be able to figure the best possible locations for landing. And because of his youth, Dr Albaz worked as secretary for some of the more senior geologists briefing reports and the like. He was complaining about the humdrum of clerical tasks to his friend one day and asked if he could attend the next geologists meeting regarding Project Apollo which will last for three days. In this meeting, geologists go to the podium to report developments of their research. In the meeting, Dr Albaz was getting bored and felt an urge to strike up a conversation. Beside him there was an old geologist who seemed to have quite a deep knowledge so he whispered him, "Excuse me, is there is any book, magazine or article about the types of moon terrains and its locations?". The man looked askance and asked, "What do you mean?". Albaz replied, "I mean a classification of the moon's terrains and its locations". The man answered back, "We already know the terrains and its locations".

Dr Albaz replied shyly, "I prefer to keep my mouth shut to avoid any more embarrassment because it seems I'm the least person who knows about the moon in this room". He quietly exited the meeting then went back to his office and asked one employee to guide him to the location where they archive the pictures and the reports of moon's terrains. Dr Albaz found piles of files and pictures full of dust and long since neglected. Dr Albaz brought tables, cleaned the pictures and arranged them according to date then began analyzing them from 9AM to 6PM. He kept doing so for the next 3 months until the next meeting. So, Dr Albaz went to the meeting and hopped on stage and to speak about the results of his research on the moon's pictures for about an hour. But those in attendance wanted to discuss with him some more and while Dr Albaz was answering questions, one of the attendees interrupted him. It was the same old man who gave him a cold answer. Dr Albaz thought the man will shame him again but this time in public. But the man did something different and said, "This young man asked me the previous meeting if we had any collective information about the moon's terrains, I answered none, but after I listened to his presentation and his results; I'd like to thank him in public. I realized that we knew nothing about moon's terrains as we thought". (29)

What drove me to tell this story is mainly its dramatic plot that manifests before me every time I face one of these situations in life:

First, when an ignoramus feels proud of his own ignorance like a pseudo-scientist who claimed he had a cure for AIDS, defending his research with unfounded claims with the highest authority of his country supporting him! It called to mind the insufficient knowledge of the senior geologist who could have caused serious harm to the NASA project. The second situation is a brave man who admitted his ignorance not feeling shame being exposed and acknowledging the fledgling and his capabilities.

****

Freedom

I was assigned to do a consultation service for a small company that suffered from mismanagement, staff mismatch, employee attrition and lack of vision. We made an organizational chart, management priority from A to Z, we categorized staff according to skills and aptitude and finally, we conducted a lecture to present and discuss the new plan. We explained the plan, many items were somehow new concepts for the staff like making visual maps of the strategic plan and the daily operations for everyone to see. Staff may add, modify it according to his area of competence, set basic goals and paths that will be translated to daily working routines. We developed a system of tracking and rectifying errors. And finally, we introduced managing staff with autonomy by granting some the freedom to choose their working hours, tasks, targets and performance as well as how to measure it even up to setting rewards and penalties for themselves.

In exchange for this wide scope of autonomy was just one thing: To keep us regularly informed of how things are going without much details of their tasks. Any comments or guidelines we shall propose will be in the form of non-obligatory advice. While clarifying this new approach, I noticed some eyes widely opened and sensed a wonder and even contempt on the faces of the staff. And that is what we always expect when we present this ludicrous proposal. While I rambled on, I noticed a lady with tears and so asked her to comment on what we proposed. This was what she said:

> My name is Sara and I have been working here a few months. I like this place and I have a desire and drive to do a great job and score amazing results but actually, I was about to submit my resignation today or tomorrow. What you are talking about now is the thing I am really missing. My manager deals with me like I'm a machine. He presses a button and I have to respond. I have no space or freedom to choose the way I do my tasks. I never know the reason why he orders me to do a certain task and just leaves me be. Although treatment is fair and the salary is competitive, but this way of managing makes me lose any desire to stay on or push harder. However, if what you propose is what will be tomorrow, I'm not leaving because I am getting back what I lost... My freedom.

Every time clients book our consulting services, the story above has the same effect on the attendees' faces. Introducing the concept of autonomy at work in a simple, realistic and personal story paves the way to discussion, debates and suggestions on how to increase productivity and innovation of individuals by allowing a certain amount of freedom. This story beats numbers and facts in reaching minds and hearts of listeners.

✻✻✻✻✻✻

Push Start Zuba

"Hisham! I need a story as soon as possible". I was stunned at the sudden request of my friend. It wasn't the fact that he needed it fast, but the fact that I'm a not a writer and he knows it. I've never written a scenario, nor have I published a novel, so I asked him why and how sure was that I would write something good. He said that he wanted to join a contest for a concept to a short movie and that he liked a the concept of a video I made for my business. He was also sure that he would get the story for free because he filmed my videos for free.

So, I accepted and asked him to come back in two days so I could focus on the project. Actually, I had an idea for a short story that I always wanted to write. It was about "Zuba", an old car in a famous TV series. It breaks down and the kids step out and push it singing, "Push-start our Zuba". So, this nice Zuba that almost every family had was good only after a push-start.

I was like this Zuba. After a push-start and some distance, the engine warms up and by then, no Japanese car could compete with its speed, not even the best German car could duplicate how it handles. So, one long night, I sat, prepared my desk and with sandwiches and cup and cups of coffee; I began seeing light from my imagination which very rarely shone. And ideas began to flow from my mind to my pen. That night, I finished one of the best stories I have ever written in my entire life. Before going to bed, I took a final look at the papers and wrote the title… "Circles". The sudden request of my friend was the push-start for me, a heavy Zuba.

"If this story does not make you weep, tear it up and never call me."

My friend was stunned when I called and said the words above. He had anticipated that he would be calling me daily but instead it was me who phoned him. The next day, the push-started Zuba was motivated to write it in English to reach more people. I was so keen to do it and take advantage of the push – the momentum I suddenly had. I took advantage of each "push" my friends gave after reading the story I wrote. And so I contracted an editor and a designer for the cover then I published in Amazon. Reaching that point, I ran out of steam – momentum.

Days passed and my story did not make any sales. The sales graph looked more and more like a flatline in a heart rate monitor. I kept checking daily, sometimes more than once hoping for signs of life but the graph was born dead. Still, I kept watch. Knowing many good books have little success making satisfactory sales within a writer's lifetime, this Zuba was about to retire in a junkyard. Nothing happened until I learned how to market my books and propagate it inside the

"Amazon" forest. Full of doubt, I offered my book for free to anyone who wanted it. If there was no benefit from it, neither will there be any harm. On the first day of the free promotion, I watched the indicator and to my surprise, it showed a leap in the number of readers from zero to couple of hundreds. It was like a dead man walking, dancing and lifting weights. The dopamine and serotonin were the first to challenge the cortisol to a fight.

After a couple of days when the promotion was done, the dead body returned to its normal state. It was like a vampire evading the sunrise which had to escape to his coffin. The Zuba began to unravel and fall apart. The cortisol was coming back tagging along his thugs for revenge and full control. Just when everything seemed done, another push-start came. I read a comment on my story from a verified reader. And at first, I thought it was a negative comment because of the silliness I wrote, but the comment is as follows:

"Some stories amuse, some provide creative escape, and a few touch the soul. This is one of those. In the span of so few pages, a life is revealed. Within that life, food for many souls. Thank you so much for writing this story. Thank you for being you and sharing who you are."

"

Top Customer Reviews

⭐ **Soul Inspiring**
By J█████████ on May 14, 2016
Format: Kindle Edition | Verified Purchase
Some stories amuse, some provide creative escape, and a few touch the soul. This is one of those. In the span of so few pages, a life is revealed. Within that life, food for many souls. Thank you so much for writing this story. Thank you for being you and sharing who you are.

This comment was like the magic wand that changed Zuba for good. From a piece of rusty and rickety metal to a modern and rigid racecar that none can compete with. This was the fateful push-start that I needed to write. From that moment on, I wrote without fear and reluctance. No other push-start was required after that. There is a Zuba in each of us, waiting for that big push-start that will let it run without breaking down again.

I never get tired telling this story to encourage others to follow their dreams and passion. It provides motivation to keep going. This funny projection has massive effect in people. If you are among the very few who do not despair or get bored whilst chasing their dreams or if your Zuba never needed a push-start, remember that many around you are also Zubas that yearn for that big push-start from that strong person who has never been once... a Zuba.

****

Investiment An Intangible

Once I met a friend who recently established his own company. And, like others before him, he committed many mistakes when he shifted from being just an employee. He got distracted from the main purpose of his company, he took on way too many side projects with no definite planning or clear results and he also hired inefficient staff. My friend was furious one day and wanted to fire everyone. That would be an impulsive decision. Although these were not the best employees, there are alternatives so I tried to dissuade him. But he was sure about what he is going to do. I told him that he could try training programs for his staff but he was persistent. The next day, we met and before I could ask anything, he told me the following;

> *"I was really determined to fire everyone today but I thought of what you told me yesterday. None of your advice seemed to penetrate but you said*

> *something which completely changed my mind and I decided to give them one more try."*

I was so curious what exactly drove him to change his mind and before I could ask, he said;

> *"It was when you told me that I had already invested trusting them. When I reflected on this, I came to a conclusion that this was the most costly investment and the most difficult to keep and nurture. Trust is an intangible investment which cannot be quantified. Intangible investments cost too much when lost yet invaluable if kept. That's why I decided to continue investing in trust and start over with them with a different approach so we can all move past this crisis."*

I use this story in the Trust Module of Manager-X because trust as a general concept does not grab peoples' attention. Of course, a good manager is expected to build trust with subordinates. But introducing trust in this concept triggers a deeper focus from the participants.

This is why many principles and values people readily accept and think they apply (when in fact they do not) rarely even raise awareness because these fundamentals remain academic – snatched from dictionaries and are just head knowledge which remain to be seen in the way we manage businesses in general.

There is no better way to make an impact on the audience except by incorporating these principles and projecting into real and personal stories which triggers reassessment and refocusing of these values into the minds and hearts of everyone in the organization.

****

Time

How quickly we can waste time especially these days is a major challenge all around the world. While many fail to combat this challenge, so many books and articles have been published to give tips on how to save time and to use it efficiently. Arabs use a smart projection about time saying, "Time is like a sword; if you don't cut it, it'll cut you off". Swords for Arabs represent numerous values so this metaphor survived the centuries. Another projection for time is as follows;

> *"Son, I now see that you know how to weave cloth and brocades. And today i want to give a valuable lesson. This brocade is nothing but warps and wefts of thread. The warp, vertical threads that gives the brocade strength; while the weft, horizontal threads that carry your art and give this brocade a certain value that enables to feed all of us. When you first started to learn weaving, your hands weren't fast enough to run warps on the loom and to string wefts. The picture was not discernable then and your brocade was worth nothing. But day after day, you were able to place all your weft threads correctly and consistently and the picture began to show more clearly. Daily, you got closer to achieving your goal until you became an artist who presents value to the people.*
>
> *This resembles your life and your time, son, the warp is time that was given to you. It's the source of your power, your development and your success. The weft is what you produce within the running warps. It's what you weave through it. And so the lesser wefts you weave, the lesser value your warps will have. And it won't benefit you nor those around you and the bin will be its destination. But when you work hard and wefts cross with warps, you become something of value and one who lived in the machine of time."*

Countless people would love this story especially those who have worked direclty or indirectly in garments industry which are abundant in developing countries. The lives of those millions of people are long hours spent with warps and wefts.

****

The Puzzle of 100

"It's all about marketing and nothing but marketing that will lead us to success"

"If I can maintain a tight grip on my subordinates, I'll get full control and that will lead me to get the best results."

"If I could just solve this matter, no other problems would bother me anymore."

The main problem in our country is education... No! The problem is justice... No, no! It's solidarity..."

Tying work, social and personal problems in a single slogan and believing that one such slogan is what is needed to solve any problem or accomplish any task may be the reason we fail solving any problems or accomplishing any task. I have met many who employ this flawed strategy.

After many discussions and arguments, I could not change the point of view of many of these people. And after finally convincing someone, I still had to go through developing a plan and then convince that someone to actually execute it. Now, everything is realigned due to a simple, clear and influential projection which aided in changing perceptions and motivate people solve problems and accomplish tasks. Altering the belief that one influential slogan or multiple ones is the sole key to success is called The Puzzle of 100.

When my friend began his own business, he fanatically believed that by just using Facebook Ads would be enough to give his venture the exposure it needed. He only focused on it and overlooked many other ways that had much more impact so I had to convince my friend as follows;

"Now, imagine that this whole project is like a puzzle which we used to play when we were kids. Imaging a picture of a castle or a face of some famous figure consisting of small pieces of cardboard. You won't finish the puzzle if you only connected the cardboards comprising the eyes because you believe those are the only important parts of the puzzle. You need all the details to complete the whole picture. But if you miss out some details, it's not as big a problem when you have most of the details in front of you. You can then stop for a certain period.

You have to approach each detail as part of a bigger puzzle – a bigger picture. Write a list which contains pieces in a puzzle that is your project. Once you finish your initial list, many other details will come up and it will be pieces to your puzzle. You will find that what you wrote is a list of things or activities that will contribute to the success of your project and 100 is just an arbitrary number.

And now after you listed pieces of the puzzles, start to weigh each according to importance. Set a relative weight for each piece that will help show the final picture in the clearest way then and immediately begin with your team to execute this puzzle beginning with the highest relative weight to the lowest. And like the way you felt when you were a child when a puzzle fits into place, you continue with enthusiasm as the piture slowly unravels before your eyes. I have witnessed this time and again when people in the organization set their priorities and execute tasks accordingly to completion, positive results are achieved. This is the best outcome of The Puzzle of 100 – to work in a correct and balanced way.

The Puzzle of 100 became a main pillar of Manager – X and maybe soon we will publish a book about it. For now, this will suffice...

****

Decision Making

Once President Roosevelt said, "In any moment of decision, the best thing you can do is the right thing, the next best thing is the wrong thing, and the worst thing you can do is nothing."

Seeking to persuade someone to make a decision is one of the most important skills everybody aims to have, like influencing people's decisions to go for something or even quit something. Logic and emotion are both involved in decision making. For example, someone is deciding to give a prize between two people depending on their answers for set of questions. Emotion does not play a part if there is no relationship whatsoever with either of the contestants. Also, if questions and answers are not related to any personal aspect that could affect or trigger any kind of emotions but rather technical questions. Add to that a prize that is of insignificant and trivial value to the one making the decision.

All the elements above will give more weight to logic over emotions in the process of decision making. In the 18th century Bernoulli stated his famous *Utility Theory* which states that people give proportional weights according to the value of the choice presented and based on the outcome of these relative weights they make their decisions by choosing the biggest relative weight. (30)

But Daniel Kahneman, a Nobel laureate in Behavioral Economics refuted of Bernoulli's theory. He cited a flaw in the theory which totally ignored the aspect of the emotion in setting up the relative weights that affect people's decisions. Bernoulli proposed that if someone offered you to choose between an 80% chance to win 100 USD or a 20% chance to win 10 USD, the relative weight respectively would be (100 x 0.80 + 10 x 0.20) = 82 USD. So, if someone was to choose between the two, 8 out of 10 times, option 1 will be picked while 2 out of 10 times will go to option 2. (31)

Bernoulli did not consider the reference point of wealth. If someone already had a million dollars, the relative weights he chooses will be completely different from a destitute man. Kahneman considered the emotional element that will cause a substantial difference in decision making for people.

Decisions that are not based on some kind of emotion represent a paltry percentage. Emotions play a significant role in decisions and most of time, emotions outweigh logic. For instance, when you have two restaurants to choose from for dinner which have competitive prices, you will go for that Italian restaurant because it reminds you of memories of Rome. Even further, emotions fully control certain decisions like when you see someone shouting at your son. You would most probably have an altercation even before finding out what your son has done. You may later learn that the man was shouting at your son who had headphones on crossing the street and a truck was about to hit him but thanks to the shouting, your son was saved.

This is why numerous research are dedicated to investigate psychology behind decision making under different emotional conditions. On such is the experiment of D Antonio Damasio. Damasio studied subjects who suffered brain injuries in parts that control emotions. They were asked to choose between items like food from a menu, and although they were able to distinguish differences for each choice logically; for instance one food item is oily, while another is fibrous and yet they could not make a decision as to what they will have. This was a landmark in the research on decision making .(32)

Providing a catalyst in order to make decision is one of the reasons that stories are powerful and widely used. Emotions that stories stir penetrate hearts and minds and influence – inspire to make the reluctant, procrastinators or the prudent decide. Many losses are because of the inability to make a decision when the time came. And in business, managers usually suffer from their inability to persuade or direct their subordinates to certain decisions so instead, they turn to power and position – threatening, coercing, stick and carrot tactic. Novice managers use these tactics because it achieves results but they do not consider that these fast catches never last and cannot be sustained in the long run. It incurs serious losses that outweigh the quick results. Turnover of the skilled and trained employees is one of them. Workers look for meaning in what they do in the organization. They should be part of the vision – add value to it, to believe in it and find ways to achieve it.

Whoever uses power and position as a strategy to deal with subordinates does not reflect concern about injecting any meaning or value to orders or views being given or conveyed. As a result, the working environment becomes vague and unconducive. Threatening people with a machine gun while giving orders may be the easiest thing to do but for how long? And what if they also had their machine guns?

If you are able to give orders to your people so they receive it with understanding and acceptance and if you trust that you have conveyed the company vision; they would have the drive and take full responsibility and make the right decisions.

What is marvelous about stories is that anyone can master it even if a storyteller has no experience in a professional setting. Stories have more impact and influence than direct orders. By converting such orders to stories, decisions will be made more quickly and in turn put it into action. One such story is by Gabrielle Dolen and Yamini Naidu,

Brussels Sprouts

'When I was a kid, I hated Brussels sprouts. Every time Brussels sprouts was served at dinner, I always left the Brussels sprouts till the end (of course I always hoped I could get away without eating them). My mother would never let me leave the table until I ate them.

One day, when Brussels sprouts was on the menu (yet again), I decided to eat them straight away so I could sit back and enjoy the rest of my meal. Do you think we could approach our quality sales leads targets like Brussels sprouts? We all know we can't leave the table without eating them. Do you think we could get them out of the way early in the week and then sit back and enjoy the rest of our week?'

Gabrielle and Yamani mentions that story above helped many top management in various companies change their view about boring and donkey works and decide to take action and tackle those boring meetings, writing memos, etc. These top management guys began to use this story on their subordinates. What is really interesting with this particular story it that it is a real situation that we all lived through. Despite different cultural backgrounds, we all can recall the kinds of healthy food our mother forced us to eat. This actually a way you can make your own personal story which will be more influential. Using the same exact theme and structure of the story would not produce impact in some other part of the world where Brussels sprouts is unknown. You would have to use a famous food that you and your audience did not like during childhood. Applying your own cultural context to the story helps to produce the impact and recall triggering emotions finally providing a catalyst to make decisions that could not be reached prior to hearing your story.

****

Modern human history witnessed several times how one story can be the main reason to change the political and social landscape in some part of the world and how it can induce nations to go into a moral battle that are memorialized in hundreds of books as a humanistic milestone. "Uncle Tom's Cabin" is an example. It was written by American writer, Harriet Stowe. She was born in Connecticut and worked as a children's teacher. She published this novel in 1852 in and around the time political moral questions were being raised about slave trade and slavery in general. The Southern States (Confederates) wanted to keep slavery legal due to their dependence on agriculture and pastoralism. The Northern States (Unionists) opposed it because of moral implications and their livelihood was more industrialized. This story left such an influence that it provided groundbreaking motivation for the American Civil war led by Lincoln and resulted in the Emancipation Proclamation. (33). The novel sold thousands of copies in the United States and about one million in the United Kingdom. They made an initiative in Scotland to collect one cent from each housewife as moral support for the issue. Lincoln met Stowe at the beginning of the war and said to her, "So you're the little woman who wrote the book which started this great war." The plot is about triggering emotions to refuse the cruelty of slavery which caused the separation of husband from his wife and children then depicts the mercy of the white man (the northern citizen) to his slaves. Stowe used family relationships that touched the heartstring of the common reader. Stowe managed to trigger the reader's emotions with the plot conveying a strong message that challenged the culture of society toward slavery.

Uncle Tom's Cabin Summary of

A Kentucky farmer Arthur Shelby faces the loss of his farm because of debts. Shelby decides to raise the needed funds by selling two of his slaves—Uncle Tom, a middle-aged man with a wife and children, and Harry, the son of Emily Shelby's maid Eliza—to a slave trader. Emily Shelby is averse to this idea because she had promised her maid that her child would never be sold; Emily's son, George Shelby, hates to see Tom go because he sees the man as his friend and mentor.

When Eliza overhears Mr. and Mrs. Shelby discussing plans to sell Tom and Harry, Eliza determines to run away with her son leaving a note of apology to her mistress.

Tom is sold and placed on a riverboat, which sets sail down the Mississippi River. While on board, Tom meets and befriends a young white girl named Eva. Eva's father Augustine St Clare buys Tom from the slave trader and takes him with the family to their home in New Orleans. Tom and Eva begin to relate to one another because of the deep Christian faith they share.

During Eliza's escape, she meets up with her husband George Harris, who had run away previously. They decide to attempt to reach Canada. However, they are tracked by a slave hunter named Tom Loker. Eventually Loker and his men trap Eliza and her family causing George to shoot him in the side. Worried that Loker may die, Eliza convinces George to bring the slave hunter to a nearby Quaker settlement for medical treatment.

Back in New Orleans, St Clare debates slavery with his Northern cousin Ophelia who, while opposing slavery, is prejudiced against black people. St Clare, however, believes he is not biased, even though he is a slave owner. In an attempt to show Ophelia that her views on blacks are wrong, St Clare purchases Topsy, a young black slave, and asks Ophelia to educate her.

After Tom has lived with the St Clares for two years, Eva grows very ill. Before she dies, she experiences a vision of heaven, which she shares with the people around her. As a result of her death and vision, the other characters resolve to change their lives, with Ophelia promising to throw off her personal prejudices against blacks, Topsy saying she will better herself, and St Clare pledging to free Tom.

Before St Clare can follow through on his pledge, however, he dies after being stabbed outside of a tavern. His wife reneges on her late husband's vow and sells Tom at auction to a vicious plantation owner named Simon Legree. Legree (a transplanted northerner) takes Tom and Emmeline (whom Legree purchased at the same time) to rural Louisiana, where they meet Legree's other slaves.

Legree begins to hate Tom when Tom refuses Legree's order to whip his fellow slave. Legree beats Tom viciously and resolves to crush his new slave's faith in God. Despite Legree's cruelty, however, Tom refuses to stop reading his Bible and comforting the other slaves as best he can. While at the plantation, Tom meets Cassy, another of Legree's slaves. Cassy was previously separated from her son and daughter when they were sold; unable to endure the pain of seeing another child sold, she killed her third child.

At this point, Loker has changed as the result of being healed by the Quakers. George, Eliza, and Harry have also obtained their freedom after crossing into Canada. In Louisiana, Uncle Tom almost succumbs to hopelessness as his faith in God is tested by the hardships of the plantation. However, he has two visions, one of Jesus and one of Eva, which renew his resolve to remain a faithful Christian, even unto death. He encourages Cassy to escape, which she does, taking Emmeline with her. When Tom refuses to tell Legree where Cassy and Emmeline have gone, Legree orders his overseers to kill Tom. As Tom is dying, he forgives the overseers who savagely beat him. Humbled by the character of the man they have killed, both men become Christians. Very shortly before Tom's death, George Shelby (Arthur Shelby's son) arrives to buy Tom's freedom but finds he is too late.

On their boat ride to freedom, Cassy and Emmeline meet George Harris's sister and accompany her to Canada. Cassy discovers that Eliza is her long-lost daughter who was sold as a child. Now that their family is together again, they travel to France and eventually Liberia, the African nation created for former American slaves. George Shelby returns to the Kentucky farm and frees all his slaves and tells them to remember Tom's sacrifice.

****

Once I wrote a book about the history of compulsory education and how it inflicts a destructive effect of the minds of many generations in the whole world. It's a real suffering for a majority of students killing creativity with the indoctrination of following and committing to as set of rules and structure with no room for thinking or questions. And what is strange is that when you ask students about their experience in school, 98% comment that this approach is flawed and parents' comments will not differ much, even members of the academe and faculty agree. Any yet no one makes a decision whether to abandon the system or find other alternatives. To make a decision to abolish something firmly established for decades is a very tough mission, but as we mentioned earlier stories like "Uncle Tom's Cabin" can contribute to change an engrained practice. Exposing the flaws of compulsory education may lead to a true change of this system.

The Frantic Race

What amazing wings I have, they lift me high in the sky, I can fly as fast as lightning. Here I am in fascinating Europe in less than five minutes. How beautiful Paris is from above.

Anyway I can't waste my time hovering over just one place, I only have twenty minutes left to watch the rest of this ancient city. I think I have to fly over now south of gree... "Midooo!". All of sudden Mido loses control of his wings. They go on auto pilot and they drive his little body at sonic speed bringing him to his homeland, Cairo. He breaks in through the window of his room, slumping his body on his nasty bed and in a blink of an eye, Mido wakes up and jumps off his bed to a loud voice resembling a military camp wake up call.

The wall clock shows 7 AM. In the background, Mido's mom continues shouting that he is late for breakfast therefore late for school. Mido begins putting books and notes that weigh several kilos in his bag. He steps out half past seven to catch the school bus. He reaches school five minutes to eight and while chatting with his friends, a deafening sound of a medieval horn blew signaling them to gather for the pep rally. Everyone stops even before they even begin and line up looking at the teachers with reverence who look back with scrutinizing eyes. The morning assembly begins with the school radio which no one listens to, then calisthenics for one and half minutes which burns no more than three to four calories. After the rally is done, students march to the rhythm of drums and tambourines – a view that resembles Auschwitz, the famous Nazi concentration camp.

The students enter their rooms to his own desk for the first class. A teacher enters and enumerates the rules of etiquette such as don't speak with your seatmate, keep eyes on the white board at all times, all are being observed and you will be held accountable for your actions, you aren't allowed to do anything without permission except breathing. With the rules out of the way, the class begins. It is literature class and each student is tasked to write a fiction of some sort. Mido stretches his imagination and stimulates his right brain to visualize a Nile cruise passing through Aswan with all the beauty it has from water, mountains, sand, temples and... All of a sudden the deafening horn blows again shutting down all the imagination and creativity in their brain because Biology class was next for the anatomy of the genito-urinary system of an amoeba.

This cycle continues every 45 minutes until the school day ends at 2 PM. Students jump from one idea to another. Students, like sailors, are flung violently by waves in their ship of dreams. They desperately cling on and those who could not is cast out and labeled a failure while those inside are called survivors. But who is the true survivor – the one who stayed inside the ship and let the waves to do whatever or those who jumped off and swam and strove in the sea till he reaches the shore with his dream.

Mido is back home at 3 PM. He can't do anything except to drop his bag along with his concerns on the floor of his room. He lays down on his bed and in a matter of minutes he falls in a deep sleep... The white shiny wings carry Mido to the highest horizon to begin a new trip toward the clouds breaking into the borders of the vast univer... "Midooo!". He falls on the floor. He answers his mom whiningly but his mother shouts again because it is 5 PM and he has to study his lessons before his dad returns and sees him sleeping. He argues and blames his mom for his failure. Mido goes out of his room and sits at his desk and begins to study as they taught him in school. He immerses in any book for about half an hour and then goes for a next one. He has thirteen books for that semester.

Mido picks up a book on geography so his mind flows to the geography of North America with its beautiful rivers, and green mountains. He takes his boat and as he nears Niagara Falls, he loses balance and falls into the quandary of a sine function with logarithmic power of a complex number but finally saves one of Priory's few remaining soldiers fleeing from the Battle of Jerusalem. Mido peruses his books until 9 PM. He sneaks into the living room to continue reading his lovely trilogy, seeking to know how the hero of planet Oranous liberated it from invaders of the evil Malingus Galaxy. Mido decides to assist his hero confront the bad guys and gets into the hero's space shuttle to do battle with the enemy in their onw galaxy. They set their laser guns and the heroes of Oranous are about to be given the green light to attack. The countdown begins, 5… 4… 3… 2… "Midooo! If you don't go to sleep right now, you won't be able to wake up for school tomorrow". The inavaders from Malingus Galaxy was no match for his shouting mother and so with shame, he retreats from the battle before it begins. He goes to his room lying on the bed, covering his face with the blanket, asking himself, what if tomorrow is the last day of my life and I was given the choice to go wherever I want. Shall I spend the last day at school as my mother wants or shall I be by the side of the hero of Oranous planet?

****

One of the false beliefs in decision making and innovation is that the best decisions and ideas are the most difficult and the most complicated. Many seek the hardest and longest path in finding solutions and many fail. Really, the simplest and clearest methods will solve any problem. To the common manager, innovation with its details in artistic formulation and execution makes it look complicated. A well-crafted story has the ability to motivate the audience in making effective decisions in the simplest manner.

The Prisoner

A prisoner was to be executed the next day at dawn. the night prior execution, the king went to him and said, "You can search for a way out in this prison, and if you find it, go. You shall be free and no one will give chase." The prisoner felt delighted to have a chance of survival and began to search. He searched inside his cell and outside as well. He went to another section that had many other cells and entered one of them. He found a torn rug on the floor and removed it. Hidden underneath was a winding staircase leading to the basement of the prison. In the basement, the stairs leads up to the other side of the prison. He proceeds with vim until he breathes the fresh air at the roof of the prison. He feels more enthusiastic and continues until he finds himself inside the prison high tower with an open window. If he jumps off from that height, he will die.

He turned back feeling sad and exhausted. But he was so sure the king would not deceive him and a way out exists if only he could find it. He lied on the floor and as he rested his feet on the wall, a stone moved with the weight of his foot. He stood up and removed the stone. He found a hole in the wall leading to a small tunnel. He could barely fit but began crawling inside and the deeper he got, the more he could hear the sound of the of the river outside the prison. He crawled faster but reached an opening barred with heavy steel bars.

He laboriously crawled back to his cell. He checked every stone in the wall. He tried looking for another way but all failed. The night finally passed and with the dawn, the king arrived, "Did you find the way out?" The prisoner replied in grief, "I spent my whole night searching, digging, and crawling but could not find the way so I surrendered". The king said, "You, fool, the gate of the prison was open the whole night but you did not even consider it, it's time for your execution."

Unfortunately, this is how we make decisions. It rarely crosses our minds that the best solutions are the simplest and most common. We always tend to go upstairs to the high tower that exhausts our energy or go downstairs to the basement that extinguishes hope believing that the solution and the exit to our problems require the biggest of effort. But the surprise is that at many times the solution is right before our eyes.

****

"A Time to Kill" written by John Grisham who originally is a lawyer. His first profession taught him the importance of storytelling in judicial proceedings. An effective story in the closing argument could influence the emotions of the judge and the jury. A ten-year-old African-American girl named Tonya Hailey is viciously raped and beaten by two redneck white supremacists. Distraught and outraged, the father, Carl Lee Hailey, consults his friend Jake Brigance, a white attorney who had previously represented Hailey's brother, on whether he could get Carl Lee acquitted if he killed the two men. Jake admonishes Carl Lee not to do anything stupid, but admits that if it had been his daughter, he would kill the rapists. Carl Lee is determined to avenge Tonya and as the criminals were being led into holding after their bond hearing, he kills both men with an M-16.

Carl Lee is charged with capital murder. He elects Jake to represent him. On the day the trial begins, a riot ensues between the KKK and the African Americans outside the courthouse. The KKK shoots at Jake one morning as he is being escorted into the courthouse, missing him but seriously wounding one of the guards assigned to protect him. They continue to burn crosses throughout Clanton. Later, they burn down Jake's house. Carl Lee did not do very well on the witness stand. The jury seem to apply double standards on Carl Lee and things look grim for him. Finally, Jake sees no way to save Carl Lee. He tells a story in his closing to persuade the jury. (34)

The Closing Argument

Now I wanna tell you a story... I'm going to ask you all to close your eyes while I tell you the story. I want you to listen to me. I want you to listen to yourselves. Go ahead. Close your eyes, please.

This is a story about a little girl walking home from the grocery store one sunny afternoon. I want you to picture this little girl. Suddenly, a truck races up. Two men jump out and grab her. They drag her into a nearby field and they tie her up and they rip her clothes from her body. Now they climb on. First one, then the other, raping her, shattering everything innocent and pure with a vicious thrust in a fog of drunken breath and sweat. And when they're done, after they've killed her tiny womb, murdered any chance for her to have children, to have life beyond her own, they decide to use her for target practice. They start throwing full beer cans at her. They throw them so hard that it tears the flesh all the way to her bones. Then they urinate on her.

Now comes the hanging. They have a rope. They tie a noose. Imagine the noose going tight around her neck and with a sudden blinding jerk she's pulled into the air and her feet and legs go kicking. They don't find the ground. The hanging branch isn't strong enough. It snaps and she falls back to the earth. So they pick her up, throw her in the back of the truck and drive out to Foggy Creek Bridge. Pitch her over the edge. And she drops some thirty feet down to the creek bottom below.

Can you see her...? Her raped, beaten, broken body soaked in their urine, soaked in their semen, soaked in her blood, left to die. Can you see her...? I want you to picture that little girl.

Now... imagine... she's white...

****

One of the toughest problems of this age is the invasion of technology in homes and in bedrooms. People suffer the inability or the desire to limit the adverse ramifications of this invasion because of dependence. Many do not consider the inherent danger of dependence on devices like the television. People believe they are invulnerable and that their children are protected from imitating what they watch. TV is one of the most dangerous devices. I personally (emphasis added) believe that networks, in majority, either directly or indirectly spread corruption, obscenity and evil. And no way are we saved from that evil unless we make a bold decision to kick (our dependence) it out of the home. In this way, the parents would take back control over the behavior of the children. One time, I listened to a short and simple but very descriptive story about the threat of television since then, I used this story and noticed how motivating and mind blowing it is.

The Stranger

The mother woke up early and prepared breakfast for her husband and kids. And after the husband went to work, kids stayed in their room playing. And during this time, the mother does housework. Suddenly, the doorbell rang. She wondered saying, "Who would come over at 10 AM?!". She carefully opened the door and saw a lanky man with a dubious look about him. He cracked a cold smile and said, "Hi, I'm your new neighbor and I moved in yesterday". The woman replied, "Welcome. How can I help you?". He said,

"Yesterday, I saw three kids playing in your back yard, are they your kids?". She answers worryingly, "Yes, they are our kids". The man asks, "So, where are they right now?". The woman close to bewilderment answers, "They are in their room". The man delightfully smiling as if finding something missing says, "Then, would you allow me to be with them in their room for a while?". The woman looked at him, stunned at his request, but eventually said, "No problem, go on, they are at the first room to your right". The man enters the room and closes the door behind him, the woman goes back to kitchen.

The story ends there. Would any mother allow a stranger to be alone with her kids? Does this woman know what the man will tell, let alone do with her children? What is the difference between TV and strangers? This is the story of the TV and gadgets with our young generation. If you feel secure about your kids in the presence of TVs and gadgets, do not be surprised of the woman in the story.

****

One of the wonders of this age is the how the family structure has drastically changed from its original makeup that held though for ages. The man used to go outside to work, while the woman worked at home to educate kids and to fill the home with morals and happiness. Now women go out to compete with the men in the workplace. That social change led to an imbalance of educating young generations when mothers quitted doing so and delegated this holy task to unqualified persons. Thus, the woman became a competitor to her husband in earnings they bring back. This led to another imbalance, that of authority. Two income households resulted to an increase in consumption and demand so both parents had to work even more. to cover those unnecessary demands, and so on. Little by little and day after day, the family structure erodes.

Many working mothers in many countries reveal the desire to go back to their traditional role in society, but the financial pressures does not allow for this. It is a bold decision to leave work and concede the extra income to go back home and care for the kids. Rachaele Hambleton, 33, posted this deeply moving message online to share how she had been inspired by a complete stranger she sees walking her children to school across Shaldon Bridge in Devon every morning; (35)

The Crazy Blonde Curly Hair Who Inspired Me

I used to be a full-time working mum.

Every morning for the past 10 years, I've driven from Torquay over the Shaldon Bridge on my way to work... and most days I've driven past a beautiful lady with crazy curly blonde hair... she started out 10 years ago walking her eldest baby to the primary school with her younger ones carried on her chest and in double buggies whilst walking a beautiful puppy retriever.

Every morning I would watch her and be in awe at how organised she was, how she could possibly manage and how happy her babies looked. I would then continue the rest of my journey to work with a lump in my throat that someone else was doing all of those things with my babies because I felt I should be at work.

This lady made me realise that actually I should work a little less, and learn to manage a little more...

So as I drove past you this morning and I saw you kissing your daughter on the forehead who once, I saw, as a tiny baby and is now a little lady... and your dog was walking at a much slower pace beside you now. He's so much older and I imagine all your other children have now grown up and go to secondary school and walk themselves to school... I just wanted to post on here, in the hope somehow it will reach you, to say

> *thank you... because of you I have now reduced my working hours... so I can spend some mornings at home doing the crazy school runs with all my babies, I make sure I go and fight back tears watching all their school plays and bake (mainly inedible) cakes for the fetes... and I love all of it!*
>
> *It's amazing that seeing a 30 second glimpse of someone else's life once a day can make yours so much more enjoyable xx*

This message was like a coup de grace to Rachaele and many others to get out of the rat race and revive their natural and holy career. What was more impressive is that the lady with blond curly hair read the message and answered Rachaele, as follows;

> *I'm absolutely AMAZED that you have noticed me for such a long time and noticed the changes in my family. I've been walking Shaldon Bridge since 2003 along with Boris the dog who's now 11 and finding it a struggle. I have had five children go to the school (my younger 3 are still there) and your (sic) right my elder two walk themselves to TCS.*
>
> *I feel incredibly honoured (along with embarrassed) to be mentioned in such a post for simply walking my children to school along with what has felt like over the years being a parent machine!!!*
>
> *That short walk across Shaldon Bridge is my little bit of therapy and how blessed we all are to live in such a beautiful part of the world! I am taking the credit for SO many other parents who do exactly the same as me so for all the other parents, that post was for you too!!!*
>
> *I know that everyone's life is different and sometimes life doesn't enable us all to spend the time with our children that we wish but I believe being there for those simple day to day moments creates long lasting memories for all!*
>
> *I have to give thanks and credit to my wonderful husband who works tirelessly which enables me to be there for our children without the need*

for grandparents or childcare so without him I couldn't do it. Let's not forget our hard-working husbands and partners!

I wouldn't change it all even if I could so hold on to all those beautiful memories you're making with your children because they won't want you going to school with them forever.... it's all over too soon.

Many, many thanks for allowing me to be part of your journey and give me a beep when we pass next so I can give you a wave!!

So touched to have made a positive difference to a stranger's life.

****

Source

Source is whether a story is from real events or fiction. Naturally, the former is more attractive and intriguing to people. This is probably why movies that are billed as "Inspired from a true story" usually have high viewership. As human beings, we have a tendency to want to know about a truth that did not witness. Curiosity is an instinct. I allowed us to survive since ancient times. Humans naturally followed traces and listen to anecdotes of hunters and adventures of travellers seeking out safer abodes and survival. A flipped and crashed van on the street is enough to tell a story of a terrible accident and the scene will not be lacking in people claiming they know the whole story.

A true story is much stronger than a fictional or imaginary one in offering proof. The story of the medical student in England, Roger Bannister, who was the first man to run a mile under four minutes. At that time, everybody believed that it was physiologically impossible to set a record. John Laundry, an Australian runner, tried to break it many times but could not. His best time was 4:02.1 but Bannister was doing his best trying to break it. As a medical student, he knew that his body would consume the lowest amount of oxygen by keeping a fixed acceleration. Mentally, he constantly imagined that he had already broken the record. In 1954 and after many attempts, Bannister did it and became the first man on the face of the earth to run a mile in 3:59.4. And hundreds followed suit just because they knew that another living human did so. John Laundry also broke the record 46 days after Bannister. The hundreds around the world who also broke the record in the subsequent months and years did not get to meet or even see Roger Bannister but heard his story. They knew it was a real man with flesh and bones achieved it which made them believe that they could do it, too. The setback was not in limited human ability but with the proof that such thing was possible. We witness this all the time. Once an athletic record is broken or a scientific milestone is achieved, we quickly go about finding ways to surpass or go beyond it. The barrier is our minds, the belief that what is impossible could one day be possible. And it seems clear that this stubborn mind swiftly submits once it hears that type of story... the true story. (36)

Many sales managers narrate Bannister's story to motivate sales teams rather than make up a completely false one where a super sales person sold the worst product in high volume. Workers, in general, need true stories that guide them and tell them that what they are seeking to reach has already been achieved by others and that there are no barriers that limit human abilities.

A true story about you has more powerful impact because people want to see and touch and interact with the hero after all the difficulties. Although there is a plethora of other people's stories, still a personal story is the best anyone can use even with its simplicity. That's why it is crucial to craft your personal stories and utilize them to what the situation may demand.

Fiction or the imaginary has a very important role in eliciting emotions and projecting reality from the imaginary which influences like a true story. If fiction has the disadvantage of leaving its audience with something less than real, it has the capacity to create that still grabs attention and trigger emotions. The first experience of children with stories is with imaginary ones and the most of what adults read is fiction. The best storytellers are those who can employ the imaginary to project actual reality. Fiction is a double-edged sword which must have a good plot and exciting elements because it has a tough counterpart in true stories. Both are powerful.

Path

Many historians view that culture and art flourished in the Renaissance then a downturn until it took a sharp rising trend in the 19th century. In the 19th century, people began to study the structure of the story. Schools included it in their curriculum. Experts and members of the academe analyzed theatrical works and novels pointing out criteria which aided in judging and qualifying a masterpiece.

Carlo Gozzi classified the dramatic situations of stories into 36 plots, amongst them is Supplication where a suppliant appeals to someone in authority and others such as Crime Pursued by Vengeance, Mistaken Jealousy, Self-sacrifice for Kin, Crimes of Love, The Enigma, The Abduction, Erroneous Judgment, etc. All in all, the story is a mix of these situations that constitute the plot. (37)

Gustav Freytag drafted a clear and simple path for a story according to its consecutive events. It was called the Freytag Dramatic Arc or Freytag's Pyramid where any story begins with the introduction then events escalate getting more complicated creating crisis and dilemma reaching the climax. The gravity of the climax is the main determinant of the strength of the plot. After the climax, the crises begins to be resolved rapidly until the ending which is most usually happy and then of course wisdom or the moral in concise phrases. (38)

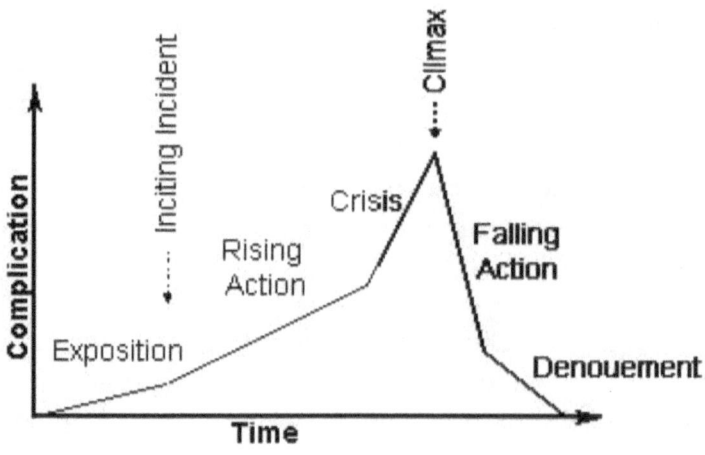

Kurt Vonnegut, while studying Anthropology in Chicago university, presented a proposal for his masters about the classification of stories in novels and plays but was rejected because the panel saw it as superficial with no value to add. Kurt decided to leave academic studies and became a writer. He turned out to be a bestseller author and his novels became very popular. His proposed classification became known where he mentioned them in a book published prior to his death entitled, "A Man Without a Country". In it, he described the path of a story through a time graph, where its vertical axis is the rate of happiness and misery and its horizontal axis is the timeline of the story. The first graph is the first type of stories he called Man in Hole. And historically, this is the most renowned plot. It shows the protagonist in good spirits and fortune until a crisis takes place then resolution with everything going back to normal ending with the protagonist in a better situation than before. Kurt says that people admire this type of story. (39)

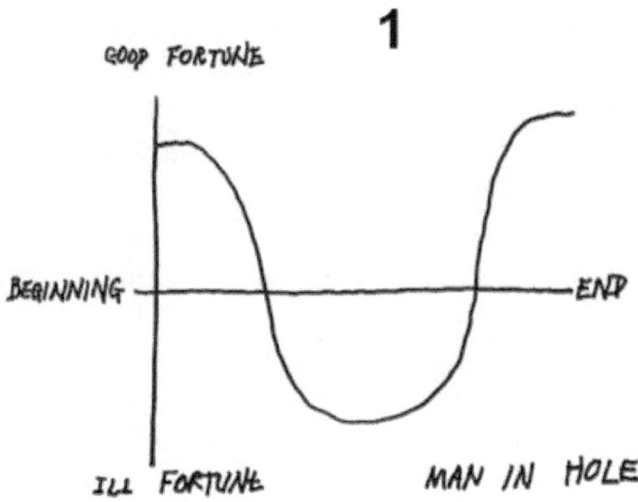

The second type is Boy Meets Girl. Events begin in a general frame where neither happiness nor misery is exposed. A normal stable life with neither advantage nor problems takes place in the passage of time until a sudden downfall takes place with a sequence of problems but ultimately success and happiness resume.

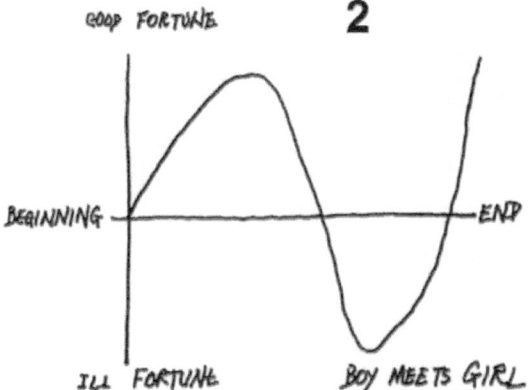

The third type is Cinderella which begins with the misery and poverty of the protagonist and when things get a little better, everything collapses instantly. But in the end, happiness comes as instantly as it disappeared.

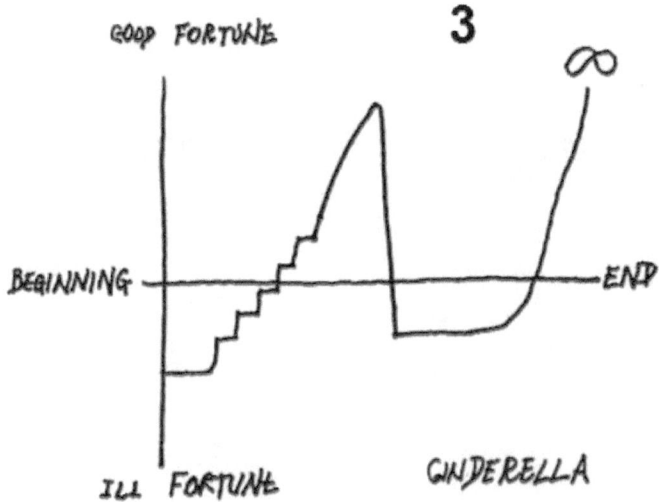

The fourth type is Kafka. Exposition begins in misery, continues and ends in misery as well. One such story is "The Garage". Naima, the wife of a property manager of an old building in downtown Cairo with seven children is abandoned by her husband. They took over running the whole building and serving its tenants. Naima learns that she has a fatal illness and will die in a few months. Her only recourse was to give up her children for adoption to different families making sure that every child knew how to reach each other so they could reunite someday. After successfully finishing her mission in securing the future of her helpless kids, she goes to her bed and dies in peace. Kafka begins with distress and culminates in depression. This kind of story has a theme of misery from the first to the last scene and yet has very deep meaning which penetrates the memory much more than happy ones. Human nature is more inclined to recall the bad rather than the good and to learn from failure more than success.

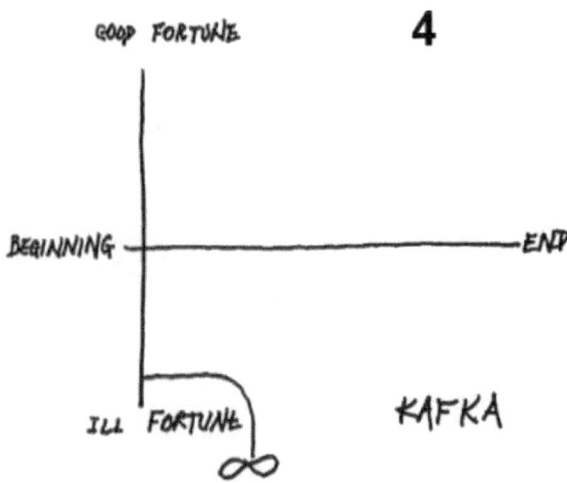

The fifth type is Hamlet. Those familiar with the story will know that it is characterized with ambiguity and obscurity from beginning to end. The reader is left hanging. Should Hamlet be delighted to encounter his father's ghost? Does he feel proud because he did not take vengeance on his uncle? The famous question is apt, "To be or not to be". Kurt referred to other types but are quite similar to the five types.

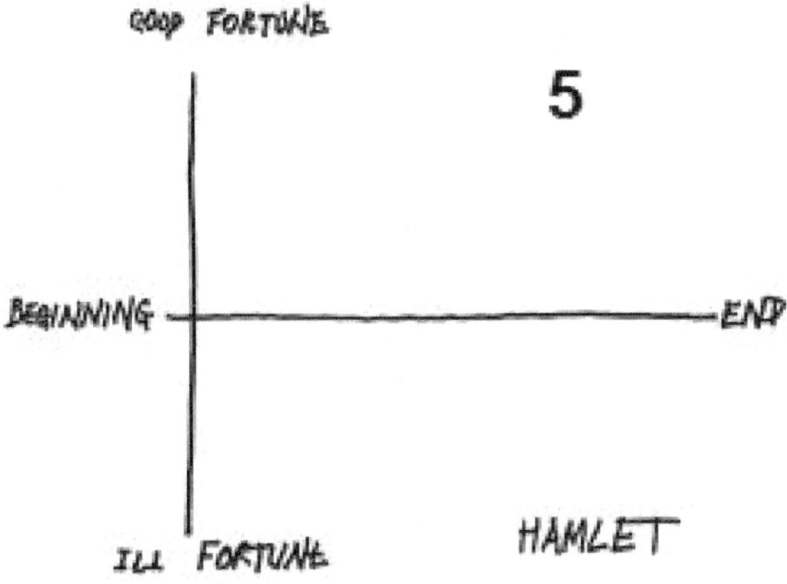

Andrew Reagan utilized technology to aid in understanding stories and the various paths, how we can spot the patterns that influence people throughout history in a better and more accurate way. In the Computational Story Lab, he collected phrases spread in social media and processes these using algorithms to deduce the emotions in a process called Hednometric or Sentiment Analysis. The millions of processed conversations are rated using a metric of happiness and are grouped per country within a certain timeline.

During the war between Gaza and Israel, Gaza was at the tailend of happy countries because conversations were about war, destruction, demolition, death and revenge. The picture shows the analysis of conversations in Twitter in the United States from Jan 2016 to April 2017. The happiness meter was very high during Christmas and quickly dipped when Donald Trump won presidential race. (40)

In 2016, they used this algorithm in a project called Project Gutenberg's Fiction, where they studied 1327 novels from the Library of Gutenberg by analyzing the words of happiness and misery, so they can extract the path the story took.

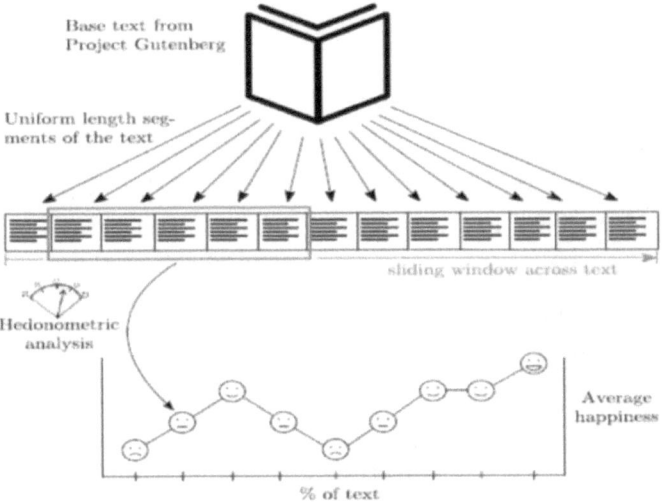

In the following diagram, the horizontal bar represents the book pages from 0 to 100% while the vertical bar represents the rate of emotions, above zero is happiness and below zero is misery. In the analysis "Harry Potter and the Deathly Hallows", it indicates the rising of positive emotions to peak levels at 15% of the pages then dips to the lowest level at 85% then finally rising until the end.

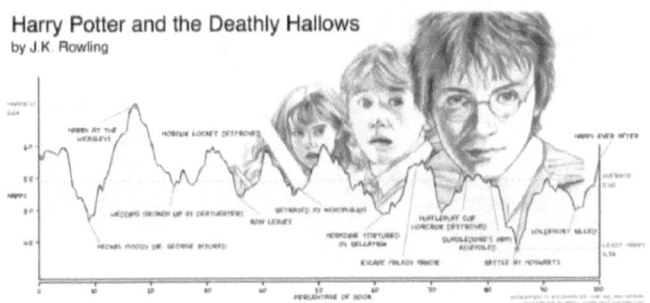

In conclusion there are six paths for a story (in accordance with emotions):

    1. Rising – Rags to Riches
    2. Falling – Tragedy
    3. Falling – Rising – Man in Hole

4. Rising – Falling – Icarus
5. Rising – Falling – Rising – Cinderella
6. Falling – Rising – Falling – Oedipus

The first path (Rising – Rags to Riches) is depicted in Alice's adventures in Wonderland. The character goes from one adventure to another filled with thrills and lessons with no suffering or misery. The second path is (Falling – Tragedy) depicted "Romeo and Juliet" filled with grief and pain from beginning to end. The third path (Falling – Rising – Man in Hole) exists in majority of stories which begins with a crisis and concludes in survival. The fourth path (Rising – Falling – Icarus) resembles the famous myth. Icarus with wings held together by wax died when he flew close to the sun. The fifth path (Rising – Falling – Rising – Cinderella) begins with happiness and continues to to the peak until Cinderella's world collapses and the graph dips until it rises a steay incline when the prince finally finds and marries her. The sixth path (Falling – Rising – Falling – Oedipus) begins with separation when Laius gives up his son, Oedipus, to a shepherd. Emotions rise in the course of the story and concludes with treachery and death.

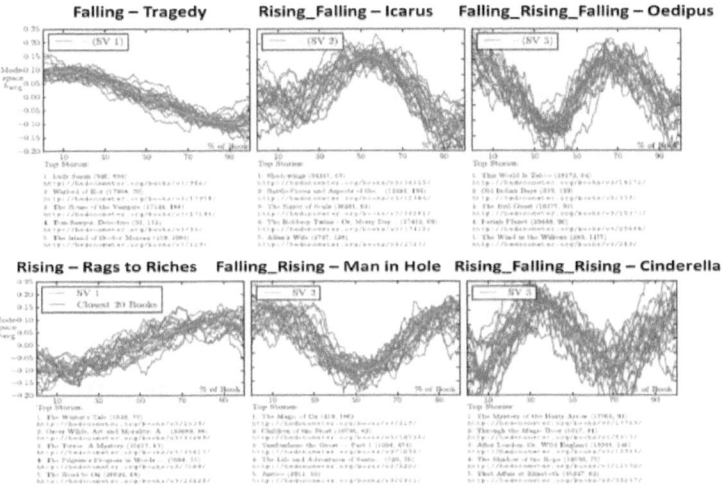

Research reveals that the sixth path is the most common plot used in stories while the fifth path comes in second. Both paths demonstrate the cycle of the rise and fall, contrasting events and situations mixing the good and the bad grabbing people's attentions. This is probably because the rise and fall of emotions move many people that causes the release of Cortisol which plays an important role in affecting people. Superficial observation would reveal that tories in this book and others you particularly like will most likely follow the last two paths.

The Content of a Path

While choosing the best path for your story, you will have to consider the details of each path. What events will take place within the rise and fall? We find the answer in "A Hero with Thousand Faces". For Joseph Campbell, stories that humans told since the dawn of time had always had similar, repetitive and unchangeable patterns that be divided in 12 stages. The first shows the Ordinary World where the protagonist lives, then comes the Call to Adventure, where the conflict is introduced. The Refusal to the Call, is where the hero refuses or hesitant to answer the call preferring to stay in the first stage. The fourth is Meeting the Mentor where the hero meets someone who grants wisdom to be able to continue the journey. Crossing the Threshold is the first adventure and the easiest in the path of the hero. (41) Sixth is the Testing Allies and Enemies, where the hero meets those who will assist him and those opposed. The 7th stage is Approaching the Inmost Cave, which is the most complicated part in the rising action. Ordeal is a sudden crisis the hero confronts nullifying all his gains. Reward is when the hero overcomes. The Road Back is the beginning of the end for the story where the hero leaves the battlefield and goes back from where he came. Resurrection is not so common but it has an incredible effect on the plot when the hero is thought to be dead but unexpectedly reappears. Return with the Elixir, places the hero back to the starting point bearing the solution to the conflict.

In her book "Resonate", Nancy Duarte depicted the twelve stages with the drawing above projected in stories that takes place in work or the household. (42) The twelve stages are crucial to note when crafting your stories. Of course, an anecdote does not require all the stages but some of the stories mentioned have three of four of the stages and yet these are enough to make impactful stories. However, Call to Adventure is a compulsory stage as well as Ordeal, which if non-existent will make for a very weak plot and of course The Road Back to provide an amazing impression to the whole story.

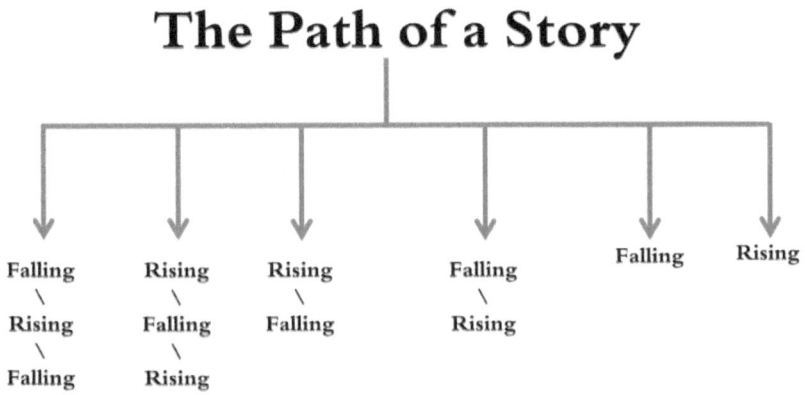

Delivery

Since ancient times, the phrase, "Let me tell you a story" acts like a magical key that can open hearts and minds of people. Stories were told and the voice, gestures, acting became part of the artform. Stories were also appreciated with the eyes so the storyteller painted on cave walls, carved on stone, inscribed columns and temples with symbols and words. This preserved stories for thousands of years to convey a message and deliver influence.

The main difference between delivering a story orally or visually is the mind's reception. If you were to choose between learning from a book or a recorded instruction, what would it be? The majority I asked chose to listen. When presented with a choice between an instructional video or a record, the majority opted to watch. Now, what if the ifnormation is so vital like the answers to your final exam? What medium would you choose? Now you choose reading over listening and make video the last option. What is the reason behind this?

The human brain on average consumes a quarter of the total energy of the body in order to perform its tasks efficiently and so the brain naturally conserves energy. The fast and intuitive path dominates majority of the brain activities in receiving, analyzing and sending information except in exigency where System 2 takes over to scrutinize the entire information in recieving, analyzing and sending. This process consumes more energy which is not better for us. That is why we are inclined to listen to information over reading it. Reading consumes much more energy. You prefer watching over listening because the photo receptors of the eyes are the least in consuming the brain's energy. This is why people are relaxed when they look at the vastness of sky, the sea or even an aqurium.

In the example above, that kind of vital information is best absorbed and internalized in written form and your mind is ready to activate

System 2. A test was conducted in Britain at the time of first Gulf War to assess the amount and quality of information people got from either watching the news or reading it. (43)

They found that the group who read the news formed a different view and attitude toward the war. This had more ability to scrutinize, memorize and analyze the situation than the group who watched the news. It is easier to compare articles you have read years than shows you have seen through the years. It is because the brain exerts more in receiving and storing this kind of information in the neuron cells. Synapses construct a diversified network of neurons which correlates with the information. Ribosomes and mitochondria along with blood cells carrying oxygen work together to energize the brain in processing. Conversely, when information is transferred on a donkey like watching, less energy required for this information and retention is short.

Technological advancement brought about tremendous improvement in visual storytelling, yet the story printed on paper still has its place. A story that is told still has a charming influence.

A written story gradually develops and conveys meaning to its readers and details can be revised from time to time as in updated versions. The challenge is grabbing the attention and retaining it.

The oral tradition is a main pillar of storytelling from thousands of years ago and its major challenge is in the storyteller – his voice, his movements, his overall performance which many dismiss nowadays which we will discuss later on.

Visual storytelling, with its spoon feeding approach, relaxes the mind which is its main advantage. When want to get your point across in shortest time possible, the most concise way is a visual presentation. An actor friend told me that he offered Aljazeera a script for a documentary but the network already had thousands of good scripts in line. He presented his proposal as a short video, they watched it and approved his script. Now he is a regular contributor to the network. Once you hook your client with the visual story, you can go for written and oral as well. But excessive dependence on visual storytelling will reduce creativity in delivering stories that affect people.

LinkedIn recently published *The 25 Skills that Can Get You Hired in 2016*. They made a study of the most prosperous jobs worldwide down to the least. Data Mining was number three in the most prosperous jobs due to the boom in e-commerce, AI and social media. There is an increasing need to make new systems to process the billions of data in the web, including the user profiles in or to patterns of behavior in their choices. Algorithms calculate and suggest ads of products or services that match user patterns in a clear and attractive way which result in business. Common in information overload is distraction and the inability to make the right decision about it .(44)

Data Storytelling emerged which is exploiting and extracting sound information from sets of the data in a form of a story that lead to a clearer understanding of such data. It became a must for data engineers and project managers assigned to collect and analyze data to learn the skill of data presentation in story form to persuade investors and shareholders to investment and approve new projects.

One application is *Infographics* which is a merge between numbers and data presented in story form that audience can appreciate. Visual storytelling became indispensable because it aided processing and made it easier to be digested.

Brent Dykes wrote "Data Storytelling: The Essential Data Science Skill Everyone Needs" wherein he quoted Dr Hal R Varian, Google Chief Economist, *"The ability to take data – to be able to understand it, to process it, to extract value from it, to visualize it, to communicate it – that's going to be a hugely important skill in the next decades."* (45)

Dykes presented these pictures that show overlapping of stories, data and visual aids. Data with stories leads to more clarity. Data in visual form expands the mind. Stories with visuals leads to engagement and captive attention. The combination of the elements would lead to three results: Explain. Enlighten. Engage. The overlapping leads to the most important result which is Change.

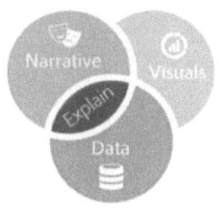 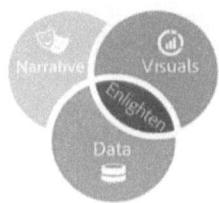 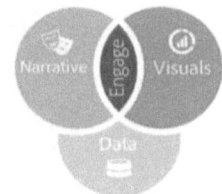

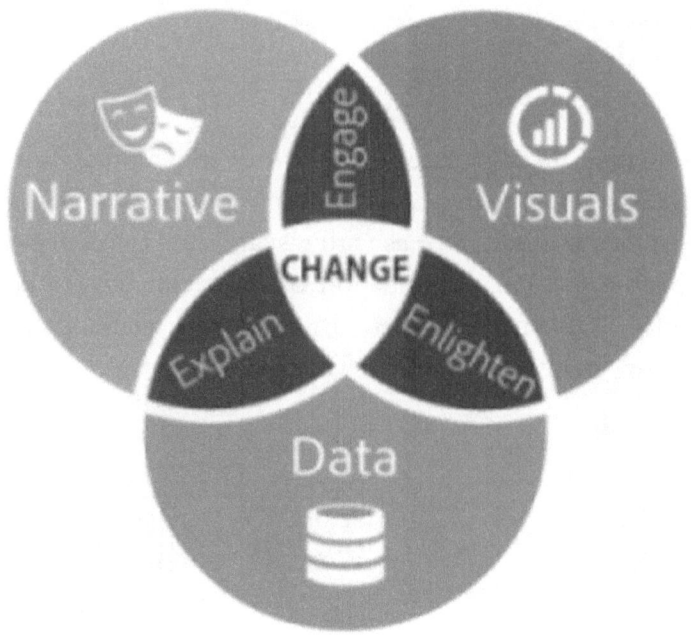

TEDx speakers use stories to get their message across about 65% of the time. Many use visual aids and tools that are handy at TEDx theater. If you think you are the type of speaker that do not need any visual aid, then you truly are a talented, not to mention brave storyteller. Being on the spot in front of hundreds watching only you makes you quite sure of yourself – your voice, your gestures and your overall performance.

But if you are an average speaker and cannot do without visual aids, be careful because the screen will compete with you. You should make sure visual aids do not take up a large part and *"To avoid killing the imagination of your audience"*. Let your story flow into the hearts and minds of your listeners. Let each of them take the thread and weave his own fabric. Allow them to make the hero bald, fat or lame. This is how they will get immersed. Showing pictures limit.

When we made the program *Manager – X*, we dedicated a special module called *Visualization*. This is what I consider one of the most important traits of any manager or leader in any field of business. Businesses suffer the lack of the ability of a manager to see the complete picture from beginning to end in a single frame. Studies show that majority of people learn things in its general and abstract form and then delve into its details. Human nature finds security in appreciating fully what is before their eyes. When meeting a person for the first time, we like to be able to see the person physically. Socially intelligent prefer full disclosure at the first meeting. When I started work in one company they were keen to familiarize me with everything that happens in the premises from A to Z and in another company, they just showed me my office.

Absence or not being able to visualize at the start of a task or project leads to distraction, boredom or abandonment. In Manager – X, we offered management many tactics that let staff visualize a whole process like a *Gantt Chart*, which is one of the oldest tools in managing a network of tasks. We also introduced *Mindmapping*, where tasks are arranged on branches like a tree. Even New York used this tool to rehabilitate Ground Zero after the 2001 attacks. We also introduced the various techniques using graphs and indicators that the manager could use as background story and allow everyone to visualize.

Chapter Three

The Story that Never Ends

The Unbearable Story

As a good story has unlimited impact potential so does a weak story have a negative irreversible impression. A good story is one that activates System 1 from beginning to end. A well-crafted story does not trigger System 2 during narration. But it is also normal that System 2 is triggered during the course of narration in order to focus and scrutinize some facts or because of a phone call. You have to make sure it does not occur too often or that the cause of the activation is a mistake while speaking or weakness of the plot.

The two reasons that trigger System 2 are disruption and ending. Disruption is the intermittent transition from System 1 to System 2.

There are various reasons for disruption. One of the most common is the inability to verbalize smoothly without stutters and long pauses. System 1 is responsible for reception and analysis the of mother tongue. The less a listener knows his second language the more System 2 interferes in recalling meanings of words let alone the context. Speaking in broken phrases and correcting right after impedes the natural flow of words and breaks its connection.

Another reason for disruption is disorder of events. How many times while telling a story have you had to interrupt yourself saying, "I'm sorry, I forgot but just before that..." It is quite easy to avoid such disorder by rehearsing your narration.

One more reason for disruption is information overload which makes your audience think and analyze more than they need to. Too much information loses its context within the story. Some examples:

1. **Names**

One of the things that make reading enlgish litreature difficult for me are names. That is why you have to take pains in choosing names that are familiar to your target audience and if an unfamiliar name happens to be in the story, better repeat it and explain its etymology or meaning. This is what many professional storytellers do. Take this example: "And while we were wandering in the desolate desert, we finally saw from a distance what we were looking for – the Valley of Mehser". Pause then explain: "They say that the name of this came from the word Hasar which in Arabic means "to bemoan" dating back to fourteen hundred years when the king of Ethiopia tried to destroy the Kaaba of Mecca. He came on a big elephant with his troops but birds flew over them and dropped hard clay and so they retreated moaning and repenting to the Valley of Mehser".

2. Numbers

Many hate mathematics but it is a language like any other and the lack of understanding is what makes it unfavorable for many. The language of math has rules and everyone has a different capacity to understand and project the language of numbers into a mental imagery. When we hear someone say, "I have been playing in this field forty years now", we can project an image of a man who has aged 40 years and may very well be in his seventies. When a speaker declares, "Finally, we made a rocket with a speed of 1200 m/hr, and only weights 2500 kg". People differ in their ability to "grasp the numbers". 1200 m/hr is fast but how fast is it? 2500 kg is heavy but it is light per rocket standards. Here we realize that numbers can be a very delicate element in storytelling because the brain scans for the right interpretation and association and as numbers get more complicated or more abstract, the more energy the brain consumes which can make the listener dismiss them.

Gabrielle Dolen is a storytelling coach. She published an article about the correct use of numbers in a story. Her friend Elise who works as a primary school teacher had to give a speech at a graduation ceremony asked for her help. Elise's original speech:

My first involvement with the 2013 graduating students was in 2009. It was my first year in grade 1/2 and one of my favourite activities was singing Peter Coombes songs such as Mr Clickety Cane and Wash Your Face in Orange Juice. I can still hear the 40 + students singing with enthusiasm and I remember these moments fondly. 2 years later, I was lucky enough to become a part of the flexible 5/6 learning neighbourhood and once again work with this cohort. What a change happened in 2 years – they were generally taller, more independent, dare I say it 'smellier' and definitely a lot more opinionated! It was clear to me that Peter Coombes would no longer be high on the list of fun activities to do. That was until our Portsea camp a few weeks ago. On the first night we all participated in a campfire sing-a-long. Whilst the ABBA songs were generally received with enthusiasm, I will never forget the rowdy rendition of 'Wash Your Face in Orange Juice' with actions and lots of reminiscing"!

A story filled with numbers. Dolan made the following modifications:

"My first involvement with this group of graduating students was when I was their grade 2 teacher and one of my favourite activities was singing Peter Coombes songs such as Mr Clickety Cane and Wash Your Face in Orange Juice. I can still hear all students singing with enthusiasm and I remember these moments fondly. 2 years later, I was lucky enough to once again work with this cohort. What a change happened in those 2 years. They were generally taller, more independent, dare I say it 'smellier' and definitely a lot more opinionated! It was clear to me that Peter Coombes would no longer be high on the list of fun activities to do. That was until our Portsea camp a few weeks ago. On the first night we all participated in a campfire sing-a-long. Whilst the ABBA songs were generally received with enthusiasm, I will never forget the rowdy rendition of 'Wash Your Face in Orange Juice' with actions and lots of reminiscing!"

If you focus on the content of both versions, you will find it a great benefit by removing insignificant numbers in the story. The ceremony was dedicated to the 2013 students. There is no need to mention this as well as others that will add nothing interesting to the story. But, Dolan left important ones that adds value like the change that happened in 2 years. This number gives a deep meaning to the passage of time.

We mentioned before about Ty bentte the storytelling coach, he got many interesting advice about how to construct you business and purposful story, where he always affirms the importance of numbers to let recpeient feel the value of events, problems, and successes, but I believe that Bennett is over obssessive of numbers, one I listened a story he told which was full of numbers that distratced my attention and affected badly my engagement, and this was his story;

"Mel Fisher was the greates treasure hunter the world has ever known, Mel Fisher was born in Hobart, Indiana in 1922, and after WII he moved to Califronia, and he bought a chiken farm, and there were in Califronia were Mel discovered the two loves of his life, his wife Dolores, and diving, he loved diving in the ocean, it was amazing for him. In 1953 Mel and Deo were married, the sold the chicken farm and they bought and the moved to Redando beach and the opened the first state's first diving shop, it was called Mel's acqua shop, it really wasn't much, but it was the only place in the state of Califronia where divers can come to get equipments, and determined to grow their business, they started to offer free dive lesson to anybody who came and buy equipments, they made modification to existing snorkeling gear and scuba gear, actually some of them is still used today, and the were some of the first people who make underwater movies, showing people the glories of the ocean, and one point Deo decided to gain publicity for their shop, she actually challeneged the current women record of staying underwater for 50 hours, so in August second, 1959, she descended into water, and she stayed for 55 hourse, 37 minutes, and 11 seconsds. They continued to grow their business, at that point Mel started diving in ship wrecks, and he found this passion in treasure hunting. Well, not long after that, they've heared about this fleet the 1715 fleet that supposebly carried tthis great treasure, and sunk of the cost of Florida, and so Mel and Deo made a decision, they closed their acqua shop, they picked up their family and they moved from Califronia across the country to Florida, and they decided to search for the treasure full time, well, the most of people think that this is nut, but all of you want to be a professional speaker, so you'd really think yes it makes a lot of sense, right? Not long into their search, they uncovered and entire carpet of gold coins on the seabed, one of the many breathtaking discoveries by the Fishers'. Well, by 1968, they discovered most of 1715 fleet, and they were looking for more treasure to find, and it was then when a friend gave Mel a copy of the guide of the treasure divers guide that was described as one of the greatest treasures that have ever been lost, according to the guide, it was lost off the coast of Califronia, so for Mel the search was on, the went and they started searching, they searched the ocean for every single day, for three years without finiding a thing, and finally one of his divers found and eight and half foot gold chain, it kept them going. But it wasn't for two more years, until Mel son's Derk found one single silver bar but it hand numbers inscribed on it that matched the spanish manifesto of the Atocha so they knew it existed. Two years after that, Mel son's Kim found five bronze cannons from the Atocha, and they thought it gotta be close, they thought they were in days to find the motherlode, but week later, a tragedy struck, one of their boats, the northwing capsized during the night, and Mel son's Derk, and Derk's life Angel and another two diveres were all killed, all in all the hunt for the Atocha claimed four young lives, But Mel kept searching, he knew his treasure existed, he just kept going after it, his persistant was almost unhuman, he searched the ocean for every single day, for more than a decade, he endured the loss of his son, his daughter in law, and two other divers, he constantly had to go and convince investors to fund them so they continue their search, and he had this amazing saying, every single day as he came up out of his cabin in the boat, he was saying, today is the day, today is the day, I know we are gonna find it, every single day.

Well, his persistance and optimisim paid off, because on July 20th 1985, a magnetometer indictated something on the seabed, and they doved down the sea, and they found they were seating on entier reef of silver bars, they found it, they found the motherlode, the Atocha, all of the keywest came to see what he found. All in all, the treasure of the Atocha was a 127,000 silver coins, it was 900 silver bars that weighted that weighted 70 pound a piece, it was 900 emeralds, 2,500 other gems, 350 pounds of discs, beds, and links of gold chain, estimates for the reached value was 400 million dollars…he done it, he kept searchcing and he found his treasure "(46)

This is such amazing and motivating story to keep chasing our dreams, the story is filled with details and problems that finally ends to get the treasure, but in a span of three minutes of narration, numbers were mentioned in this short story for about 20 times, and they are very fatiguings numbers for the mind to percieve. I bet you would propose omitting many of those numbers and keep the most crucial ones, so start doing it.

3. Complex Details

Details are solid and important elements in a story but complex and too much of it may be detrimental. Novice storytellers tend to stuff their narratives with so much details thinking that it will do the work of engaging their audience still other novices forget to place any detail at all. Leaving out details as well as excessive details both lead to a weak story. If you are telling a story to your employees about a worker in the factory who saved his friend from getting caught in one of the machines, details about the place, the position of the worker and the circumstance are very improtant and represent the backbone of the story but dwelling on the description of the worker or his personality may not be the best details to focus on.

4. Ending

Another reason for making a story weak is the ending. If a bad start or exposition could harm a story, for sure a bad ending could just as well. A wise Arab once said, "It's not about the shortcoming of a beginning, but the perfection of the ending". Also, Prophet Muhammad said, "Verily, (the rewards of) the deeds are decided by the last actions (deeds)". He also said, "When Allah wants good for a slave, He puts him in action. 'It was said: How does he put him in action, O Messenger of Allah?' He answered, 'By making him meet up with the righteous deeds before death'".

Ending is a universal law, as we profess in the Islamic faith. The best time for praying are the last hours of the night before dawn and the best supplication to Allah is Friday in the last hour before sunset and the best deeds of a man is before his death. Endings are like fruits of a deeply rooted tree, dangling and bringing benefit to humanity.

Endings are about two things. First, it is about the last events of the story. Second, is about the last words or the wisdom behind the story. Many storytellers fail to use these two effectively. The stroyteller should determine the ending from the onset like that of Nancy in the Obamacare speech and The Closing Argument in "A Time to Kill" or that of "Uncle Tom's Cabin" with a heartbreaking scene with Goerge on his deathbed with his final words. So, when ending your proposal, you have to be keen to add some kind of shock that induce people to make change or hope that motivates audience to take action.

A friend used to tell customers the story of the tremendous pains we went through with our first import cargo and how customs refused to release it until finally we found a solution after several weeks. I was thinking our customers were aksing themselves, "And what has that got to do with me". This friend told a follow up story of how he was quite patient with an outstanding payment from a client. This made our customers settle their accounts on time and our suppliers very patient in collecting outstanding payments. The story, indeed, had something to do with our audience. The ending carried the message my friend was conveying.

The Bearable Story

The bearable story has many elements stacked on top each other like bricks. This is the result of using of what God granted humans like imagination, voice, mobility, curiosity, diligence, etc. In this chapter we will discuss sixteen elements make the oral, written and visual story an unforgettable experience. Of course, there are many other elements, but we identify the most common and influential.

1. Ping Pong
2. Zeigarnik Effect
3. Repetition
4. Contrast
5. Numbers
6. Ambiguity
7. Sound
8. Silence
9. Gestures
10. Messages of the Eyes
11. Humanize It
12. Influencers
13. Ending
14. Unexpectedness
15. Details
16. Handful of Words

Ping Pong

Come & Go!

Once the famous billionaire Zalata Kabonga wrote in his diaries:

> "Don't get despaired with any work you do. Amassing wealth can be the result of practising what others see as trivial. I began making my own wealth when I was nine years old picking apples traders discard which I clean and sell at very low prices to poor people like me. Many people mocked me for it, but I was persisting and ambitious and kept doing it for couple of years. When I had sufficient money, bought good quality apples directly from the farmers accumulated wealth for the next 35 years. And then something cataclysmic happened in Brazil, that famous billionaire drug dealer died, who turned out to be my uncle. I was his sole heir and all of a sudden I became a billionaire… Please don't ever be fooled to think that discarded apples would make you a billionaire one day".

I am impressed with table tennis aka Ping Pong, especially with the incredible talent of the professional player as if directing his opponent wherever he wanted to with the ball. The same is true with some of the best stories. They captivate and take you wherever the storyteller wants. One of the hidden powers of a story is its capability to manipulate focus and emotions of listeners, moving them like puppets.

One example of Ping Pong projection that can elicit laughter so easily is as follows,

Eight planets, seven seas, seven continents, 809 islands, 204 countries and I'm still single.

These jokes are considered the best of its kind because of its capability to grab focus.

The story of Stranger is a clear example of Ping Pong. His emergence accompanied with his strange request regarding the children and the unexpected reaction of the mother drew mixed emotions then it was redirected to the main point and voila! The Frenetic Race began with an ambiguous dream and in a single line, reality surfaced.

An intriguing element to the story is its uncertainty leading the audience reluctantly but excited because of the unexpected. A creeping interest and enthusiasm to know the relation between incoherent incidents until the end of the story. People fear uncertainty but are always curious. Ping Pong stories reduce anxiety in learning new things. One friend kept a correspondence with a man from Hungary. He had many questions about Islam when he came to visit Egypt. When he went back to his country, he emailed my friend more questions. He had a copy of the Quran but was anxious to read it so we encapsulated my friend's answer in a simple story:

Dear Mark,

Let me share a story and I hope you focus. Two men in a prestigious company were awarded a weekend vacation for reaching their sales targets. The trip had both staying in antique wooden hand built huts in front of an amazing beach in one of the most beautiful and exotic Caribbean islands with a long and marvelous beach that extends over the horizon with white sand, crystal clear water and beautiful corals and trees of coconut and bananas. On the flight, the first man was handed a leaflet which listed all the information and the activities on the island. The second man was handed the same leaflet and he read an extra information in the footnote – a warning.

Animals considered to be dangerous sometimes wander to the beach coming from the island's jungle at sunset. Caution is advised although there has not been a single incident recorded. Both reached the island. The weekend went by so fast and both went back home. Come Monday, their colleagues asked them how their weekend was. The first man swore it was one of the most incredible weekends he had ever spent in his entire life watching the marvelous white sandy beach, experiencing the pleasant climate, sunbathing, jumping in the water, lying on the sand, watching the shining stars. When they turned to the second man, he declared that the weekend was one of his most awful, pathetic and sleepless weekends ever in his entire life. They were confused with his answer. How come the second guy had such a terrible time when both of them had identical accommodations? The second one explained that he was afraid one of those wild animals in the warning might come and eat him. And because of his strong instinct for survival, he was extra alert for the possibility that the wild animals would hunt even before sunset. As a result, he didn't experience the island as the first man did.

You're the second man, Mark. We tend to perceive things based on what we focus on. You were already focusing on conflicts, wars and monsters that you were convinced would be in the book. These monsters exist only in your mind and consequently your mind overlooks hundreds of other things that are exists in the Quran like love, sacrifice, bravery, mercy, charity, honesty, solidarity, etc… So I advise you to re-read and reflect without prejudice, without any fear. Prejudices accomplish nothing but prevent you from knowledge. The message of Islam that is clear and devoid of any evil. Make up your mind, Mark and abandon your monsters.

****

Mark did not answer for many days. My friend thought that the monsters may have gotten to his mind, but one day, my friend shared the answer he received from Mark:

> *I think we've reached a point too much arguing and unclarity. I feel we better stop this communication. But, actually your answer to my question has changed my mind and I decided from today to read and explore The Quran.*
>
> *Mark*

Mark's answer was a shock to me (a positive one of course). It was one of my first direct proofs of the immense power of storytelling. A story that encapsulated facts but smoothed in the edges and coated with sugar that made it more intriguing to the mind and the heart. This is one of the best examples of Ping Pong. Mark was waiting for a direct and argumentative answer but when he read the first line and realized it was a story, he accepted it and he swallowed the candy; then the facts started to work settle. The story subtly brought him to the Caribbean Islands then at the last lines brought him back to the essence of the issue.

Zeigarnik Effect
Will Be Right Back

Once I began a lecture differently:

"Today I want to tell you three short stories: A train is running at maximum speed when the engineer sees three people lying tied on the railroad tracks. Our hero sees the train and the hapless victims from a bridge. Our hero thinks how he could save the people. He doesn't have enough time to reach and free them. He sees someone on the edge of the bridge. This man was the largest man he ever saw in his life and so he thought that if he pushed the man onto the railroad track, his massive size could stop the train before it could kill the three people. But surely it would kill the fat man and he would be responsible. Our hero has passed the point of no return because the train had already reached the bridge. Tension rises and his eyes dart from the train, the fat man and the three bound victims when all of a sudden he makes up his mind and…

A young French guy was walking alone at one of the avenues in Paris when all of a sudden a pretty girl rushes toward him and says, "S'il vous plait, monsieur, those five men stole my handbag, please stop them!" The guy sees to the five men looking like tough, heavy set criminals and so he is hesitant but then the young girl is so pretty and remembers he is single. He is encouraged but then is hesitant again. And in between the feelings, the guy makes up his mind and…

An American guy in New York City, while jogging, spots a wallet on the ground, picks it up and finds it filled with money. Looking for identification, he rummages through and sees a small folded paper. He opens it and reads. It was a letter by the owner of the wallet begging whoever finds his wallet in cases he loses it to return it. The guy quickly dials the number on the paper with his cell phone but just before he presses "dial", he becomes hesitant and thinks of taking the wallet and the money inside. He glances at the letter again and then makes up his mind and…

And know, let us begin our lecture where we will tackle…"

With that, the attendees looked at me in bewilderment and soon ask me the endings of the three stories. Nonchalantly, I asked them to remind me to tell them at the end of the lecture then I began the two-hour lecture but for the first time, I noticed an exceptional increase of attention that I had not witnessed before.

This act I borrowed from Prof Robert Cialdini, the Godfather of Persuasion science. He mentioned in his last book "Pre-suasion" that he began a lecture with a unfinished story and when the lecture ended, the students didn't close their notes and leave their desks like usual, but they all sat waiting for the end of the stories that was suspended for two hours. (47) It was an amazing feeling to finish my lecture thanking everyone and pretending to leave, but as expected, the students urged me to end the three stories.

Kurt Lewin, the German psychologist and so-called father of social psychology, once invited his students for lunch at one restaurant in Berlin. Among the students was a Lithuanian named Bluma Zeigarnik. A waiter came to take orders and to their surprise, the waiter did not write down the orders but instead memorized them. The waiter didn't make a single mistake with each of the order. They wanted to further test him and covered the table and asked him to enumerate the orders of each person.

The waiter failed to accurately recall what he had just served. The conventional explanation is that memories fade with time, but it was not accurate because they tested the waiter merely minutes after he served the last plate. So, Bluma Zeigarnik came up with a more accurate explanation. Human beings tend to retain details of their task for as long as they are not finished yet. Once done, the memory cells tend to discard much of the details in order to make room for future tasks. This phenomenon is called Zeigarnik Effect to honor the coiner. (48)

There are more than six hundred scientific studies conducted to test Zeigarnik Effect in different circumstances and contexts. One observed people watching TV shows or listening to the radio being bombarded with commercials household products. The subjects are tested on the ability to recall details of the commercials. They found that the commercials with high retention are those which finished five to six seconds earlier than its original ending. The subjects recalled those ads even two weeks later. (49) In another experiment, they asked some children to perform activities while they interrupted them couple of times. Ninety percent of the children emphatically insisted to continue the activities they already started. (50)

I recall TV series ending with this magical phrase "To be continued..." meaning the story is not finished yet and we all have to wait for the next episode to see the rest of it. This anticipation is very different from waiting for any other episode. There is this eagerness and yearning for the conclusion of the suspended story as it is human nature to finish what we have begun. Without the trigger of achievement, the guards of the dopamine warehouse will not allow release of the hormone. This why we die for the last 2% even if does not have much effect on the final outcome. And as we exert effort to do so, the more we recall details of the events that preceded the unceremonious interruption. The influence of that story will be more lasting than traditional ones.Zei garnik Effect is not just confined in delaying a story's ending .It is heavily used by filmakers and called *Suspense*. The reason behind is something to hang on to. When a scene is reaching the peak of interest, they suspend and continue later. It has become a standard in many novels and documentaries.

Stories and anecdotes in meetings can use Zeigarnik Effect. The more you get experience in storytelling, the more your ability increases in utilizing suspense as an element. For example, when you introduce your company to investors or clients, you may begin narrating its successes and the biggest challenges your company faced, but prior to the topic that turned everything upside down, steer the talk to something else about your company for one or two minutes then go back and continue your unfinished story. Upon getting back to the original flow of the story, the listener suffers from an abrupt disruption due to the sudden transition from one topic to another (Ping Pong). The listener would need a few seconds to be able to recall the first part of the story and some more time to immerse back. Going back hastily increases disruption and would lead to resistance. This element necessitates a quick pause enough for the audience to recall the first part of the story. For now, we are done with Zeigarnik Effect..

****

Well, thanks for reminding me. In the train story, our hero is standing on the bridge, contemplating whether to push the large man off the bridge to stop the train or do nothing and let three people die. This dilemma was presented to a group of people and majority refused to push the large man. The same was presented to another group but a high percentage agreed to push the man off the bridge. How come? The dilemma was presented to the first group in their native language while the second group was presented the same using their second language. The conclusion, therefore, is when someone hears in his native language, System 1 is more active. When a person listens to the dilemma in his second language, System 2 is activated that trigger the memory cells to recall synonymous and relate it with its native language. System 2 understands and analyzes the situation in a more pragmatic way. It computes the life of one to the other three. The tragedy of three lost lives is greater than one. From there we know that activating either one of the two systems will lead to different decisions, and a good speaker knows when to trigger either to benefit his persuasion.

In the story of the French guy, two types of guys were asked to help. The first type refused to help the girl fearing the five thugs. The second type of guys were willing to help the girl and confront the men with a simple change in the parameters of the experiment. She asked guys primed and ready for love. This changes the behavior and action of the second type. This is an example of how priming focus and emotions could compel a person to do requests that are not readily performed.

For the American guy who found a wallet full of cash, two groups were used as subjects. In the first group, a higher percentage returned the wallet than in the second group. The letter used for the first group was written in perfect New Yorker style that portrayed the owner as a local while the second group read a letter written in a broken English that indicated the owner was an immigrant. Familiarity and affiliation heightened the desire to return the wallet, while absence of these reduce empathy to the owner. Affinity is very instinctive in all human beings and there are hundreds of tactics to draw this out from your audience and lead to compliance and less resistance.

Zeigarnik Effect can backfire if the second half of the story is less interesting than the first half or it does not have the element of surprise people expected. Going back to the secret of how our company survived the financial crises, we could say that we took out a loan and improved the processes and everything went well afterwards. This is a terrible way of using the Zeigarnik Effect but narrating it this way is better:

> *"Amid this extremely tough crisis when everyone settled that what was coming next is worse, all of a sudden, a noble person emerged out of*

nowhere. He believed in what we did and we could do good for people, and we can make a profit together. He decided to inject funding to our company and with him, we moved past the crisis. We have tripled our growth in the last ten years. The man decided to focus on his private business while we continued. He recently passed and his sons continue his ventures. This person is the main reason after God why we are standing here today offering our services to you. This man is Mr Hanson Clark, the founder of your esteemed company."

Quite rare coincidence, but this just an example of making an impactful second part against the first part of the story.

Repitition

Say it Again!

One of the implications of using System 1 majority of the time is that the mind receives input and processes automatically. The woman who routinely prepares food for her kids executes it automatically almost unconsciously assuming the end result thinking that food will satisfy her children. But when she tastes it, she finds that she unintentionally put more salt than she should have. She begins adjusting the ingredients so the food could be acceptable at best. The mind has switched from autopilot to analytical thinking which is focused and scrutinizing. And the assumption – the imagined picture or end result of the family on the dinner table has been removed. System 2 has taken over.

If the main purpose of the story is to trigger System 1, stimulating System 2 in some parts is beneficial breaking the monotonous flow of the mind and allow it to spot details and extract meaning. Repetition technique stimulates System 2. For instance, when telling a story with numbers like gains and losses or numerical milestones, the audience's minds needs a pause to think about the figures. A storyteller can narrate this way, *"The wrong decisions prevailed until the losses exceeded Three million Dollars, US (pause)… Three million dollars US!"*. In the story of the Himalayan wise man, when the events reached climax with Tao Su's, *"It's up to you, little boy… you who will decide whether this small bird will live… or die"*. The repetition of *"You"* has an intriguing effect on the listeners. When the wise man approached the boy while all were silent and said, *"But I…"* and all of a sudden he opened the boy's clasped hands and released the small bird. Tao Su continued, *"But I prefer it alive"*. The repetition of *"But I"*, has a powerful effect and provided a milestone that increased the desire to know what comes next.

Repetition has stronger effect when it appears sporadically – scattered in several phrases as in "The Closing Argument". After the lawyer horridly described the rape of the young girl, he hurriedly asked, *"Can you see her? Her raped, beaten, broken body soaked in their urine, soaked in their semen, soaked in her blood, left to die. Can you see her?"*. This repetition style was resonant to the audience.

Another amazing style of repetition is placing a phrase in different parts of the story then end the story with the same. We see this in the story of The Milk Crate, *"One week we decided to bring along an old milk crate… The following week we brought along the milk crate again… few other people had also brought along their milk crates… everyone had a milk crate… we need to constantly be on the lookout for our next milk crate"*.

Another type of repetition is to repeat a whole sentence in the beginning, the middle and the ending. Repetition is one of the most interesting methods to keep and grab attention to certain parts of the story. But if you do not carefully or strategically place the repetition, the audience may not digest it. Finally, the repeated word, phrase, sentence or part must be varied which we will discuss later on.

Contrast

A Gap of Difference

One of the most prominent features of creation is dynamism. Even the Quran states this about God, *"Every day He is bringing about a matter"* Al-Rahman 29. Night comes after day, death after life, light follows darkness, planets swims in the vast universe. Humans are mercurial. We go from sadness to happiness, from hate to love, from cowardice to bravery, from quitting to persisting, from retreating to attacking. God made the state of the nations to be in continuous change, from defeat to victory, from shrinking to conquering, from fractured to consolidation. Even in the creation of animals and the inanimate, He created small and big sizes, positive and negative, prey and predators, even atoms are constant movement.

Stillness and inactivity are characteristics of death while movement and change are characteristics of living matter. But human beings tend to violate this nature by favoring either of the states. He sleeps under the sheets on a cold night and does not wish to get out of bed to begin a new day. If he is at play, he never wants to finish and do something serious. And if he is doing something serious, he never stops and enjoy its benefits. If he is up, he does not want to sleep. If he sleeps, he does not want to wake.

When a person realizes that by running contrary to the fiber of his being led him to failure in many aspects of life, he begins to change and imitate successful figures. He finds a common characteristic of these figures is that they are never inactive whatever the circumstance. A story has to embrace this characteristic, always changing in its events and having contrast. What makes jokes such an amazing piece of literature is the contrast between situations. Normal does not grab attention as compared to an extremely contrasted situations where laughter is elicited. What makes thrilling movies enticing is the contrast of the hero's situation between normal and calm to sudden crisis until he resolves the conflict going back to his normal and calm state. Earlier, we mentioned several paths and showed graphs of happiness and misery in a story that are always in a state of change. And how the most famous novels utilize more than three shifts from happiness to misery and back again. But, what about the very details inside the plot itself? And what about the simple projection that wears the cloak of a story delivered in couple of seconds? Here lies the value of contrast to a story.

In "Resonate", Nancy Duarte dedicated a special section to analyze the famous speeches that inspired millions of people, like the "I Have a Dream" speech of Martin Luther King, Jr and presentations of Steve Jobs. These were built on the concept of contrast. The whole talk was about what is and what could be.

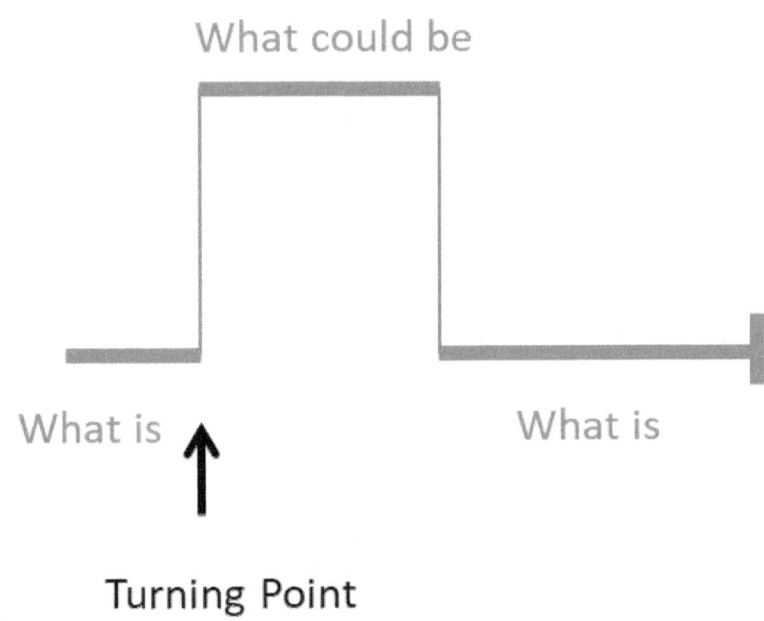

When people tell stories; they narrate present struggles, past failures, achievements or they narrate visualizing their future, how they see their social and professional lives. Yet, the best of stories are those contrasting between what is and what could be in a dynamic manner. These have the power to elicit sympathy then tranquility, excitement then disappointment, sadness then happiness. The speeches that motivate people are those that direct people to focus on their current situation and visualize what they can achieve. In the speech of Obama about Nancy, he tried to present this kind of contrast between her status before and after Obamacare.

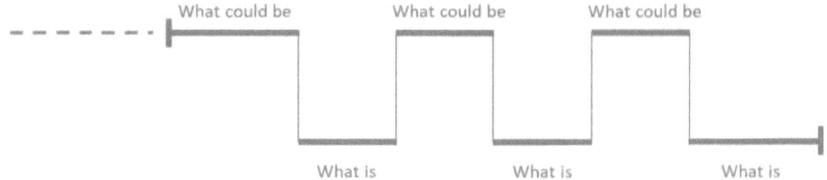

The "I Have a Dream speech coincided with mass protests of African Americans against racial discrimination. It had global resonance and Martin Luther King, Jr employed many projections that made it evocative which maybe led to his assassination in 1968. He successfully contrasted between the miserable reality Afro-Americans are living and the near future of equal rights in society. The main theme of Martin Luther King, Jr's speech was the contrast between two realities, present and future, and here is his speech outlined what is and what could be;

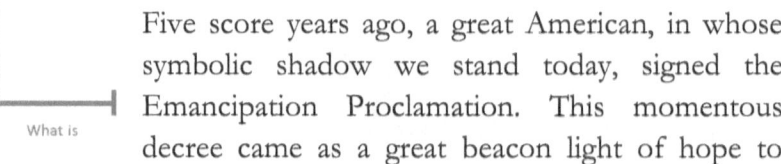

> Five score years ago, a great American, in whose symbolic shadow we stand today, signed the Emancipation Proclamation. This momentous decree came as a great beacon light of hope to

millions of Negro slaves who had been seared in the flames of withering injustice. It came as a joyous daybreak to end the long night of their captivity.

But one hundred years later, the Negro still is not free. One hundred years later, the life of the Negro is still sadly crippled by the manacles of segregation and the chains of discrimination. One hundred years later, the Negro lives on a lonely island of poverty in the midst of a vast ocean of material prosperity. One hundred years later, the Negro is still languished in the corners of American society and finds himself an exile in his own land. And so we've come here today to dramatize a shameful condition.

In a sense we've come to our nation's capital to cash a check. When the architects of our republic wrote the magnificent words of the Constitution and the Declaration of Independence, they were signing a promissory note to which every American was to fall heir. This note was a promise that all men, yes, black men as well as white men, would be guaranteed the "unalienable Rights" of "Life, Liberty and the pursuit of Happiness." It is obvious today that America has defaulted on this promissory note, insofar as her citizens of color are concerned. Instead of honoring this sacred obligation, America has given the Negro people a bad check, a check which has come back marked "insufficient funds."

> *What could be*

But we refuse to believe that the bank of justice is bankrupt. We refuse to believe that there are insufficient funds in the great vaults of opportunity of this nation. And so, we've come to cash this check, a check that will give us upon demand the riches of freedom and the security of justice.

What is

We have also come to this hallowed spot to remind America of the fierce urgency of Now. This is no time to engage in the luxury of cooling off or to take the tranquilizing drug of gradualism.

What could be

Now is the time to make real the promises of democracy. Now is the time to rise from the dark and desolate valley of segregation to the sunlit path of racial justice. Now is the time to lift our nation from the quicksands of racial injustice to the solid rock of brotherhood. Now is the time to make justice a reality for all of God's children.

What is

It would be fatal for the nation to overlook the urgency of the moment. This sweltering summer of the Negro's legitimate discontent will not pass until there is an invigorating autumn of freedom and equality. Nineteen sixty-three is not an end, but a beginning. And those who hope that the Negro needed to blow off steam and will now be content will have a rude awakening if the nation returns to business as usual. And there will be neither rest nor tranquility in America until the Negro is granted his citizenship rights. The whirlwinds of revolt will continue to shake the foundations of our nation until the bright day of justice emerges.

What could be

But there is something that I must say to my people, who stand on the warm threshold which leads into the palace of justice: In the process of gaining our rightful place, we must not be guilty of wrongful deeds. Let us not seek to satisfy our thirst for freedom by drinking from the cup of bitterness and hatred. We must forever conduct our struggle on the high plane of dignity and discipline. We must not allow our creative protest to degenerate into physical violence. Again and again, we must rise to the majestic heights of meeting physical force with soul force.

This was the rhythm of the speech that went between both extremes of the bitter reality and the desirable future. Other unprofessional storytellers would enumerate all the reality and then speak about the future. Narrating a list of problems and tragedies could dishearten an audience. A succession of desirable outcome in the future could result in boredom. Contrasting in chunks over the storyline would be like heartbeat to the body in rhythmic synchronicity.

Dr Robert Cialdini in his book, "Influence: The Psychology of Persuasion", told this story which illustrates the power of contrast, (51)

Dear Mom and Dad,

Since I left for college, I have been remiss in writing and I am sorry for my thoughtlessness in not having written before. I will bring you up to date now, but before you read on, please, sit down. You are not to read any further unless you are sitting down, okay? Well, then, I am getting along pretty well, now. The skull fracture and the concussion I got when I jumped out the window of my dormitory when it caught on fire shortly after my arrival here is pretty well healed now. I only spent two weeks in the hospital, and now I can almost see normally, and only get those sick headaches once a day.

Fortunately, the fire in the dormitory and my jump was witnessed by an attendant at the gas station near the dorm, and he was the one who called the fire department and the ambulance. He also visited me in the hospital. He is a very fine boy and we have fallen deeply in love, so we got married at once, and I left the dormitory and we moved to his apartment. It's really a basement room, but it's kind of cute. At the beginning of the marriage, we used to fight a lot, but discovering that I'm pregnant has calmed us down and my husband quit beating me. Yes, Mother and Father, I am pregnant. I know how much you are looking forward to being grandparents, and I know you will welcome the baby and give it the same love and devotion and tender care you gave me when I was a child. Supplicate God that the baby comes in good health and not infected with the rare virus his dad has. Although I was infected with his virus, the doctors said it's not a big risk that the baby will catch it, too. This is all I've gone through since we last talked. What about you?

Now that I have brought you up to date, I want to tell you that there was no dormitory fire. I did not have a concussion or skull fracture. I was not in the hospital. I am not pregnant. I am not married. I am not infected, and there is no husband fireman in my life. However, I am getting a "D" in History and an "F" in Chemistry, and I want you to see those marks in their proper perspective.

Your loving daughter,
Rosa

Rosa were extremely successful in devaluing the incident of failing grades by magnifying other incidents that the family would not expect their daughter to go through. Rosa then ended her letter by negating all the incidents and to confront them with the truth wherein if she wrote about it at the beginning, her parents' reaction would be much worse.

Numbers
Count it!

Numbers in some ways could inflict harm on the content of a story, yet it still represents an important factor to increase focus and influence. Numbers are like antibiotics, a large dose harms while controlled usage brings benefits. At work meetings, everyone is eager to get to specific facts. The "work story" is most likely formulated, translated and composed of numbers or sets of it. The story of Mil Fischer would not be complete without mentioning the exact value of the treasure he finally found after the great effort of searching for ten years which was 400 million dollars. It is always advisable to turn successes and achievements to an easy round number to trigger System 2 for easy comprehension.

The goal of injecting numbers must be to encourage imagination and reflection. When we say, "Since fifty years...", the purpose must be to recall a memory existing in the mind of the listener. However, mentioning a hundred fifty years ago is almost the same as three hundred years, and quite so to four hundred years. They are all similar to those who did not exixt at the time. It is better to say, "More than a hundred years...". It is enough to trigger a mental imagery of that time. In most cases determining the date does not serve the story like saying, "In 1963..." but becomes very important when dates refer to an important detail like saying, "In the year 2000, the beginning of the second millennium..." or "In 2011, the Egyptian revolution" or "In 1776, the Declaration of Independence...". One of the benefits of numbers is deepening the feeling of pain, happiness, or worries, etc like saying, "We waited for this life changing phone call for more than three hours". It is better than, "We waited for this life changing phone call for a long time". Also saying, "I felt the pain for ten long hours", "And all of a sudden this person came back after he disappeared for three months".

Finally, numbers that positively serve the purpose of the story are those that trigger System 2 to aid the recipient to imagine the value or size of a thing then to go back rapidly to System 1. Numbers that do not serve the story are the numbers that trigger System 2 but fails to project a mental image of what the number represents derailing the smooth transition to System 1 resulting in distraction.

Ambiguity

You're Weird

When I think of the reason why the story is so popular as a method of transmitting ideas summed up in a simple statement or in one line, I think of a village which with the most marvelous surroundings. Wherever you look, nothing but lush green plains, hillsides and clear streams that run all over and through the village. Amidst all this nature, exists an old abandoned train tunnel. Strangely, tourists hike in the village and choose to pass through this abandoned, spooky tunnel rather walk past it. The desire to delve in the ambiguous and strange is a natural instinct. The projection in general, should lure the listener to something strange and ambiguous and then return him to the natural, clear, and usual. When you revise your story, you have to check the places of ambiguity, are they mentioned enough? Is the ambiguity is overstated? I remember that the biggest challenge in every story I told people was to begin it with ambiguity because this captivates recipients. Ambiguity should simply aims to produce several conjectures from the audience about a scene, or the plot so it generates a desire to wait out the unraveling and focus.

> *"Have you once asked yourself how tough this life is? Do you know that your stomach inside your own belly is ever ready to digest itself if it stops even once the secretion of mucous..."*

> *"Once upon a time, I was returning home walking at night, and fortunately or unfortunately, rain fell down heavily at unusual time, and while I was running to one pub for shelter, all of a sudden I find..."*

> *"The prey was finally a few inches from the jaws of that lion, but for one reason or another, it was able to flee for the tenth time in a row..."*

These kinds of beginnings represent ambiguity that make recipients ask what will come later on. And this is one of the best catalysts that triggers System 1 for the long periods of time and immerse the listener.

****

The Magic of Riddles

Besides the Unfinished Story, I also use a more powerful method to keep minds clinging. A riddle works the mind until it finds the solution. It is one of the most joyful stories, the strongest to grab attention and the best to inculcate meanings and values.

Several years ago, I had an idea to use a new technique teaching foreign language and called it "LingoMind". My main goal in the program is to increase focus of students to the highest levels which will result in accelerated learning. Originally, I do not have certification to teach any language nor have I taught, but I am fascinated with the human brain and I always had the passion to discover and understand it. I finished designing the program and we opened it. We accepted students. I was challenging myself to produce an educational system that trumps the traditional education modules (at least in my country).

Several trainees from different backgrounds attended. All the trainees had already gone to other language institutes and most agreed on the high quality and the exceptionality of LingoMind. Most attested it was different, weird, and yet very effective. One student sent me a message a year later saying he still remembers many of the details we discussed in class and wanted to continue training.

LingoMind centered on a single story for each module which immersed all with focus and emotions. LingoMind presented stories in the form of a riddle which had a better effect on memory retention. A lecturer narrates a relatively long story that contained a riddle with the answer hidden within the lines. The trainees had to focus on each word and phrase. Applying other various tactics in isolating the trainee from any distraction to correlate phrases and sentences with mental pictures made the program all the more successful.

If you are telling a story to begin your talk, a joke can perk up an audience or a riddle can grab attention like the following story a lecturer used to begin his Error Management session;

> *"I'll tell you a riddle and the first one to get the right answer, I'll give my pen as a prize. Once there was a head of state who had a personal guard. The ruler wanted to travel by airplane to some place. But the previous day, the guard slept and dreamt that the plane crashed and the head of state died. He advised his boss not to travel. The head of state told him that if he was correct, he will be generously rewarded with money; and if not, he will be executed. The plane did crash so his boss thanked him and gave him sacks of money but then fired him. Why?"*

The attendees thought and analyzed but could not get the right answer. The lecturer continued;

> *"The guard's dream saved his boss, but falling asleep during duty could also endanger the life his boss. And this is what usually happens in the workplace. Your failure to recognize a small error can lead you to commit a big catastrophe sooner or later."*

Sound

Rhythm

I met this young man barely in his twenties with a knowledge of his field that may surpass his seniors. We were presenting lectures with this young man. People were happy and content with the man's knowledge, but we noticed that many attendees do not stay for the entirety of the lecture and sneak out. We asked and their answers revealed that most of them had a problem listening to the guy's voice.

I started to listen to his delivery and found I could not for more than ten minutes. It was not the quality of his voice, it was normal, but it was static, fixed, and pegged in monotone. It had neither variation nor dynamic rhythm. Actually, it was the first time I realized that the human voice had an incredible ability to repel people within minutes if the speaker does not employ the natural characteristic of the beautiful and complicated sound. I then started to listen to people who mastered using their voices and it was also the first time I realized that the voice can attract people to listen for it for hours with full attention.

I began trying to help my friend. Of course, at that time I did not know exactly what I had to do but I followed my instinct and so I asked him to do his lecture. I stopped him from time to time (actually all the time) to give advice and directions such as increasing his pitch in some parts, lowering it in others, slowing down the pace to emphasize a crucial point, and speeding up on unimportant details, and mimicking if required. The basic instructions worked and improved his delivery and I did not feel monotonous resonance in his voice.

It seems that one of the drawbacks of this technological age is the continued decline of the use our voice. We traded speaking to texting and watching a flat screen for hours a day. The humans of today speaks lesser than his ancestors. Therefore, the sensitivity of in our voices is getting less and less. Rehabilitation must be done to perfect one of the main pillars of the story.

Everyone would admit how voice affects the mood of people. God created in humans a complex auditory system that has the ability to distinguish among millions of sounds, and to detect emotions accompanying these sounds. One of the best sounds is the recitation of Quran. When those twenty-eight Arabic letters are laced together and recited in a special rhythm, it produces an effect that no other sound in the universe could match.

Some researchers suggest that sounds can affect and change human behaviour. In Acoustic Influences on Consumer Behaviour, Klemens Michael listed some past researches that proved the influence of special types of sounds in increasing the consumption rates of customers in retail stores. He played music in a hypermarket with a variety of fast and slow tempo in major and minor mode. The slow tempo in minor mode combination made customers stay and spend more by 12.10% while a similar study reached 38.20%. Sounds coupled with human voices stimulate the mind and stir emotions to make unexpected decisions and help to deliver variety of meanings to the audience. In other words, understanding and influence vary with the variety of voice. (52)

Here, I believe that the best storytellers are those who can switch effortlessly from normal speaking voice to a voice of a character in the story. This technique grabs attention quickly immersing listeners. Changing the rhythm and tone of your voice to resemble a character will have a better effect than a monotonous one.

But when narrating an event, there are many factors to sound that can enhance delivery like pitch, tone, melody, or gravity. Generally, the human vocal cords can produce hundreds of sounds and rhythms. Choosing the right rhythm for this or that sentence is a natural instinct and with people high voice sensitivity can manage well. Yet it is possible to train yourself. This can be done by writing a story in lines then marking and denoting the first letter of each line with the most important rhythms and to shadow the parts where the voice will be altered. Rehearsing this way will make you more sensitive. Let us take "The Closing Argument", there were six types of rhythms and tones:

1. Slow
2. Fast
3. Alto
4. Low
5. Rattle
6. Warm

The Closing Argument

I'm going to ask you all to close your eyes while I tell you the story.

(Slow, Low)

I want you to listen to me. I want you to listen to yourselves. Go ahead. Close your eyes, please.

(Warm, Slow)

This is a story about a little girl walking home from the grocery store one sunny afternoon.

(Fast)

I want you to picture this little girl.

(Warm, Slow)

Suddenly a truck races up. Two men jump out and grab her. They drag her into a nearby field and they tie her up and they rip her clothes from her body.

(Fast, Alto)

Now they climb on. First one, then the other, raping her,

(Slow, Low)

shattering everything innocent and pure with a vicious thrust in a fog of drunken breath and sweat. **(Fast, Alto)**

And when they're done, after they've killed her tiny womb,

(Slow, Low)

murdered any chance for her to have children, to have life beyond her own

(Fast, Low)

they decide to use her for target practice.

(Slow, Low)

They start throwing full beer cans at her. They throw them so hard that it tears the flesh all the way to her bones.

(Rattle)

Then they urinate on her.

(Slow, Low)

Now comes the hanging. They have a rope. They tie a noose.

(Slow, Low, Rattle)

Imagine the noose going tight around her neck and with a sudden blinding jerk she's pulled into the air and her feet and legs go kicking. They don't find the ground. The hanging branch isn't strong enough.

(Slow, Alto)

It snaps and she falls back to the earth. So they pick her up, throw her in the back of the truck and drive out to Foggy Creek Bridge. Pitch her over the edge. And she drops some thirty feet down to the creek bottom below.

(Slow, Low)

Can you see her? Her raped, beaten, broken body soaked in their urine, soaked in their semen, soaked in her blood, left to die. Can you see her?

(Slow, Alto)

I want you to picture that little girl.

(Slow, Low, Rattle)

Now imagine she's white…

(Fast, Alto)

Listen to the actor's performance. You will find that he switches from the six rhythms which helped to make the story unforgettable.

Silence

Keep Your Mouth Shut

Some people would ask what silence has to do with storytelling. Actually, silence is a crucial element that gives a story a very interesting dimension. The moments of silence while telling a story has two effects. First, it allows the mind time to relax, especially after successive information like, "I went to ask help from my neighbour on the first floor but he refused on the pretext hat he was busy and so I went to a second one who did not even open the door, off I went to a third one who answered me from inside that he was not home. I went to the physician on third whom I forgot had already passed away two days ago…". A pause here would be best to allow the listener to recollect and digest all the information and also smile or laugh. The second effect is intensify shock value like so;

> *"And the result of this human error was when this humble employee went to withdraw his meager savings from the bank, he found that he had about twenty million dollars added to his three thousand dollars savings account…"*

> *"Do you know the sole reason that ruins this company… It is I, you, and everybody like us who are lost without proper guidance…"*

"And finally, I remind the first words of the hero in our story... When we don't realize the essence of this life, we would never realize the essence of that death..."

You notice the silent moments in the stories are denoted using ellipses. In the story Obama narrated, it was as follows, "And for a while she had temporary insurance that covered her multiple sclerosis...", "But starting today, she can get coverage for much less... because today's new plan can't use your medical history to charge you more than anybody else", "She's been uninsured ever since... So she pays all of her medical bills out of pocket, puts some on her credit card, making them even harder to pay...", "Six months ago, she was diagnosed with a brain tumour... She couldn't afford insurance on the individual market, so she hasn't received treatment yet... Her daughter LeNaise, a student at the University of Maryland, is considering dropping out of school to help pay her mom's bills...", "Well, starting today, thanks to the Affordable Care Act, Tranaise can get covered without forcing her daughter to give up on her dreams...". And in the story of the wise man of Himalayas, "It's about you little boy... you who will decide whether this small bird will be live... or die", "But I... prefer it alive", also in The Closing Argument, "Can you see her...? Her raped, beaten, broken body soaked in their urine, soaked in their semen, soaked in her blood, left to die. Can you see her...? I want you to picture that little girl. Now... imagine... she's white..."

These silent moments varied between suspense, relief, leaving enough room for shock or wisdom to sink in and let emotions run to its maximum degree. Silence used efficiently brings about distinct effect.

Gestures

Silent Messages

People everywhere find great difficulty acquiring a second language, so many theories emerged discussing the best way to learn a language. One of them is called The Direct Method, where a teacher focuses on speaking in the second language without considering grammar or translation to ensure complete immersion. Another technique is Communicative Language Teaching (CLT), where a student is asked to give descriptive details of many situations. There is Audio-Lingual technique, which is repetition of several words patterns in different situations. Suggestopedia focuses on removing mental barriers students involuntarily place in their minds making the training more intriguing.

All those techniques have relatively contributed to improved learning of second languages, but a big dilemma the reception of students of the techniques. There is a need for assessment to determine the best technique for a particular student. Still the best technique in practice and fits people is Total Physical Response (TPR). A technique invented by James Asher, a psychologist at San Jose University in the United States, where a student receives phrases in the second language and using bodily gestures explains its meaning. This technique inculcates phrases and meanings in the mind of students faster than any other method. TPR stimulates the motor cortex so more neurons and synapses embed the word in the mind.

Some white papers proposed the effectiveness of using storytelling in learning the second language by adding nonverbal performance as an extra tool. Beth Decker in "The Effectiveness of Total Physical Response Storytelling (TPRS) in Secondary Foreign Language Instruction" published that benefit and pleasure have exceptionally increased which helped in better acquiring the second language. (53)

Charades is an example. Each movement however trivial it may denote an important meaning, so a team has to frantically recall words that match the gestures.

The element of nonverbal gestures being added to professional storytelling may be the best element that would make a story last in the memory of recipients. The storyteller has to rehearse his story, taking into consideration how to use his limbs for a strong influence and deep meaning. We shall tackle the arms and hands, which move unconsciously while a person speaks. Sometimes their movement is beneficial to the story and sometimes keeping them dead still is better.

The most commonly used gesture types are the following: (54)

Iconic gestures

Iconic gestures depict a characteristic of the actual object, person, action or event being described. Examples include an upward movement of the hand accompanied by the words "he climbed up the tree". Another example would be a throwing motion, when someone in the scene throws a ball. Iconic gestures benefits the story as it deepens the felt emotions of an audience, also it increases the credibility of the speaker. This is why whoever is not speaking the truth involuntarily use excessive iconic gestures.

Metaphoric gestures

Metaphoric gestures describe abstract concepts and relations. As the term implies the gesture depicts the metaphor of the concept or relation. Examples would include depicting a group by moving both hands in a ball shape, or progress by moving the hands around each other in a circular fashion. Metaphoric gestures are the most difficult to use as they need creativity and good imagination to transform an abstract into meaningful gestures.

Deictic gestures

Deictic gestures are pointing gestures. They might point to real objects or persons, but quite often, they point to entities in the imaginary world of the scene that is being described. Deictic gestures are unconscious movements a speaker makes, but they still represent a meaning for the listener. If they are absent, the audience would think there is something wrong about the story.

Beat gestures

Beat gestures are generally small, short movements which are used to emphasize certain parts of speech, or sometimes serve as fillers where no other gestures can be used. An example could also be the gestures people make when they cannot think of a word. Beat gestures are a bit of an exception in that they do not refer to anything like the other types of gestures do. Beat gestures help add emotional impulses as they are sudden and high in frequency. They help swiftly grab attention. Also, they help generate emotions of enthusiasm, happiness, or laughter. It is one of the gestures that has to be determined prior delivering the story because they act as double-edged sword when misused. A speaker may look like a buffoon desperately grabbing attention.

Rehearse your gestures in front of a camera and then watch your own performance, correcting and enhancing each time until you are satisfied. At the beginning it may be difficult to focus on your story along with your gestures and maintaining a dynamic voice rhythm. It resembles learning to drive a car as the amateur driver has to focus on the elements of driving separately. A skilled driver can diversify his focus while maintaining good driving. Soon all elements can be blended in one harmonious motion and that is how storytelling talent grows. At first, the practitioner stumbles in focusing on the essential parts that build his story, but after a period of training, elements come together to produce a smooth and sound story.

Progressively, a storyteller will feel which gesture is best employed for this or that situation. Many will come to realize (especially introverts) that gestures have the upper hand in producing a powerful impact for their stories.

The Myth of Mehrabian 55-38-7

- In order to be a good communicator who can influence people, you have to know that studies revealed 93% of the influence of your message has nothing to do with the words you verbalize. Your voice tone represents 38% of the influence and your body gestures represent 55% with total 93%, yet the words of your message represent only 7%. What you have to do is...
- Excuse me! When and where was this study published?

The speaker is stunned with the question of a young man which no one had asked before and so the lecturer stammers,

- "It's a very famous research," the lecturer answers nervously.

The young guy responds

- If it was famous, so should its title be and the name of the researcher, too.

By that time, the attendees began chiding the young man for interrupting the amazing lecturer. They asked him to go so they may enjoy the lecture with scientific and... anonymous studies.

This renowned theory was published in 1967 by Albert Mehrabian, the professor of psychology at California University, entitled Inference of Attitudes from Non-Verbal Communication in Two Channels. Seventeen participants listened to the word "Maybe" in various voice tones (Like, Neutral, Dislike). They informed the participants the voice is from person (a) directing his talk to another person (b) and they have to figure out the attitude of the first person

(a) toward the second person (b) just through the tone of voice. Then they randomly showed three pictures for three girls with facial expressions showing either like, neutral or dislike while participants listened to the word "Maybe" in different voice tones. The pictures had the strongest effect on the participants when interpreting the attitude of person (a) toward another person (b) 2/3. (55)

Then the second study was done in the same year entitled, "Decoding of Inconsistent Communications", where he focused on the inconsistency between the spoken words and voice tone. They divided participants in three groups and each group to listened to three sets of messages. For the first group, the three messages denoted liking, such as (Honey, Dear, Thanks), the second group listened to disliking such as (Don't, Brute, Terrible), and the third group listened to neutrality, such as (Maybe, Really, Oh). The voice tones of the nine messages were varying between positive, neutral, and dislike. The result that the voice tone outweighed the meaning of the spoken words by 2/3, which means that participants tended to feel hostility toward person (b) if the voice tone of person (a) is hostile even if his spoken word was "dear" or "thanks". In addition, the word brute that was accompanied with a positive tone of voice gave an impression of a positive attitude between person (a) and (b). The words of either amiability or hostility accompanied with neutral tone of voice led to the inability of participants to determine the emotions of person (a) toward person (b). The result of the study was that the tone of voice has stronger effect than the words on interpreting the type of emotions even if the words are contrary to the tone of voice. (56)

What Albert Mehrabian did then is that he combined the two studies, and got a correlated value of the effect of spoken words, tone of voice, and the nonverbal communication (i.e. facial expression, body language) so it was 0.07 for words, 0.38 for tone of voice, 0.55 for nonverbal communication. Prof. Mehrabian published two books discussing the results of his studies, one is "Silent Messages", and the other is "Nonverbal Communication".

One criticism of this study is that it measured results on single words and not varied long sentences because perceiving emotions out of the context of a single word will not be so accurate as a full sentence. Another criticism is the absence of the previous relationship between person (a) and person (b) in the participants who had to guess the attitude whereas history would allow for more accurate results.

Mehrabian, in "Silent Messages" stated that this result is confined when person (a) speaks about his own personal emotions to person (b) and is not valid or tested on any other communication out of this context. This seems logical because when a person speaks about his personal memories or anything related to his emotions or desires, we notice that people receiving such messages tend to focus more on the speaker's body gestures and their ears are more attentive to the speaker's tone of voice so as to judge how honest or how strong or weak the person is. Recall how you focus on someone when he begins telling his personal story and compare it when he speaks of another impersonal matter. You will detect a difference on your focus in both cases. For example, when you watch the daily news on TV, you neither listen attentively to the presenter's tone of voice to judge his honesty, nor focus on his facial expressions and body gestures so to measure how much he was influenced by a massacre or tragedy. And because he is a third person, your focus is just drawn to the spoken words.

In Mehrabian's studies, we find a great benefit to storytelling, because a story in its entirety is a process of a communication and narration of personal memories and personal emotions where the focus of an audience is drawn to the facial expressions and body gestures of the storyteller. Maybe it does not always match Mehrabian's ratio, but that is academic.

According to Mehrabian studies, the critical parts of your story are those where you reach the peak of emotions like saying, "At this particular moment, I felt a complete breakdown". This is a crucial moment in your story where your oral performance and body gestures are key to elicit intense emotions from such words. Also, when seeking the confirmation for your words in saying, "And this was the moment I risked my life and jumped into the raging river to save this helpless child", the focus of your audience will be involuntarily drawn to your face, limbs, and tone of voice searching for the truth in your amazing words. Write a draft of your story and highlight crucial parts where you need to enhance with action because more attention will be on your tone of voice, facial expression, and body gestures during those moments boosting audience's emotions and increase focus and belief.

Peak of Emotions
One of the hardest missions of any storyteller is to incite peoples' emotions shedding tears, cause laughter, as this needs a good plot and effective oral performance, yet bodily remains as the most important element to bring those emotions to the hilt.

Marc Mero, a famous professional wrestler, has famous video with students giving instructions on how to act good. He hopped on stage and told hundreds of students a personal story of his mother, how she was the only person who believed in him but he always used to embarrass and belittle her when he was young. And one day Mero travelled to Japan to participate in a wrestling tournament when all of a sudden he received a call from home informing him that his mother passed away. Mero says that he dropped the phone and left the hotel running aimlessly in the streets. He could not believe that his mom is not there and will never be again. He hurriedly went back to his country and stood before her coffin, and kept saying, "Mom! Please wake up!". Mero ended his story saying to the school kids that life is short and they have to take care of each other because it is not about what you have in your wallet but rather what you carry in your of emotions. (57)

Once Anthony Robbins told a story about the first charity work he did when he was young. He began telling his personal memories when he was a small child and his father was jobless then someone came to their house in Easter bringing them food, but his father refused and was harsh with the man because he does not take charity. The man said to him, "Don't let your kids starve because of your ego". Years after this incident, Robbins decided to be like this good man. Every Easter, he buys lots of food and goes to one of the poor neighbourhoods where Mexicans live and enters one humble house where he is met with laughter and tears of joy for his unexpected gift. Robbins leaves the house, remembering when he was in the same place as those kids looking at the good man stepping into his van. Now he fulfilled his dream and became the man in the van, but it is not just one van. Robbins' foundation distributes millions of meals to poor people around the world, their goal is to feed the poor whoever and wherever they are. (58)

When I watched both videos, I observed the gestures and overall physical performance of Mero and Robbins that made the audience shed tears and be intensely influenced with the content. Mark Mero kept moving on the wide stage, his hands amazingly described the death and pain of losing his mom. Robbins gave a masterful performance using his body and facial expressions to deliver his story. When he reached the point where he placed the bags of food on the table, something hit his right leg making a bang and another hit his left leg making another bang! When he looked down, the kids rushing for the food all excited and happy after a long fast and misery. Robbins almost used his four limbs to describe that situation and other situations in the story until he himself shed tears. Yes, physical performance is exhausting, hard, and needs a continuous training, yet it remains the best way to draw in people and affect their emotions.

Messages of the Eyes
Cornea's Chat

The eyes are one the most beautiful things God created in the human body. In it contains many and many a secret. Since early ages, humans perceived eyes as windows to the soul. When someone recalls, his/her eyes move in all directions. This is an automatic reaction of the brain searching for information. Claims state that eye movement serve as a catalyst to activate areas of the brain that contain a particular information. This is similar to the instinctive reaction of rubbing the forehead when recalling something or scratching the nape in worry or confusion, activating parts of the brain that has something to do with such states of mind.

Eye movements were observed while thinking and patterns emerged. You learn a great deal from the eye movement patterns of a speaker such as personality and even honesty. Generally, when recalling a visual memory, eyes move up to the left. When imagining or creating a new picture in the mind, eyes move up to the right. Investigators use this technique along with polygraph. They note that when recalling an actual memory, the interviewee's eye move up to the left corner. Conversely, it moves up to the right, when creating a visual picture which was not experienced. Eye movement sideways to the left generally happens when recalling an auditory memory like the voice of parents. Looking sideways to the right generally means creating a sound that has never been heard before like imagining a strong Russian accent. Looking down to the left is like looking to the heart and happens when a person is talking to himself. Finally, looking down to the right usually happens while imagining a kinesthetic feeling like touching. When a victim speaks about torture, the eyes look down to the right. (59) Some eye movement patterns are shown in the illustration.

In an experiment, we noted the accuracy of eye movement patterns. We asked volunteers sets of questions and the results are shown in pictures.

1. What is the colour of your bedroom door?
2. Imagine how you'll look 15 years from now?
3. Recall the best three voices you've ever heard.
4. Speaking with a sponge in your mouth, how would you sound?
5. When speaking to yourself, which voice do you use?
6. Recite the multiplication table of 8?
7. Describe what you feel when you take a hot shower?
8. If you fall in a freezing river, what would your body feel?

We asked these questions to four volunteers, and took pictures of their eyes to document the pattern of each subject. The eyes move in various directions so it is important to capture its instinctive movement. The first volunteer registered usual patterns in all questions except recalling visual memory where his eyes went up to the right. During internal monologue and kinesthetic feeling his eyes went up left, and again for kinesthetic feeling his eyes did not move at all maybe because the question did not trigger enough emotions.

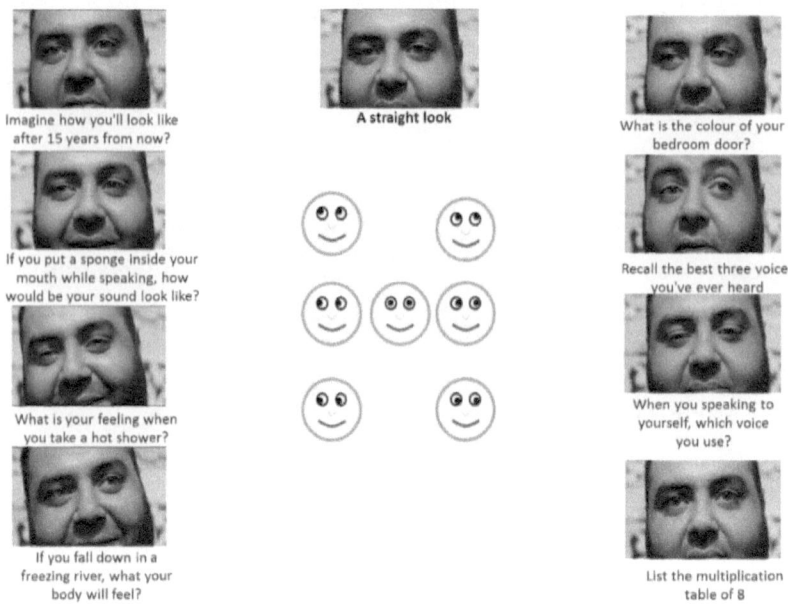

The second volunteer moved his eyes down to the left for a majority of his answers being extremely introverted.

Imagine how you'll look like after 15 years from now?

If you put a sponge inside your mouth while speaking, how would be your sound look like?

What is your feeling when you take a hot shower?

If you fall down in a freezing river, what your body will feel?

A straight look

What is the colour of your bedroom door?

Recall the best three voices you've ever heard

When you speaking to yourself, which voice you use?

List the multiplication table of 8

In the third volunteer, we noted that majority matched the pattern but some of questions needed to be deeper as he did not move his eyes. When we asked him item 8, he moved his eyes randomly but quickly fixed his eyes down to the right which shows sometimes we have to filter out random movements.

Personally, I know the last volunteer to be very active, dynamic, extroverted, and quite sociable. These traits affect his ability to focus intently. He is also the type that does not to recall all the things he did in his extreme social life. His eyes were fixed at the centre for half of the questions. We had to rephrase questions many times to get his pattern.

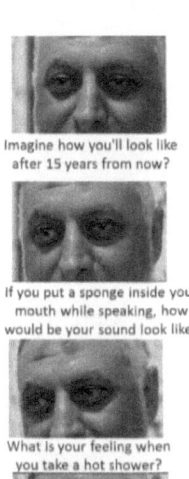

Therefore, be keen in telling your story, as your eyes will have a very powerful effect on the audience, especially when combining with moments of silence. For example: I remember one day... (silence, eyes up to left). I remember one day when I was a small kid sitting with my mom on the beach looking at the sunset. She told me, 'Your life will be the same as the tide. Go with it then come back, but... (silence, eyes down to right)... but endure the pain of the tides and the nostalgia of the ebb tide so one day... (silence, eyes down to left)... So, one day you may came back before letting the raging sea of life take you away from your beloved ones'.

In conclusion, eyes have fixed movement patterns which vary from one person to another and the eye movement patterns of left-handed people mirror those of right-handed people. By practicing close observation, you will get more insight on one's mind and verify authenticity, and ultimately respond more persuasion.

Humanize It!

I'm Vulnerable

"Taxi!"

Muhammad yelled and waved to the next cab waiting at the arrival terminal in San Francisco airport. The cab approaches then stops and Muhammad rushes to the trunk to put his bag, gets in then told the driver, "Silicon Valley and speed up please!"

The African American cab driver drives faster than he usually does, and Muhammad sat behind, switched on his laptop and focused on the screen mumbling what he was reviewing. From time to time, the cab driver looked at Muhammad noticing his worry and anxiousness, but he keeps quiet. After thirty minutes, the taxi reaches Silicon Valley and stops at one of the biggest IT companies. Muhammad pays the fare and quickly leaves the taxi, rushing toward the entrance of the building.

The cab driver yells, "You forgot your bag!"

Muhammad returns to the car and thanks the driver who told him, "In case you finish your meeting in a couple hours, I can wait to bring you back to the airport".

Muhammad knits his brows wondering and asks, "And how did you know that I'm having a meeting for a short time?".

The driver smiles showing white teeth and says, "Majority of my customers are young talented people like you whom I pick up at the airport to present ideas to giant companies in Silicon Valley".

Muhammad is amazed at what the driver said and said, "Well, but I have one other company after I finish and then I go back to the airport".

The cab driver waits in his car for more than an hour reading the newspaper when all of a sudden Muhammad opens the rear door not feeling very satisfied and said, "I'm done, let's go to the next one".

The driver just goes to the next destination and looks at the distracted Muhammad. Within moments, his phone rings and begins speaking Arabic in a low voice while the driver observes. After the call, the driver said to him, "My mom died the last month, she was a great woman"

Muhammad looks at him in astonishment and says, "I'm sorry but how could you have known I was talking to my mother?"

The driver smiles and says, "I guessed".

Muhammad continues, "But I was speaking in Arabic, do you speak it?".

The driver said, "Not a word. And now if you don't mind, tell me how you did at your first meeting so I may advise you".

Muhammad began feeling comfortable with the man and says, "I study programming in Texas University, and I'm on a project to develop a new management system for e-commerce. I communicated with several companies to fund my project. Only two companies in Silicon Valley responded and today I'm presenting my project to both and I would have to wait for their acceptance or rejection".

The driver asks, "And how did it go with the first company?".

Muhammad said, "I made a good presentation as far as I'm concerned. I spoke about all the benefits and strengths of the project, but I think they didn't care much".

The driver says, "Did they ask you anything personal?".

Muhammad knits his brow and asked, "Did you work at one of these companies before?". The driver smiles and doesn't respond, so Muhammad continues, "Actually, they did. They asked me many personal questions and that bothered me a lot but how did you guess?".

The driver let out a deep sigh looking right straight at the road, and said, "Thousands of young men come to Silicon Valley year after year. They present their ideas and inventions seeking to turn it into profitable ventures. In the beginning many of the projects failed and companies lost although they invested in products and people who were very talented and unique until finally entire companies collapsed and failed".

Muhammad said in astonishment, "Then they did fail?"

The driver responded, "Because their entire focus on the idea and the project. They forgot to give the person behind the idea the same attention. The human is the main factor to make the idea flourish and prosper. That's why these companies are now giving more attention to check and scrutinize the presenter more until they reach a decision that this is the person we want to share success with".

Muhammad reflects deeply and then says, "You're right. I spent many months focused on my project. Days and nights I did nothing but to concentrate on its technical details. I never thought of talking about myself or to present it in awesome way. What a misery if this thing will fail...".

The driver suddenly interrupted him, "How did you speak with your mom about your project?".

Muhammad wondered at the question, but hesitantly answered, "My mom and I are so close even though we are thousands of miles apart. We talk on a daily basis and although she knows nothing about computers, I tell her all the details of my project from the first day and..."

The driver swerves at high speed and at the same time interrupts Muhammad, "This is what I want you to do. In your next meeting, leave your laptop here and present your project that same way you do to your mom".

Muhammad panics at the driver's advice and says, "What did you just say! I'm a programming engineer and I'm going to meet a programming company, and you ask me to leave my laptop here. So what shall I say to them, shall I tell them stories?".

The driver smiles, and says, "Yes, and I promise you I won't steal your stuff and leave, except of course if you make me wait too long".

Disapprovingly Muhammad says, "Do you want me to talk to them like I talk with my mom? You want me to tell them about moments of my suffering, misery, and failure. Do you want me to reveal to them my weakness that only my mom knows? How do you think things out, man?!".

With a wide smile, the driver says, "Those people may become your second mother – the care they'll give you if you're accepted will be like your mom's, but for the sake of profit, of course. So, if you want them to act like a second mom, you have to show that, in return, you're ready to be a loyal son to them".

Although Muhammad couldn't believe the driver, he had a feeling that this man had wisdom and vision, so he asked, "Well, how shall I present?".

"That company you just presented to and the company you're about to go to have extensively studied your idea, otherwise they wouldn't invite you and pay for your flight. They want you to say why they should become your partners, why they have to give a bunch of cash, and why they should open their gates to you. Majority of the people who come here return with tails between their legs because they think they are gods. Companies here hate gods. They don't hire gods, and they don't have the least bit desire to work with gods," the driver answered.

The taxi stops at the entrance of the new company turns his torso to Muhammad saying, "Yes, these companies make their profit from machines, yet they still prefer to work with humans – humans who commit errors then innovate, humans who lose then triumph, humans who fear but never back down".

The driver looks from his side window to the facade of the company's tall building and continues saying, "Those people want to work with other people who are honest the same way you are truthful to your mom and this honesty is what prevents losses and gain profits".

Muhammad dropped his jaw staring and driver pointing to his wristwatch said, "Those people hate latecomers. I promised to get you here on time and you less five minutes to get your butt inside, go!".

Muhammad startled leaves the car, and at the building's entrance, remembers his laptop. Turning back, he sees the driver with a firm look so he goes inside hearing the driver shout, "Humanize it Muhammad!".

More than two hours passed. A knock on the window of the taxi wakes the driver. Muhammad sits beside the driver this time.

The driver asks, "Have you done well?"

Muhammad nods his head in confusion saying, "Many would say I am out of my mind going to the most important meeting in my life without my presentation or even my laptop. And many would truly believe that I lost it when I followed your advice and talk about my failures instead. But I did ".

The driver smiles and says, "Don't worry. The companies of Silicon Valley are never late to tell that one is a lunatic, so keep checking your email...".

Muhammad laughs sarcastically, and the man started driving and continued saying, "Or stick to your cell phone".

The taxi goes to the highway to the airport. Halfway, Muhammad puts his cell phone in his bag and leans back shutting his eyes saying, "I believe I need nothing but a quiet rest. I have a long trip to Texas".

The driver smiles and says, "Yes, it shall be a long trip".

Muhammad turns his head to the driver and says, "Could you guess what happens next?".

The driver answers, ""Have you read the story 'It Always Happens at N75'?".

Muhammad said, "No. What is it about?".

Before the driver could answer, Muhammad's cell phone rings inside the bag he placed on the car floor. He bends down to get it, but it was buried and he got frustrated and said, "Better answer later".

The driver's smile disappeared and he said, "What if it was your mom? Pick up the phone now!".

Muhammad rummages for his phone and before he could pick it up, the driver swerves to an exit and mumbles, "It Always Happens at N75, I bet you are the starring in this story soon, Muhammad".

Muhammad was astonished and asked the driver, "Why are you turning back?!".

The driver said calmly, "Nothing, I'm testing the refurbishments on Exit N75. Now answer before the caller quits".

Muhammad's hand finds the phone and answers it. He shivers, stutters, and was about to drop his phone in jubilation.

The driver kept looking at the road in calmness and said, "Goodbye Texas and welcome Silicon Valley". Then he looked at the cracked windshield and said, "My wish was to fix you, but I think I'll buy a new one for today".

****

After college, began work in different organizations. I avoided coworkers for no particular reason and being a proud introvert, I tended to focus on my tasks, but sometimes knowing the technical skills at work has the lower hand in career development as compared to building good relationships. I noticed that coworkers were avoiding me, some even revealed that they feared although I treated them well. But being ambiguous gave a bad impression. Some thought I was arrogant, others thought that I was trying to set them up, and others thought I had a grudge against them. I was stunned to know the awful traits my colleagues thought of me and I was even more stunned with the fact that innocent silence could cause negative connotations turning the working environment into a breeding ground for hostility.

As expected, this Mamdouh was a mere tireless storytelling machine, particularly his personal tales. Listening in on a conversation, he cuts in the thread to add his POV with a story of a similar incident which happened to him. He begins with a story, asks with a story, and of course answers with a story. No wonder, like others I felt comfortable with him. I never figured out and neither did others the reason for this feeling. I came to realize that it was his personal touch in storytelling. The stories were like a magnet which no one can see its power, but we all were drawn by its effect.

I focused on his stories, studying and analyzing them. And I found that he had an instinctive and extraordinary ability to compose his story that leaves listeners with their jaws dropped even if sometimes it does not last more than a minute. Mamdouh's stories had many powerful elements, but at that time I could not grasp them all as I knew so little about the skill of storytelling. I began listening to others looking for common features. Sometimes it was a good plot, a sudden twist of events, an inspiring tone of voice, intriguing body gestures or an influencing end. I found that a combination and integration of all these elements create a masterpiece that leave the audience wanting more. Although I thoroughly studied the elements, I had a nagging feeling that there is another less obvious element. After long evaluation, it was *Vulnerability*.

Each language has its own idiosyncrasies and uniqueness in its ability describe things. In Arabic, it is impossible for some phrases to even have synonymous meaning in other languages. For example "lion" in Arabic has more than hundred names and each name, the lion is described in a certain position and situation. Some English words carry other meanings. One of these words is "vulnerability" which means to be exposed to the possibility of being physically or emotionally harmed. It is hard to find the exact meaning for vulnerability because it is one of the rare words used in literature and especially rare in Western culture because admitting to vulnerability is not a very good idea in a world where competition and struggle is the main rule for survival. Life is hard and tough, and it has no place for the faint-hearted.

Some researchers studied effects of vulnerability on the behavior and attitude of people. One of them is Dr Brené Brown. Her books on vulnerability are bestsellers like "The Power of Imperfection". She also spoke in TEDx about "The Power of Vulnerability". Dr Brown lists misconceptions on vulnerability in "Daring Greatly" like pairing vulnerability with weakness. While weakness refers to the inability to confront attacks, it does not necessarily follow that one who is vulnerable cannot handle attacks because the bravest and strongest people who can confront shocks and attacks are vulnerable people who at any time might get hurt, injured, or even breakdown, and get defeated too. A brave person is not one who never fears but one who admits his fears because he is a vulnerable human being who does not allow fear to block the road toward his/her goals. (60)

One of the results of Dr Brown's research is people fear exposing their vulnerability because they associate it with shame, and this is the fiercest enemy of vulnerability. Shame has the power to silence and no one dares verbalize it. This is why the best incubator for this disease are people who seek perfection in everything. It is very easy to silence them out of fear of shame directed at them. Confronting shame and facing the emotions of disgrace inside is the biggest challenge to your vulnerability. When you have gone through barriers, your vulnerability becomes a womb that gives birth to love, belonging, joy, and tranquility.

Vulnerability is the shortest route to empathy. As mentioned earlier, one of the reasons of the power of storytelling is its ability to trigger emotions of empathy between the storyteller and the listener, and empathy comes shortly after vulnerability. When you see someone being stabbed, you twitch because your mirror neurons put you in the person's position. Also, all the sad situations that inflict a hero, like calamity, defeat, fear, and disappointment have a major impact that trigger empathy, which in turn makes the story a memory in people's hearts.

Maybe one of the reasons that made me avoid showing vulnerability is a natural instinct that all humans have, which is concealing humanistic weakness for the sake of safety. The human brain has at its base the Amygdala which is responsible for making decisions in dangerous situations. It overrides rational thinking and reacts quickly. It works to hide a person's weakness from the eyes of an enemy until reaching a state of physical and emotional safety. The Amygdala's function evolved from times of danger to a perpetual state of hiding weakness which became the norm. In this age of capitalism, people go as far as hiding their weakness even from themselves so much so when they look in the mirror, they do not dare confront themselves about moments they fell. They fool themselves with the illusion they are invulnerable and go out to face life in pieces with other human debris. These pieces and debris never heal because we were raised that it is a shame to cry showing weakness. But the real shame is living in a society that only cheers strengths while negating vulnerability.

This is what I realized later on. My colleagues wanted to perceive me as a simple human being the same as they were. They did not care about my strength as much as they did my vulnerability in order to feel safe around me. This is why I named this part Humanize It. Your story should be more "human". And nothing would make it more human than stating your vulnerability in the story.

The former Egyptian President Anwar Al-Sadat was featured in one Egyptian magazine. The article showed very detailed pictures of his personal life, some were even in the bathroom in his underwear shaving. This allowed the masses to see him as a normal human being and therefore identified with him. Al-Sadat in his book, "In Search of Identity", shared personal aspects of his life like attending religious festivals in his small village, life in prison and his impoverished years. Of course, these things would not come up at the beginning of his presidency, or when he sought power, or during The Yom Kippur War but after he emerged victorious in 1973; it was just the right time to show some vulnerability for the sake of more approval.

The United States President perceived to be the most powerful man on earth tend exaggerate vulnerability. For example, Barack Obama was keen to project himself as a father talking about his daughters Malia and Sasha, and the strong emotions he felt seeing them as adults wearing high heels. He always talked about his past and suffering during childhood and how this past gave him strength and perseverance to chase his dreams.

Prophet Muhammad, although he became the most powerful man in the entire Arab Peninsula as he was the first one to ever reunite it under one leadership, was the one God referred in the Quran, "Indeed, you are of a great moral character" Al-Qalam-4 and yet kept reminding his companions and all Muslims that he was a mere human being, but receives a revelation, "Say, I am only a man like you, to whom has been revealed that your god is one God. So, whoever would hope for the meeting with his Lord - let him do righteous work and not associate in the worship of his Lord anyone" Al-Kahf-110. The vulnerability of Prophet Muhammad was reflected in his saying, "I am Allah's servant, I eat like a servant and sit like a servant". Prophet Muhammad meant to correct any misconception about him being a god that may result to a deviation from the principles of Islam.

Derived from human nature, the more power and authority we attain the tendency to show vulnerability increases because when harsh events in life become old memory, it becomes preferable to speak out about it. Have you ever thought why people tend to be guarded in the first meeting? When you get on a bus or a train and sit between two strangers, do the three of you talk and get to know each other, or is it a rare incident? People fear rejection and do not easily trust strangers. On the flipside, people avoid interaction because they lie about themselves and fabricate stories of success and selfless acts. Why people tell such stories and lies is the tendency to hide weakness exaggerate strength. People are generally extremists so when they avert weakness, they are excessive in strength; although our lives is a somehow a balance of both. A satisfactory achievement and a severe failure should be the balance of our stories.

It is sad to note that 95% of the people I met begin their stories bragging about themselves and their good fortune in anything they did, many of whom were colleagues. The remaining 5% are those who leave an imprint in my memory – emotions and personality through their very natural stories. These people cared less about their successes than their failures and defeats. Only after enumerating the latter do they mention their achievements which take up a minority of the time.

Mamdouh always mentioned his failure with his own business and how he exerted effort to keep it afloat but could not. He had to become an employee in this company. Mamdouh does not shy away from sharing his failure but is proud that he tried over and over and maybe his testimony was the reason to land this prestigious job. Mamdouh never felt embarrassed about his divorce and did not blame anyone except himself, promising to be more patient and compassionate with his new wife. Mamdouh and people who are like him do not ever fear vulnerability, they are truly brave human beings. This is why their stories deserve to heard and more so to be imitated as persons.

There are infinite aspects of vulnerability you may use in your story. The story of a single success is accompanied with scores of setbacks, defeats, and failures so you will never find difficulty weaving vulnerability to the fabric of your story. But, it is not that easy for humans to do so. It is exactly like a phobia from rats, and all a new graduate of psychiatry can do is lock a big brown rat in a room with the patient saying, "Face you fear".

This feverish psychological struggle between what you've been believing for decades and between your initiative to speak out about your vulnerability wouldn't be ever an easy thing to do. It will face resistance from your ego and many times you will not be able to continue as planned. You will feel embarrassed, frightened, and ashamed. But over time, you will surprise even yourself at your ability to publicly verbalize words that you do not even dare think. You will be amazed as much as the patient who finally caught the rat and kissed it (depending if the patient is still alive). You will be amazed how your vulnerability has made you invulnerable. You shall stand firm telling your story which will be remembered. Years later, your listeners neither recall your name, nor where you are from, but they will remember your story – your role in it... a vulnerable human being.

Influencers

Vibrating Words

A Day

At one storytelling lecture, I asked attendees to listen to a recitation of Qaf, a chapter in Quran and note the verse that left the deepest effect. They mentioned different verses, but as expected a majority chose "On the Day we will say to Hell, 'Have you been filled?' and it will say, 'Are there some more?'" Qaf-30. Some said that they immersed into the meaning of this verse as if they lived it, while others actually wept upon hearing it. So I investigated the matter some more and asked them to clarify the reason why they chose such verse and did not choose others. We finally concluded that "Day" triggers the mind to open the gates of thinking, reflection, and immersion. It is a window leading to projection and imagination. So, when a reader or a listener perceives the word of the day, it directs all consciousness in the past or the distant future. This is why it is not a coincidence that storytellers through the course of history used the word day to begin stories.

In my previous book "The Persuasion Matrix", I mentioned that one the most famous technique is Priming. It is a tool that has been mentioned excessively in academic studies in the recent years as it has a deep effect in persuasion attempts in various channels. Priming is about stimulating the mind with swift and small information so the mind involuntarily anchors to this information and the person's next decision will be heavily associated with such information. For example, a client enters a mobile phone shop and buys a Samsung, in coming days, clients buy iPhone. No one notices that the past days, Samsung ads were playing in the background and in the following days, iPhone ads played. The information was received by the clients through the channel of System 1 and it affected their purchasing decisions. Priming in stories has various approaches, one of them is beginning with the word "day" or whatever may refer to it, so that the mind begins to associate that word with the most accessible meaning in his mind going deep in the past or distant future. And both are very interesting to anyone who listens to a story. (61)

The storyteller may use variety of expressions denoting "day" like saying, "I recall that one day...", "I can see in the near future that a day will come where...". Mentioning a certain day in the past or future gives a wide space and freedom to imagine place and time. On the other hand, not mentioning "day" would lead the focus to a general frame of the plot without delving into a specific place or time which is in the storyteller's control.

Mentioning a specific day has a good effect when you want to get a hold of the audience's memory of that date like saying, "In 1990, in one of the December's very cold days...". Here the listener's mind goes back to 1990 which he may have experienced, immersing more in the story. Some storytellers would give a more specific date saying, "In 25th of February 2010..." because it represents something important to the storyteller which may not be the same for the audience and may interrupt System 1 cutting immersion because the mind will scan for that particular date which has no special meaning to the listener. Dates are the quickest detail students forget in history class. They recall the events in battles and treaties as it contains drama, struggles, victories, but dates do not carry substantial meaning for them, so they drop it. It is quite funny how schools still test students on dates knowing students have a hard time retaining them. A professional storyteller should say, "A thousand years ago...", "In a time in history...".

And Finally

Storytelling is like swimming in the middle of a vast ocean where the shore is nowhere in sight. Sometimes swimmers do not feel the need to go ashore if they are enjoying the swim, but at times need a glimpse of the shore for enthusiasm and stamina not abandon the swim back. "Finally" is the glimpse of that shore. It is the sign that we are about to finish, so better pay attention because it will not be long until we reach the ending. "Finally" has the ability to reinvigorate the bored listener who keeps checking his wristwatch. "Finally" connotes shorter distance to the ending. It denotes the last 25% more or less of the story. But never use it twice because it would be absurd.

What no one ever expected

Why would people remain and listen to a long story that could otherwise be abridged and told not longer than a few minutes? A story provides ecstasy which abstract information cannot. And what intensifies ecstasy is the moment of change. As we saw earlier in the graphs that depict Story Path, ecstatic moments always follow sudden change in the graph. This is why people are keen for words implying sudden change like, "What nobody expected was...", "And this was the moment when...", "All of a sudden...". Almost all the stories in this book have a change event which has been described using various word and phrases.

Ending
A Wise Wisdom

The goal of a reasonable story is to impart but a little wisdom that cause change. "The Shame", "The Beast's Race" and "El-Keif" (The Drugs) are three Egyptian movies that had a tremendous echo in Egyptian society in the late eighties. One common feature of the three is its wisdom that encapsulate the entire story in the mind.

"The Beast's Race" is about four people and God's destiny. The first did not accept God giving him wealth, but making him sterile. The second did not accept God blessing him with many children but not enough wealth. The third, a physician who did not accept God's creation. He had knowledge which he used to change the nature. Finally, the fourth one accepted and submitted to God and so the other three made fun of him. The physician convinced the rich man to give the poor one money for his frontal lobe which is according to the physician's research would enable him to have babies. But the rich man fell ill and could not have sexual intercourse to make the baby he paid half of his wealth for. The poor man became so rich but feared that something wrong happened to his brain and all the money he had could not treat him. With this, the reputation of the physician was ruined. The only one saved was the fourth man who from the beginning accepted God's will, and with his voice in the last scene he said, "And whoever exchanges the favor of Allah after it has come to him - then indeed, Allah is severe in penalty." Al-Baqarah-211".

"The Shame" is about three brothers with a rich and pious father who dies in a car accident travelling for a business deal. The big brother threw a fit over his family claiming that their father was not the pious man they thought he was, rather he was a drug dealer. And with all the money their father accumulated over the years, he bought a cargo of drugs on a ship which will be somewhere off the shores of

Alexandria. The three of them have to collect it themselves because the assistant of their father died with him in the accident. They stand to lose everything if they do not. After a feverish internal struggle for the brothers, the middle one who worked as prosecutor quit his job as he does not see himself fit for the honorable profession. The same goes with the youngest brother who is a psychiatrist treating drug addicts and witnesses their sufferings and pains. Their only sister had to break off the engagement with her fiancé who is a policeman as she does not see herself deserving to marry a man who day and night puts his life at risk to chase drug dealers. Finally, all three brothers go and retrieve the cargo from the sea. In the end, they contact the buyer to sell the cargo which was hidden deep a salt lake. The salt water leaked into the cans and they lost everything – the cargo, their wealth, their jobs, and their honor. In the last scene inside the boat, the eldest brother jumps in the lake searching for any hope inside the empty cans, the middle brother shot himself and the psychiatrist completely loses his mind. The scene is blurs out and a singsong voice recites, "And by the soul and He who proportioned it. And inspired its wickedness and its righteousness. He has succeeded who purifies it, and he has failed who instills it with corruption" Ash-Shams-7-10.

"El-Keif" (The Drugs) is a story between a successful chemist with a steady job and happy family and his younger brother, a loser and a deviant confined to his desires and caprice. Despite efforts of his older brother to remove him from his filthy lifestyle, he does not respond. Constantly reminding him of the morals that their father used to teach them, the elder brother visits his younger sibling in the house of their dead parents. In one visit, the elder brother sees an old and dusty frame with a famous poem hanging precariously on the wall. He fixes it and reads it, "Nations flourish as long as their morals flourish, yet if they perish, they perish". He is inspired and decides to help his younger brother to quit smoking Hashish. He uses his expertise to concoct something similar to Hash without the harmful materials, yet leaving a similar effect. When the younger brother found out, he insists that his elder brother make more so he could sell it and make profit. Initially the elder brother refuses but finally gives in as he is also in financial crisis. This new fake drug spread all over Egypt and when the elder brother mistakenly smokes it and gets high, he realizes that the buyer added other materials to it. He analyzes it in his laboratory and he gets the shock of his life. The buyer added one of the most dangerous toxins that rapidly destroys the nervous system. He is overcome thinking of the evil he produced and he decides to stop. But the buyer abducts the two brothers and tortures them. The thug injects the elder brother with high doses of cocaine making him addicted to it. This way, he will produce his profitable fake Hash whenever he was told. Finally, both brothers lose their lives because of the evil they created. In the last scene, a singsong voice narrates, "Nations flourish as long as their morals flourish, yet if they perish, they perish".

Normally, the wisdom comes at the end of the story, but it is savvy to connote it in the middle of the story sometimes in a repetitive way. For example, a story aiming to instill in the team to acquire a value. They might be told a story with a wisdom in the beginning, "My father taught me to never sell what I don't own...". Continue narrating and finish with the same wisdom, "...So, the result of this achievement was shaped by the words of my father I mentioned earlier... Never to sell what I don't own". Usually it is good to repeat the wisdom twice and separate them with moments of silence let the audience digest and remember the words of wisdom.

Unexpectedness

Surprise Me!

Once a friend called me on the phone and right after I answered, this friend out of nowhere said, "Do you know that I'm going to change your name on my phone from Hisham to The Heart Hunter?". It was very unexpected and within seconds, laughs and a nice talk. Moreover a closer and tighter a friendship with that man who does not only make a powerful argument but has a smart way of talking and an extraordinary ability to create surprises resulting in cheer.

I do the same thing now. When someone calls who has not communicated for a while, I would answer, "Do you how long I have waited to see your name on my phone?" or I would answer this way, "Before you say anything, interpret this". The caller wonders and asks, "What thing?!". I continue, "Why does my phone vibrate in happiness especially when you're the caller?". Sometimes I greet in riddle like saying, "Hello, before you say anything, if you and I are in the forest and two lions are chasing us and I have in one hand a rifle loaded with one bullet, which lion shall I shoot?". The caller answers, "Of course, the one chasing you". And I answer in a sad tone, "Unfortunately you're wrong my friend. If you don't trust my chivalry, how shall I care going out with you anywhere tonight? And how shall I trust that you are fine lending me your car tomorrow morning?". With that, he changes his answer, "I guess you'll shoot the lion chasing me". So, I revert, "Then, I think the one who you sacrifices his life for yours and saves you from a fierce lion deserves some cash like a thousand dollars... Please deposit the amount in my account first thing tomorrow, see you...".

In their groundbreaking book, "Made to Stick", brothers Chip and Dan Heath mentioned this nice story that happened on a flight going to San Diego. While preparing to depart from Dallas airport, the stewardess Kareen Wood made this announcement; (62)

"If I could have your attention for a few moments, we sure would love to point out these safety features. If you haven't been in an automobile since 1965, the proper way to fasten your seat belt is to slide the flat end into the buckle. To unfasten, lift the buckle and it will release. And as the song goes, there might be fifty ways to leave your lover, but there are only six ways to leave this aircraft: two forward exit doors, two over-wing removable window exits, and two aft exit doors. The location of each exit is clearly marked with signs overhead, as well as red and white disco lights along the floor of the isle. Made ya look! Located in the seat-back pocket in front of you or to the side of you in the lounge area, among the peanut wrappers, coffee cups and newspapers, you should find an emergency information card supplementing our safety features. Take note on the back that in the event of a water evacuation, your bottom — your seat bottom, that is, can be used as a flotation device by removing the cushion, holding the straps underneath it, and choosing your favorite stroke. Please check at this time to make sure your seat belts are securely fastened, seat backs and tray tables are in their full upright and most uncomfortable position, and all the carry-on luggage you've brought in is crammed underneath the seat in front of you, or in one of the overhead bins. FAA regulations require passenger compliance with all lighted passenger information signs, posted placards, and crew member instructions, regarding seat belts and no smoking. In other words do exactly what we say! Speaking of smoking, there's never any smoking aboard our flights. You know what happens if we catch you smoking here at Southwest, don't you? You'll be asked to step out onto our wing and enjoy our feature movie presentation, "Gone with The Wind." There is never any smoking, even in lavatories. Finally, although we never anticipate a change in cabin pressure, should one occur, four oxygen masks will magically appear overhead. Immediately stop screaming, please deposit a quarter, and unlike President Clinton, you must inhale! If you're seated next to a child or traveling with someone who is acting like a small child, secure yourself first and then assist him or her. Please continue wearing the mask until otherwise notified by a uniformed crew member – yes, believe it or not, these are uniforms! And we do need to tell you that the bag does not inflate, but you still are receiving oxygen. Sit back, relax and enjoy a one-hour flight to San Diego on the best airline in the universe – Southwest. Southwest Airlines is determined to offer positively outrageous Service to customers" "

In another flight departing to San Francisco, the flight attendant announced prior take off;

Hello and welcome to Alaska flight 438 to San Francisco. If you're going to San Francisco, you're in the right place. If you're not going to San Francisco, you're about to have a really long evening. We'd like to tell you now about some important safety features of this aircraft. The most important safety feature we have aboard this plane is . . . The Flight Attendants. Please look at one now. There are 5 exits aboard this plane, 2 at the front, 2 over the wings, and one out the plane's rear end. If you're seated in one of the exit rows, please do not store your bags by your feet. That would be a really bad idea.

Please take a moment and look around and find the nearest exit. Count the rows of seats between you and the exit. In the event that the need arises to find one, trust me, you'll be glad you did. We have pretty blinking lights on the floor that will blink in the direction of the exits. White ones along the normal rows, and pretty red ones at the exit rows. In the event of a loss of cabin pressure these baggy things will drop down over your head. You stick it over your nose and mouth like the flight attendant is doing now. The bag won't inflate, but there's oxygen there, I promise.

If you are sitting next to a small child, or someone who is acting like a small child, please do us all a favor and put on your mask first. If you are traveling with two or more children, please take a moment now to decide which one is your favorite. Help that one first, and then work your way down. In the seat pocket in front of you is a pamphlet about the safety features of this plane. I usually use it as a fan when I'm having my own personal summer. It makes a very good fan. It also has pretty pictures. Please take it out and play with it now.

Please take a moment now to make sure your seat belts are fastened low and tight about your waist. To fasten the belt, insert the metal tab into the buckle. To release, it's a pulley thing — not a pushy thing like you're car cause you're in an airplane, hello! There is no smoking in the cabin on this flight. There is also no smoking in the lavatories. If we see smoke coming from the lavatories, we will assume you are on fire and put you out. This is a free service we provide.

There are two smoking sections on this flight, one outside each wing exit. We do have a movie in the smoking sections tonight, hold on, let me check what it is . . . Oh here it is, the movie tonight is 'Gone with the Wind'. In a moment we will be turning off the cabin lights, and it's going to get really dark, really fast. If you're afraid of the dark, now would be a good time to reach up and press the yellow button. The yellow button turns on your reading light. Please don't press the orange button unless you absolutely have to. The orange button is your seat ejection button.

We're glad to have you with us on board this flight. Thank you for choosing Alaska Air, and giving us your business and your money. If there's anything we can do to make you more comfortable, please don't hesitate to ask.

If you all weren't strapped down you would have given me a standing ovation, wouldn't you?

;And after landing, she said

Welcome to the San Francisco International Airport. Sorry about the bumpy landing. It's not the captain's fault. It's not the co-pilot's fault. It's the Asphalt. Please remain seated until the plane is parked at the gate. At no time in history has a passenger beaten a plane to the gate. So please don't even try. Please be careful opening the overhead bins because shift happens."

Here is one by a southwest flight attendant giving safety instructions assisted by three others;

I'd like to pretend to have your attention for just a few moments. My ex-husband, my new boyfriend and our divorce attorney are gonna show you the safety features on this 737-800 series. It's been a long day for me. To properly fasten your seatbelt, slide the flat end in the buckle. To release, lift the buckle. Position your seatbelt tight and low across your hips like my grandmother wears her support bra. If you get mad and wanna take your toys and go home there's six ways to get there. Two forward exit doors, two over wing window exits, two rear exits. There are signs overhead and lights on the floor near each exit.

Everybody gets a door prize in the seat back pocket in front of you along with dirty diapers, chewing gum wrappers, banana peels and all other gifts you leave for us. Right on top is a safety information card. Take it out, check it out, you'll notice in the highly unlikely event that the captain lands us near a hot tub. Everybody gets their own teeny-weeny yellow Southwest bikini – one size fits all. Take it out only when told to do so. Place it over your head, put that strap around your waist, buckle it in front, pull it tight and once outside, pull the red tab to inflate.

My attendants are coming by hoping you'll tell them how good looking they are. They're gonna make sure your seat backs and tray tables are in their full upright and absolutely most uncomfortable position possible. And your carry-on items are crammed and shoved completely under the seat in front of you leaving absolutely no room for your knees or feet. As you know, it's a no-smoking, no whining, no complaining flight. It's a "please" and "thank-you" and "you are such a good-looking flight-attendant" flight. Smoking is never *allowed onboard at Southwest. If you are caught smoking in a lavatory the fine for that is $2000. If you wanted to pay that for your airfare, you should have flown somebody else.*

If we do make you that nervous in the next hour and a half, you're more than welcome to step outside. We don't discriminate at Southwest, we have a special smoking section just for you. We'll even show you a movie tonight. We have "Up in the Air." And the flight attendant serving you is Wendy and her motto is "if you can light it, you can smoke it." It's against the law to tamper with or disable any smoke detector in the lavatory. Federal aviation regulations about passenger compliance and are on passenger information signs and posted on placards. Basically, just do what we say and nobody gets hurt.

And although we never anticipate a loss in cabin pressure – if we did, we certainly wouldn't be at work tonight. But if needed, 4 oxygen masks come out of the compartment overhead. Stop screaming, let go of your neighbor, pull until that plastic tubing is fully extended, place the mask over your nose and mouth and breath normally. To activate the flow of oxygen simply insert $.75 for the first minute and $.50 for each additional minute. Although that plastic bag may not inflate, you are receiving lots and lots of gin. Oxygen, that is. And if you're traveling with small children… we're sorry.

If you're traveling with more than one child, pick out the one who you think might have the most earning potential then proceed down the line. And if you're traveling with somebody needing special assistance – like your husband – bless his heart, or your wife put on your mask first. That's it for the do's and don'ts of show and tell. So, sit back and relax or you can sit up and be tense, either way. It's a one and a half hour flight, gate to gate, the clock's already ticking. Seriously, if there is anything at all we can do to make your flight more enjoyable please tell us… just as soon as we land in Salt Lake City. And if there's anything you can do to make our flight more enjoyable, we'll tell you immediately. We're not shy in Southwest.

> *That's what we call very cheap entertainment. Nobody had to pay extra but you certainly don't get a refund. Thank you for choosing Southwest, welcome aboard!*

These three flight attendants did very well in sparking interest with the unexpected delivery from the usual safety instructions passengers ignored scores of times, and for sure it added overall satisfaction of the passengers and left a powerful impression on the quality the airline.

The ability to include unexpectedness in your talk has an extreme effect on the emotions of the audience. Unexpectedness in a good story is all about placement. We quickly lose interest in stories that do not have surprises, shock, or sudden shifts. Unexpectedness can be categorized in the following:

1. Jokes

Jokes are the best types of projections. It is the oldest way to generate warm emotions and break the ice with people. Jokes, like aspirin, are very small in size but have great effect. Jokes provide an intense dose of ambiguity and contrast between two events, so the listener would assume a close relationship of both events, then finally flips things over and laughs follow the unexpected surprise.

Three hunters challenged each other in a forest. The first one went deep inside and returned with hands soaked in blood. The two asked him what happened and he replied, "Do you see the tree over there?". They said, "Yes". He said, "Right there I killed a rabbit". The second one went and returned with arms soaked in fresh blood and he said, "Do you see the big rock right there?". They said, "Yes". He said, "I killed a deer right there". The third went and came back with his face drenched in blood, so he said, "Do you see the pole placed right there?". They said, "Yes, we see it". He said, "I didn't".

That unexpected surprise with the third hunter and the stark contrast from the other two are reasons why people love such type of jokes.

2. The relation between the last correlation first

One of the most amazing and subtle types of unexpectedness is constructing correlation between events or characters then little by little reveal the relationship of both until the end of the story like a man in need in the first part of a story who happens to be the one to give a hand to the hero at a crucial time retuning the favor the hero did for him earlier. This draws "Ah" and "Oh" from the audience. The more you gain experience in storytelling, the more you can construct this correlation in a subtle way. When your story lacks some of the other elements, correlation can save it. An example is the Uber story which we already tackled.

****

Allah Almighty, in Quran tells the story of Prophet Joseph. "We relate to you, [O Muhammad], the best of stories" Joseph-3. Many scholars comment it is the best story in the entire Quran as it encompasses many elements that make it fascinating. It was revealed to Prophet Muhammad at a time he felt most sorrowful to comfort him. Here, we will focus on a single charactristic in the story:

Young Jospeh tells his father, Jacob, his dream. He saw eleven planets along with sun and moon all prostrating to him. His father knew then that Joseph will be the greatest amongst all his sons. Joseph is the one who inherited Prophethood. Jacob feared his other sons would envy Joseph and ordered him to keep it between them. Joseph's brothers observed the great love Jacob felt for their brother so they conspired to kill him; but the eldest brother adviced, they throw him in a well for someone else to find and be rid of their for good. After they did so, they returned to their father and showed him his clothes soaked in blood claiming that a wolf killed him, but their father knew that something else had happened and he keeps calm.

A caravan passes from the eastern desert of Egypt, stops at the well and finds Joseph. Delighted, they take him and sell him as a slave. Joseph grew up a handsome youth, so the wife of his master seduced him, but he refused and ran and in doing so, she grabbed him and ripped off a piece of his garment. When the master returns, she accused Joseph of attempting to rape her. After it became clear to the master that Joseph was innocent, he orders Joseph to keep silent and the wife to repent for he sin. Then, the wife brings in someone women to spread rumors and gives them knives. She summons Joseph and because of his beauty, they cut themselves.

They finally throw Jospeh in jail where and he remained for nine years. Two of the inmates had dream. One of them said, "I have seen myself pressing wine". The other said, "I have seen myself carrying upon my head bread, from which the birds were eating". He interpreted their dreams where the second one will be crucified and the first one will be released and return to his post back as the pharaoh's bartender. Joseph tells the first one to mention him to the pharaoh, but the devil makes him forget to do so. Then the pharaoh has a dream that none of his courtiers could intepret and so the bartender remembers Joseph. He goes to him in the jail and narrates the dream of the pharaoh. Joseph interprets it to be a famine in Egypt for the next seven years. He adviced them to store grains to save Egypt. The pharaoh likes the advice of Jospeh and summons him to court. Jospeh asks the pharaoh to reinvistigate his case which threw him unjustly in jail. The wife of his former master finally confesses.

Joseph asks the pharaoh to oversee saving grains in the storehouses of Egypt. The brothers of Jospeh come from Palastine seeking to buy grains for their tribe. He knows them but they do not recognize him.

He summons them to court and asks them to bring him their youngest brother otherwise he will not give them a share the next time they come for grains. They go to their father and ask to let their youngest brother go with them, but he refuses so they would not do to their youngest brother what they did to Joseph. They plead to their father and take him to Joseph. He talks to him alone in the palace and lets him know that he is his missing brother. Joseph orders one of his servants to hide a gold measuring cup in the bag of his youngest brother. Upon leaving, the soldiers stopped and inspected their bags found the gold cup in the bag of the youngest brother. They sieze him and the older brothers go to Joseph pleading but he refuses. The eldest brother is afraid to go back to his father without his youngest brother and decides to stay while the rest go and tell their father what happened. The father goes blind out of grief. They return to Egypt and face Joseph, who finally who he really was. The brothers repent. Joseph gives them his shirt which he wore when they threw him in the well and orders them to return with all the tribes of Israel.

Upon their return, Jacob smells Joseph. They cast the shirt over his face and he regains his sight. The tribes of Israel migrate to Egypt. Jacob, his wife and sons step into the court of Joseph. He takes his parents and raised both upon the throne and his brotheres bowed to him in prostration. In these moments, the hearts tremble and eyes shed tears when Joseph finally says, "O my father, this is the explanation of my vision from before. My Lord has made it reality" Joseph-100

The reader gets immeresed in the rapid and successive events and forgets Joseph's dream then unexpectedly it is mentioned again is the relation between the commencement and the ending of the story which brings the audience to ecstacy and engrave the memory in their hearts and minds.

****

Who is Muhammad? People often ask me wherever I go. I used to answer it by enumerating information and facts: Muhammad is the last Prophet, he is from Mecca, he migrated to Medina, etc. The information above are important but for those who do not really know him, he is a "need to know the man with a story" type. Recently, this is how I answer that question:

> Let me tell you a story that happened fourteen hundred years ago; when the whole world was in chaos and misguided, when weak people and nations were held between the jaws of two immense civilizations – the Byzantine Empire on one side, where slaves were thrown to hungry lions to entertain kings, and collecting taxes was the rule. And the other side was the Persian Empire that subdue and humiliate its people. The men entering the king's palace had to lay flat on their stomachs, injustice and the enslavement of the people were the prominent features of this old kingdom which was immersed in luxury, abundance and power. But in one exceptional night, in the middle of the Arabic peninsula, the harshest desert on the planet where no human wishes to be, in a small place called Mecca, a man went up to a mountain facing the stars, isolated himself from everything, stayed in a cave on that mountain and reflected on the universe and searching for God when suddenly what he knew later as the archangel Gabriel descended to him inside the cave and recited something he did not understand at the beginning. The archangel ordered him to recite, but he was scared and he said that he could neither read nor write. The archangel repeated his order and the man repeated his argument but then he recited to him what later was known as the first verses of the Quran – the last and the only doctrine from God sent to the entire human race to be followed until the day of judgment. Muhammad descended the mountain in the middle of the night shivering and

shaking, he ran out in the open but everywhere he looked he saw Gabriel blocking the entire horizon. He went to his house calling his wife Khadija saying, "Cover me, cover me". He narrated what happened and told her, "I fear that something may happen to me". She answered him, "Never! By Allah, Allah will never disgrace you. You keep good relations with your kith and kin, help the poor and the destitute, serve your guests generously and assist the deserving calamity-afflicted ones". Then she took him to her cousin called Waraqa who used to read the old scriptures of Jesus and other Prophets. He was an old man over ninety years old, blind and lived alone. He narrated all that happened and while Muhammad was speaking, the blind eyes of Waraqa was glistened and tears began falling. He then said to Muhammad, "This is the law, the law that has been sent to Moses, you're the final Prophet sent from Allah to the entire humanity, and I wish I would still be alive when your people drive you out from here". Muhammad surprisingly asked, "Shall they drive me out?". Waraqa said, "No Prophet has what you have except that their own people drove them out as well and I wish I could live to that time so I could be at your side".

After they finished, Muhammad left and within few months Waraqa passed away as if he lived long enough just to convey such message to Muhammad. And from that night, the journey of calling people to the guidance of Allah had started – a journey full of sacrifice, hardship and pain. Prophet Muhammad remained in Mecca for thirteen years calling people to Islam and the Muslims suffered a lot – torture, boycott, segregation and even death. But they kept firm and strong, believing in the truth revealed to their Prophet. Some fled to Ethiopia while others endured until the order came from God for the Muslims migrate to Medina 400 miles north of Mecca. The Muslims snuck out of Mecca leaving their homes and wealth – some with nothing to ride on and so traveled the distance by foot. One night when the majority of the Muslims had fled, Gabriel came to Muhammad. He went out of his house in the middle of the night and walked in the alleys of Mecca until he reached a small house and knocked on the door. It was opened by his dearest friend and follower and Muhammad said, "Now my friend, I've been ordered by Allah to migrate tonight".

Earlier that same night, the leaders of Mecca were gathering to decide the case of Muhammad. They all agreed to kill him that particular night. They brought men to stab him. They surrounded his house waiting him to come out and a great miracle happened. Muhammad stepped out and walked past them. No one could see him while he was passing few feet away from them. Allah temporarily blinded them. Muhammad and his friend snuck out of Mecca taking different routes that do not directly lead to Medina in order to confuse their pursuers. The news spread fast among the leaders of Mecca. They knew how firm and strong the belief of the Muslims are and they knew that if Muhammad reached Medina and establish the first community of Islam, it will be a serious threat to their authority and business. They were furious and had consultations. They offered a hundred camels to those who could bring back Muhammad dead or alive. The bounty was mind-blowing for all the tribesmen. A flood of adventurers and desert tracers prosecuted Muhammad and his friend, searching all over the way to Medina, searching in the caves, mountains, using magic and bribery, but all their efforts resulted in nothing, except the effort of one man – a man from Mecca, a strong and smart cavalier called Suraqa. He was an ambitious man and believed that he is the one who will earn the prize. He is over fifty years but as strong and passionate as a twenty yearold. He prayed to his idols to help him find Muhammad. He rode his horse into the vast desert using every skill he had in his life. He kept searching for days and before the despair could take over, he saw them – Muhammad and his friend each on a camel toward their destination. Suraqa, energized already seeing a hundred camels being given him, poked on his horse and went running after Muhammad, raising his sword, ready to shed the blood of the Blessed Prophet of God. Muhammad's friend saw him from a distance and recognized him and told Muhammad, "Suraqa following us". Muhammad saw him and did nothing but raise his hands to the heaven saying, "O Allah, protect us from Suraqa". Once Muhammad was done with his supplication, it was like the heavens and earth obeyed him. While Suraqa was fast approaching, all of a sudden he was thrown off his horse violently falling on the ground. The hooves of the horse were buried in the sand. Suraqa could not believe what had just happened to him. It had never happened to him even when he was a young amateur cavalier. And the smooth soil of the area can never cause a horse to stumble. Furiously, he jumped on his horse again pursuing even faster than before but again, he is thrown off for the same reason. Suraqa, desperate, retrieves his dice game from his bag to use as an omen. He places two arrows in a pot with one marked "Do it!" while the other with "Don't do it!". If he rolls and he gets either, it means the gods answered him to pursue Muhammad or otherwise. Suraqa looked to the heavens supplicating to all the gods he knew and all he did not, then he shook the pot and retreived one of the arrows, and it was "Don't do it". All of a sudden he insulted all the gods he knew and all he did not. Contrary to tradition, he rolled again and he got one arrow and very slowly and hesitantly he looked at it, and again it was "Don't do it". In wrath and anger, he tried for a third and last time believing that the gods would not abandon him for a third time along with some of the camels as a blessed sacrifice for them. It was a fair deal, he thought. He took out an arrow and his scream of victory abated and instead preceded by a cry of frustration because he drew "Don't do it". Even if he tried a thousand times, it would not help. Suraqa did not know that the earth and heavens and what was in between were assigned to protect the man.

Suraqa threw the dice game and decided to make a last try. He is now disobeying his gods. He took his horse and pursued Muhammad. This time, he gained distance. The hooves of his horse sparked from friction of the steel horseshoes and the rocks. Suraqa thought the bad omen left him when he got rid of the dice. He was a few feet behind the two when for the third time his horse told him "No" the only way it knew how by throwing him off. This time it was not just his body that suffered the blow but his mind, heart and soul. He realized that Muhammad is protected beyond his imagination and power. He called to him and Muhammad looked back saying, "Suraqa? Would you accept going back and in return I will give you bracelets of Khosrow the Persian king?". He is apparently a weak man running, escaping persecution in the scorching ruthless desert; his attacker a few feet away with sword and spear ready to finish his mission, and yet he promises bracelets of Khosrow. Trading the moon for his salvation would be more logical. Suraqa looked intently at Muhammad and then spoke out, "I accept, so write it down for me!".

Countless would fall down laughing with the response of Suraqa who took the contract and left Muhammad to continue on his way. But Suraqa did it, took his horse and went back to Mecca. And the horse never threw him off again. Going back, something fell from him which he never stopped to pick up, abandoning it forever — his false dice game. Suraqa hid the contract in a safe place in his house and kept the secret of Muhammad in a safe place in his heart. Muhammad finally reached Medina. The first Islamic territory was established wherein the Muslims can perform their rituals freely far from oppressors. From the second year of its establishment, incursions from Mecca and other tribes becan. Muslims bravely defended their religion. Conquering lands and subjugating evil, after eight years since the first day of migration, Muhammad overcame Mecca and forgave its people. He then returned to Medina and shortly his soul went back to its Keeper. Prophet Muhammad died while Islam was ruling the entire Arab Peninsula. And his dearest friend, Abu Bakr, who was his companion in the Migration ruled the Islamic nation and led several battles against the settlements of Romans in the Levant and the Persians in the northwest reaching their old capital. After two years of ruling the Islamic State, Abu Bakr dies and his successor Omar ruled the state for ten years. He continued the battles and conquests until he conquered Jerusalem. Its priests voluntarily handed him the keys of the city and for the first time Omar ends the influence and the existence of the Byzantine Empire in the Levant and moreover he conquered Al-Mada'in, capital of the Persian Empire. He ended the Persian Empire which existed for a thousand years, an empire that was built on subjugation, humiliation and enslavement of peoples, preventing those who want to know the truth about God and to choose his own path. Shock rippled across the world for the victory this young and unknown nation accomplished. Bounties of the Khosrow was brought to Medina. Unimaginable quantities of treasure were placed at the central mosque of Medina, large carpets, gold and silver and other luxurious materials that the people never saw in their lifetime. And while the bounties were being counted and distributed, all of a sudden Omar's eyes spotted the bracelets of Khosrow. Omar who loved Muhammad more than himself, more than anyone in his life did not just see the bracelets but saw Muhammad. He saw the promise Muhammad made to Suraqa. This moment was one of the best moments in Omar's life, a moment fulfillment, a moment of paying back. He ordered all the people to gather at the mosque and bring Suraqa right away. The people gathered. They did not know what was about to take place but they expected to witness something great. Omar was standing at the center of the mosque. Suraqa enters, all eyes were on him. He was an old man in his late eighties, could hardly walk and bowed stature. He could have died a long time ago because of the many things that had transpired in his life but the heavens and earth preserved him, delivered him to witness this moment. Omar calls Suraqa to come closer, people are watching eagerly. Omar raised the bracelets of Khosrow and loudly said, "This are the bracelets of Khosrow, this is the promise of Prophet Muhammad and now it is fulfilled by the will of Allah". And he handed Suraqa the bracelets and continued, "Go, Suraqa, walk all of Medina and tell her people, this is the promise of God's messenger, it has been fulfilled, the promise of Muhammad has been fulfilled. Allah promised to grant victory to Muhammad and to his followers and when Muhammad made this promise, it was Allah's promise and it had no way but to be fulfilled."

****

3. A Different Answer

I Shall Pick Up the Phone

While writing this book, there were moments where my mind could not take any step further. Once inclined to quit, I go back to a process of gathering information to move the stagnant waters in my mind. One turning moment was when I was at my desk engrossed in writing and a colleague came to my office and began chatting about some of his success and failure stories. I could not resist and directed my entire focus toward him. He told me how he started working in shipping business for about twenty years in various companies gaining experience throughout which qualified him to apply for a job in a big multinational logistic company as regional sales manager. The job will be a culmination of years of diligence. He went through many interviews and tests. It filtered to just two and he was one. He said, "The final interview was the criterion for my acceptance or rejection. The regional manager from headquarters traveled to meet both of us and choose the best qualified. After meeting the first guy, I believed that I still had a chance if I answered well". My friend leaned back on his chair and stared at the ceiling, recalling the memory and continued, "He asked me about everything for about two hours. Some of the questions were repetitive. As the interview progressed, I felt I didn't give good answers that satisfied the manager."

My friend looked me straight in the eyes and continued, "And then the man told me, Mr Muhammad, I'll ask you my last question. I paid close attention and summoned all mental powers to ready myself for what I thought was a lethal question. The manager said, Mr Muhammad, our company AB Logistics is on of the biggest in the world, we are spread across a hundred and fifty countries. We own about two hundred and thirty cargo ships, thousands of containers with a hundred thousand trucks, twenty five freight trains and seventy thousand employees. This is AB Logistics, what shall you do in middle all this?".

My friend told me that each time the manager mentioned a figure, he thought that the question was about it until the man interrupted his assumption with the question. He told me, "While my mind worked in full capacity formulating a winning answer in a matter of seconds, I felt that the man's patience wearing out waiting for my smart answer. I saw him take a deep breath about to release it by saying I'm out of the race. As the sigh was coming forth followed by deadly words of rejection, my mind sent my tongue the signal I've waited for what seemed so long. Involuntarily and quickly, I said I'll pick up the phone. The man knit his brows in amazement and confusion, leaned on the desk asking me, "What!". I said I'll pick up the phone and say I'm one of AB Logistics success contributors, may I help you". My friend told me that the man almost jumped off his seat, pointed at me looking to the board directors also in the room and yelled, "This is what I want".

****

The Stumbling of Carol

"How will you support your claim that you will be able to perform the job, although you don't have enough experience?". The question was like a sledge hammer. After passing previous interviews and after satisfying other hard questions, I was stunned by the company owner, who initially wanted to hire me but was hesitant due to my tender age. Also, my friends, who were already in told me that the owner was partial to creative employees over traditional hardworking ones thus obsessed with good and rapid answers that reveal that characteristic. So, I knew that I had no more than a few seconds to fathom my mind and give an answer. While doing so, memories popped up in the speed of light then suddenly time stopped and I said loudly, "The Stumbling of Carol". The man wondered and asked, "What?". I leaned on my side of his desk with both arms focusing my eyes to his and after a moment of silence, I said, "I was wondering how my little daughter, Carol, barely a year could keep up with me running in our small garden with her fragile legs unable to walk or even stand. I looked at my wife and considered picking Carol up and play an easier game or go back inside the house certain that she isn't fit for such games. But, in a second, I decided otherwise. The stumbling of Carol was exactly what I aimed for because after she was able to stand and keep her balance, after few more trials she was able to take steps and after a few minutes she was able to run. This happened before she reached her first year. I am certain the stumbling of Carol was what led her to rapid success, and my eyes that encouraged her were far better than my hands that could balance her". I looked at the man who did not show any emotion, then I stood up and said, "Shall you walk me through the duties of my new job or will you leave me to discover it by myself... and stumble for a while?".

NB
The owner was impressed and decided to hire me in a better position. One sly guy whispered to him showing my curriculum vitae, "Sir, according to his CV, he is single". It was a good story to tell in my next interview.

******

A Plumber on the Moon

What does Essam Heggie do in NASA aside from Taking Pictures of Rocks?"

The article above was written by a pro dictator journalist during that regime in Egypt discrediting the Egyptian scientist due to the latter's continuous criticism of the same. Although the same newspaper hailed him as an honor for the country for his participation in sending a space shuttle to Mars, its stance changed when his political views did not match theirs. They began humiliating him in a pathetic way claiming that he was just a photographer as if NASA went to a studio and asked him to take pictures of rocks!

Although such an article required no reply, Dr Heggie did deliver a marvelous answer in story form:

> "In 2002, I received my PhD from Paris University in the discipline of discovering water on planets with Grade A and before I worked in NASA, my parents insisted that I go to Egypt and visit my grandma in our small village. When my grandma knew that the Doctor (she used to call me so) will visit her, she decided to invite many of the villagers to our humble house. And when I came, I was stunned with the number of people that came with prescriptions, medical imaging sheets and medical analysis. My grandma told them that her grandson (The doctor who just came from France) will treat everybody. When I told my grandma who was born in 1918 and didn't get any education that I'm not a

physician; rather my PhD is in discovering water on planets, she told me, "Discovering water, Son! Do you work as a plumber on moon?!". My greetings to your esteemed newspaper.

Dr Heggies could simply answer by writing an article that exposes the obtuseness of the journalist. But the story had an effect that amplified the stultification of the journalist by comparing his knowledge with that of the grandma who was born in 1918 and did not get an education comparable to the former. Using stories to give an answer than what the audience expects strengthens one's argument and keeps mouths shut. And this is one of the best ways of using stories to deliver indirect messages to an opponent – reading or listening until he is hit with its ending, finding that it carried a rebuttal that was never expected.

****

Details

Delving Into

A common medical advice is to drink lots of water as it has numerous benefits health, yet there are few advice about excessive and unnecessary consumption. The same goes with piling details to a story. Mentioning enough details will help your audience to visualize, but what many do not tackle is reducing details in some cases, or quit providing any detail at all. No example fits as perfectly as the repetition of Prophet Moses' story in the Quran. When his story appears in many chapters of the book, some details were added and some were omitted. Chapter Taha provided details about the direct conversation between Moses and God, while In Chapter of The Stories, the focus was on the details of Moses' childhood - his time in Pharaoh's house and the exodus. The entire story was summarized in just two verses, "And We had certainly given Moses the Scripture and appointed with him his brother Aaron as an assistant. And We said, 'Go both of you to the people who have denied Our signs.' Then We destroyed them with complete destruction." Al-Furqan-35-36. The diversity of details in the Quran draws focus to certain parts while removing some pulls it from unnecessary situations in order to deliver certain meanings.

Providing details draw attention or trigger emotions, while omitting them keeps focus in one direction or guarantee a particular emotion. Details comprise o characters, places, or events. So, if the storyteller wants to create a rapport between a character and the audience, details of the character is necessary. When telling a story about a manager who exercises bad management, you shall be keen to delve into details about the appearance and behavior of this manager to immerse your audience on the issue projecting the bad appearance, behavior and attitude. The audience will perceive details of his bad appearance as a proof of his bad performance and in the case of detailing perfect appearance, they would perceive hypocrisy or wrong orientation of the manager.

The same goes with details of places. You have to ask why you should provide details about a place? Will this description serve your story or not doing so is better? Some people would describe places in detail then all of a sudden introduce another rendering the details of the former verbose. Finally, in events, mounting details would prime the audience for the climax. Giving details about your first set of failures then in more detail your second set so on and so forth then reeling it back with lesser details about succeeding setbacks to avoid onset of boredom. Human instinct adheres to details over instructions. By rehearsing, you shall know the right dose of details better each time.

In "We Already Know", the event that had the most details was in the conference where Dr Albaz talked with the geologist about the moon's terrains. In "Freedom", focus was on the appearance of attendees – their surprise and condemnation because the emotions of audience were the turning point. In "The Stranger", details were provided for the appearance of this stranger to induce emotions of worry and anxiety. In "The Closing Argument", details were excessive on the event of the rape of the little girl excluding details of her rapists, although these could be considered important.

Handful of Words
A Less bla bla bla

Traders used to say, "Two words are more blessed than ten". Arabs used to say, "The best of words is that which is short and to the point". Also, a famous English proverb states, "Brevity is the soul of wit". Stories can, likewise, take a very short but eloquent path that serve its purpose and leave an impact. The Quran showed how a handful of words could have a major influence on people. God mentioned in the Quran, "And these examples We present to the people, but none will understand them except those of knowledge" Al-Ankabut-43, "And they do not come to you with an argument except that We bring you the truth and the best explanation" Al-Furkan-33, "And Allah presents examples for the people that perhaps they will be reminded" Al-Furkan-25, "O people, an example is presented, so listen to it. Indeed, those you invoke besides Allah will never create [as much as] a fly, even if they gathered together for that purpose. And if the fly should steal away from them a [tiny] thing, they could not recover it from him. Weak are the pursuer and pursued" Al-Haj-73.

Examples in Quran are meant to show facts in different perspectives that make it more conducive for people's intellects. These are short projections aimed to transform abstract fact into something real or imaginable with an example at the end affirming and making it more familiar. To illustrate, "Have you not considered how Allah presents an example, [making] a good word like a good tree, whose root is firmly fixed and its branches [high] in the sky? It produces its fruit all the time, by permission of its Lord. And Allah presents examples for the people that perhaps they will be reminded. And the example of a bad word is like a bad tree, uprooted from the surface of the earth, not having any stability. Allah keeps firm those who believe, with the firm word, in worldly life and in the Hereafter. And Allah sends astray the wrongdoers. And Allah does what He wills." Ibrahim-24-27. Metaphors are very visual and meaning is seamlessly transmitted.

Mathematical equations appear hard until represented with examples so they are easier to digest. The same goes with project managers who suffer explaining to stakeholders procedures in executing plans, especially when requesting additional resources. Metaphors help project the meaning like, "Getting the job done with these tools is like asking me to dig ten meters deep using teaspoons". While some would not understand the capacity of heavy machinery, most would know the capacity of teaspoons. Such example is enough to guarantee an understanding of the setback. When arguing with a colleague with a different discipline about technical issues, you could say, "You've been a senior civil engineer for two decades, it's impossible to argue with you about the quantity of cement and steel this building would need. The same goes with me, it's hard to argue with me about what I've been doing for two decades as well".

Nothing could describe the true nature of usury of banks as accurately as a lady did. It was a very powerful metaphor that projected this awful fact. She said, "The moment you get the loan from the bank is the moment where you start to race a train on its track. If you're a good, fit athlete, you'll easily maintain enough distance the chasing train. But once you stumble over a rock or feel some exhaustion, the train will never wait even for a fraction of a micro-moment. Neither will it pity you, rather it'll mash your flesh and grind your bones below its metal driving wheels. And it won't leave your remaining shreds so your family could bury them, but it'll take them all as reparation for arrears!"

Our dear Prophet Muhammad use the best metaphors. He described himself saying, "My similitude in comparison with other prophets before me, is that of a man who has built a house nicely and beautifully, except for one brick in a corner. The people go about it and wonder at its beauty, but say: 'Would that this brick be put in its place!' So I am that brick, and I am the last of the Prophets". A simple kind of metaphor that can easily transmit to commoners the mission of prophets and their solidarity to deliver the same message.

Rhymes

Rhymes have an amazing effect to allowing words to linger in the mind. Beginning a story with a rhyme and placing the wisdom in the rhyme format would provide an outstanding resonance like, "If it's to be, it's up to me". Proceed with the story of your struggle then end the story with the same rhyme, "... and by achieving so, I had the merit for the first time in my life to say... If it's to be, it's up to me".

Epilogue

Finally, when you're done with this book, you ought to take action on the hundreds of projections and stories around you. One of the unique skills a storyteller exclusively has, is the ability to hunt for stories around him and choose the best then scrutinize, modify or rectify them with a good beginning, ending, wisdom, and/or rhyme. All, without exception, receive scores of stories each day but few people are able to use these stories in his life or business. We live in an age where stories are everywhere – movies, series, commercials, and reality TV, a billion dollar industry. In the meantime, our natural ability to extract meaning and wisdom from such has exponentially decreased compared to our ancestors. Maybe what made Facebook addictive to millions around the world is its ability to jump from one story to another, suggesting another event is better and more thrilling than the previous one so on and so forth (in just sixty seconds). You go from a story to another, not finishing most because you are sure that there are many waiting for you like quenching your thirst with sea water.

To acquire the talent of our ancestors in influencing masses using meaningful projections and stories demands letting go of some of the technological advances and begin immersing mind and heart in stories that deserve listening to and reading.

Of course, this seems irrational, new and extremely difficult in the beginning but with practice it becomes something pleasurable. When the day comes you shed the cloak of introversion and your tongue freely speaks your mind – when stories become a way of thinking, chatting, listening, loving, working, persuading, reconciling and softening hearts. By then, we become human again – a person who has a story that everyone wants to listen and immerse into – a meaningful projection of many mazes that initially a listener would feel lost inside but at its end would wish to get lost within.

References

1. **McGregor, Douglas.** *The Human Side of Enterprise: 25th Anniversary Printing.* New York : McGraw-Hill, 1985.

2. **Ariely, Dan.** *Predictably Irrational: The Hidden Forces That Shape Our Decisions.* s.l. : Harper Collins, 2009.

3. *Dual Process Theory.* **James, William.** 1910.

4. *Dual-Process Theories of Higher Cognition.* **Evans, Jonathan St. B. T. and Stanovich, Keith E.** 3, s.l. : SAGE Journal, 2013, Vol. 8.

5. *Reflective and Impulsive Determinants of Social Behavior.* **Strack, Fritz and Deutshc, Rolan.** s.l. : Personality and Social Psychology Review, 2004.

6. **Kahneman, Daniel.** *Thinking Fast & Slow.* 2012.

7. **Csikszentmihalyi, Mihaly.** *Flow: The Psychology of Optimal Experience.* s.l. : https://www.amazon.com/Flow-Psychology-Experience-Perennial-Classics/dp/0061339202/ref=mt_paperback?_encoding=UTF8&me=, 1990.

8. *The power of the mind: the cortex as a critical determinant of muscle strength/weakness.* **Clark, BC, et al., et al.** 112/12, s.l. : Journal of Neurophysiology, 2014, Vol. 15. 3219–3226.

9. *Reading cinnamon activates olfactory brain regions.* **Gonzalez, Julio, et al., et al.** 32/2, s.l. : Journal of NeuroImage, 2006, Vol. 15. 906 – 912.

10. *Metaphorically feeling: comprehending textural metaphors activates somatosensory cortex.* **S, Lacey, R, Stilla and K, Sathian.** 3, s.l. : Brain Language Journal, 2012, Vol. 120. 416-21.

11. *Grasping Ideas with the Motor System: Semantic Somatotopy in Idiom Comprehension.* **Boulenger, Véronique, Hauk, Olaf and Pulvermüller, Friedemann.** 8, France : Journal of Cerebral Cortex, 2008 , Vol. 19. 1905–1914.

12. **Tyndall, John.** Scientific Use of the Imagination. 1870, Vol. https://books.google.com.eg/books?id=mdEEAAAAYAAJ&redir_esc=y&hl=en.

13. **Sinek, Simon.** *Leaders Eat Last: Why Some Teams Pull Together and Others Don't.* s.l. : https://www.amazon.com/Leaders-Eat-Last-Together-Others/dp/1591848016/ref=tmm_pap_swatch_0?_encoding=UTF8&qid=&sr=, 2017.

14. *Why Inspiring Stories Make Us React: The Neuroscience of Narrative.* **Zak, Paul J.** s.l. : Cerebrum Journal , 2015 , Vol. 2.

15. **Buckingham, Marcus.** What Great Managers Do. *HBR: Harvard Business Review.* https://hbr.org/2005/03/what-great-managers-do, 2005, Vol. 3.

16. **Hart, Michael.** *The 100: A Ranking Of The Most Influential Persons In History* . s.l. : https://www.amazon.com/100-Ranking-Influential-Persons-History/dp/0806513500, 2000.

17. **Seymour, Martin.** *The 100 Most Influential Books Ever Written: The History of Thought from Ancient Times to Today.* s.l. : https://www.amazon.com/Most-Influential-Books-Ever-Written/dp/0806520000/ref=sr_1_1?s=books&ie=UTF8&qid=1513639530&sr=1-1&keywords=100+Most+Influential+Books+Ever, 1998.

18. *A Wandering Mind Is an Unhappy Mind.* **Killingsworth, Matthew A. and Gilbert, Daniel T.** 6006, s.l. : Science Magazine, 2010, Vol. 330. 932.

19. **Callahan, Shawn.** *Putting Stories to Work.* s.l. : https://www.amazon.com/Putting-Stories-Work-Shawn-Callahan/dp/0992338565/ref=tmm_pap_swatch_0?_encoding=UTF8&qid=&sr=, 2016.

20. **Booker, Christopher.** *The Seven Basic Plots: Why We Tell Stories.* s.l. : https://www.amazon.com/Seven-Basic-Plots-Tell-Stories/dp/0826480373/ref=sr_1_1?s=books&ie=UTF8&qid=1513640372&sr=1-1&keywords=The+Seven+Basic+Plots, 2006.

21. **M.R., Stephen and Merrill, Rebecca.** *The SPEED of TRUST: The One Thing That Changes Everything.* s.l. : https://www.amazon.com/SPEED-TRUST-Thing-Changes-Everything/dp/1416549005/ref=sr_1_1?s=books&ie=UTF8&qid=1513640423&sr=1-1&keywords=The+Speed+of+Trust, 2008.

22. Lessons from an oil spill: how BP gained - then lost - our trust. http://theconversation.com/lessons-from-an-oil-spill-how-bp-gained-then-lost-our-trust-40307, 2015.

23. **Sobel-Lojeski, Karen.** The Subtle Ways Our Screens Are Pushing Us Apart. *HBR: Harvard Business Review.* https://hbr.org/2015/04/the-subtle-ways-our-screens-are-pushing-us-apart, 2015.

24. **Bennett, Ty.** *The Power of Storytelling.* s.l. : https://www.amazon.com/Power-Storytelling-Ty-Bennett/dp/1936631083/ref=sr_1_1?s=books&ie=UTF8&qid=1513640848&sr=1-1&keywords=The+Power+of+Storytelling, 2013.

25. Uber. *https://www.uber.com/en-EG/our-story/*. [Online]

26. **H.Pink, Daniel.** *Drive: The Surprising Truth About What Motivates Us.* s.l. : https://www.amazon.com/Drive-Surprising-Truth-About-Motivates/dp/1594484805/ref=sr_1_1?s=books&ie=UTF8&qid=1513641035&sr=1-1&keywords=drive, 2011.

27. **Welsch, Jack and Welch, Suzy.** *Winning.* s.l. : https://www.amazon.com/Winning-Jack-Welch/dp/0060753943/ref=sr_1_4?s=books&ie=UTF8&qid=1513641138&sr=1-4&keywords=Winning, 2005.

28. **Denning, Stephen.** *The Leader's Guide to Storytelling: Mastering the Art and Discipline of Business Narrative.* s.l. : https://www.amazon.com/Leaders-Guide-Storytelling-Mastering-Discipline/dp/0470548673/ref=sr_1_1?s=books&ie=UTF8&qid=1513641196&sr=1-1&keywords=The+Leader%E2%80%99s+Guide+to+Storytelling, 2011.

29. **El-Baz, Farouk.** https://www.jsc.nasa.gov/history/oral_histories/El-BazF/El-BazF_11-2-09.htm. [Online] 2009.

30. **Bernoulli.** Expected Utility Hypothesis. *https://en.wikipedia.org/wiki/Expected_utility_hypothesis.* [Online]

31. *Prospect Theory: An Analysis of Decision under Risk .* **Kahneman, Daniel and Tversky, Amos.** 2, s.l. : Econometrica, 1979, Vol. 47. 263-291.

32. *Emotion, Decision Making and the Orbitofrontal Cortex.* **Bechara, Antoine, Damasio, Hanna and Damasio, Antonio R.** 3, 2000, Vol. 10. 295–307.

33. **Stew, Herret.** *Uncle Tom's Cabin.* s.l. : https://www.amazon.com/Uncle-Toms-Cabin-Wordsworth-Classics/dp/1840224029, 1852.

34. **Grisham, John.** *A Time to Kill.* s.l. : https://www.amazon.com/Time-Kill-Novel-John-Grisham/dp/0440245915/ref=sr_1_1?s=books&ie=UTF8&qid=1513642285&sr=1-1&keywords=A+Time+to+Kill, 1988.

35. **Ward, Victoria.** School run stranger inspires mother to spend more time with her own children. *http://www.telegraph.co.uk/news/newstopics/howaboutthat/12135425/School-run-stranger-inspires-mother-to-spend-more-time-with-her-own-children.html.* [Online] 2016.

36. John Bannister. *https://deepenglish.com/2015/10/the-power-of-belief-2/.* [Online]

37. **Gozzi, Carlo.** The Thirty Six Dramatic Situations. *https://en.wikipedia.org/wiki/The_Thirty-Six_Dramatic_Situations.* [Online] 1806.

38. **Freytag, Gustav.** Dramatic Arc. *https://en.wikipedia.org/wiki/Dramatic_structure.* [Online] 1863.

39. **Vonnegut, Kurt.** *A Man without a Country.* s.l. : https://www.amazon.com/Man-Without-Country-Kurt-Vonnegut/dp/081297736X, 2007.

40. *The emotional arcs of stories are dominated by six basic shapes.* **Reagan, Andrew J, et al., et al.** 31, s.l. : EPJ Data Science, 2016, Vol. 5.

41. **Campbell, Joseph.** *A Hero with Thousand Faces.* s.l. : https://www.amazon.com/Thousand-Faces-Collected-Joseph-Campbell/dp/1577315936/ref=sr_1_1?s=books&ie=UTF8&qid=1513674682&sr=1-1&keywords=A++Hero+with+Thousand+Faces, 1949.

42. **Duarte, Nancy.** *Resonate.* s.l. : John Wiley & Sons, 2010.

43. *MASS MEDIA AND ATTITUDES TO THE GULF WAR IN BRITAIN.* **SHAW and CARR-HILL.** 1, s.l. : The Electronic Journal of Communication, 1991, Vol. 2.

44. **Linkedin.** The 25 Skills That Can Get You Hired in 2016. *https://blog.linkedin.com/2016/01/12/the-25-skills-that-can-get-you-hired-in-2016.* [Online] 2016.

45. **Dykes, Brent.** Data Storytelling: The Essential Data Science Skill Everyone Needs. *https://www.forbes.com/sites/brentdykes/2016/03/31/data-storytelling-the-essential-data-science-skill-everyone-needs/.* [Online] 2016.

46. **Bennett, Ty.** The Story of Mel Fisher. *https://www.youtube.com/watch?v=syoSgZ8M8s4.* [Online]

47. **Cialdini, Robert.** *Pre-suasion: A Revolutionary Way to Influence and Persuade.* s.l. : Simon & Schuster, 2016.

48. *Das Behalten erledigter und unerledigter Handlungen.* **Zeigarnik, B.** 1-85, s.l. : Psychologische, 1927, Vol. 9.

49. *The Zeigarnik Effect in Advertising.* **Heimbach, J. T., and J. Jacoby.** 746–57, s.l. : Third Annual Conference of the Association for Consumer Research, 1972.

50. *Undermining the Zeigarnik Effect: Another Hidden Cost of Reward.* **McGraw, K. O., and J. Fiala.** 58–66, s.l. : Journal of Personality, 1982, Vol. 50.

51. **Cialdini, Robert.** *Influence: The Psychology of Persuasion.* s.l. : Harper Collins, 2009.

52. *Acoustic Influences on Consumer Behavio: Empirical Studies on the Effects of In-Store Music and Product Sound.* **Knöferle, Klemens Michael.** Germany : University of St. Gallen,School of Management,Economics, Law, Social Sciences,and International Affairs, 2011.

53. *Body Language: The Effectiveness of Total Physical Response Storytelling in SecondaryForeign Language Instruction.* **Decker, Beth.** s.l. : EDUC, 2008, Vol. 480.

54. *Gestures in the Storytelling Domain.* **Niesink, Luke.** s.l. : Semantic Scholar, Vol. https://pdfs.semanticscholar.org/6cc0/836818e2a41fadafa4c1f091a6f221554fb0.pdf.

55. *Inference of Attitudes from Non -Verbal Communication in Two Channels.* **Mehrabian, Albert and Ferris, Susan R.** 3, s.l. : Journal of Consulting Psychology, 1967, Vol. 31. 248-252.

56. *Decoding of Inconsistent Communications.* **Mehrabian, Albert and Wiener, Morton.** 1, s.l. : Journal of Personality and Social Psychology, 1967, Vol. 6. 109-114.

57. **Miro, Marc.** The Simple Message That Brought This Middle School Class to Tears. *https://www.youtube.com/watch?v=WI0Twlt1aek.* [Online] 2015.

58. **Robbins, Anthony.** https://www.youtube.com/watch?v=CN3wXSU-oO8. [Online] 2013.

59. *Eye movements and NLP.* **Dilts, Robert.** s.l. : Langley Porter Neuropsychiatric Institute, 1977.

60. **Brown, Brené.** *Daring Greatly: How the Courage to Be Vulnerable Transforms the Way We Live, Love, Parent, and Lead.* s.l. : https://www.amazon.com/Daring-Greatly-Courage-Vulnerable-Transforms/dp/1592408419/ref=la_B001JP45BA_1_3?s=books&ie=UTF8&qid=1513679988&sr=1-3, 2015.

61. **Ezzat, Hisham.** *The Persuasion Matrix.* s.l. : http://www.hishamezzat.com, 2018.

62. **Heath, Chip and Heath, Dan.** *Made To Stick.* s.l. : https://www.amazon.com/Made-Stick-Ideas-Survive-Others/dp/1400064287/ref=sr_1_1?s=books&ie=UTF8&qid=151368012 6&sr=1-1&keywords=Made+To+Stick, 2007.

63. *I know what you are doing.* **Umilta, M.A., Kohler, E., Gallese, V., Fogassi, L., Fadiga, L., Keysers, C., & Rizzolatti, G.** 155-165, Vol. 31.

64. *Action recognition in the premotor cortex.* **Gallese, V., Fadiga, L., Fogassi, L., & Rizzolatti, G.** 593-609, 1996, Vol. 119.

65. *Activation of human primary motor cortex during action observation: A neuromagnetic study.* **Hari, R., Forss, N., Kirveskari, E., Salenius, S., & Rizzolatti, G.** 15061-15065, 1998, Vol. 95.

66. *Evidence for mirror neuron dysfunction in autism spectrum disorders.* **Oberman, L.M., Hubbard, E.M., McCleery, J.P., Altschuler, E.L., Ramachandran, V.S., & Pineda, J.A.** 190-198, s.l. : Cognitive Brain Research, 2005, Vol. 24.

About the Author

Hisham Ezzat is all about what you have read above…

Communicate through:

http://www.hisham-ezzat.com
eng.hesham.ezzat@gmail.com
https://www.facebook.com/h.ezzat818
http://www.amazon.com/author/hishamezzat

www.ingramcontent.com/pod-product-compliance
Lightning Source LLC
Chambersburg PA
CBHW020632220526
45464CB00001B/115